Greek in the Carolingian Age

SPECULUM ANNIVERSARY MONOGRAPHS

THIRTEEN

Greek in the Carolingian Age

The St. Gall Manuscripts

Bernice M. Kaczynski

THE MEDIEVAL ACADEMY OF AMERICA 1988

The publication of this book was made possible by funds contributed to the
Medieval Academy during the Semi-Centennial Fund Drive.

Contents

Plates

Acknowledgments

Perhaps more than other books, a first book reflects debts of gratitude incurred over many years. I began the work that led to this one as a student in the Department of Medieval Studies at Yale University. Jaroslav Pelikan drew my attention to the problem of Greek in the West. Walter Cahn and Cora Lutz persuaded me that it was a pleasure to forage among manuscripts. Deno Geanakoplos supervised the doctoral dissertation in which I began to broach the questions that have occupied me since.

In recent years there has been a quickening of interest in western Greek, and I am indebted to the scholars whose welcome contributions have enabled me to focus more sharply on the St. Gall sources. I should like to give special thanks to Edouard Jeauneau, of the Pontifical Institute of Mediaeval Studies, Toronto, and the Centre national de la recherche scientifique, Paris. He heartened me with his encouragement and inspired me by his example. I am grateful, too, to John Contreni of Purdue University and Michael Herren of York University for much conversation and correspondence on Carolingian matters. For advice and good cheer I am grateful to Maureen MacGrogan.

My colleagues in the Department of History at McMaster University in Hamilton, Ontario, have helped in many ways throughout the writing of the book. It is a pleasure to thank them, especially Daniel Geagan, Richard Rempel, John Trueman, and Edith Mary Wightman. The Arts Research Board of McMaster University gave financial support for travel and for assistance in the preparation of the manuscript.

I am deeply grateful to Dr. Msgr. Johannes Duft for the generous welcome I received when I first came to work in the Stiftsbibliothek of St. Gall. More recently Dr. Peter Ochsenbein answered queries and gave valuable assistance. For permission to consult additional manuscripts and for courteous help I am indebted to the Bayerische Staatsbibliothek, Munich; the Bibliothèque Nationale, Paris; the Deutsche Staatsbibliothek, East Berlin; the Staatsbibliothek, Bamberg; and the Zentralbibliothek, Zurich. After my travels I have always returned to the library of the Pontifical Institute of Mediaeval Studies, and I should like to take this opportunity to thank the staff of that hospitable institution.

Jacqueline Brown supervised the preparation of this volume and resolved numerous difficulties presented by the unusual setting of the Greek type. I am very grateful to her and the Medieval Academy of America for the great care they have taken in the production.

Finally—and above all—I wish to thank my parents, to whom this book is dedicated, and my brothers and sisters, William, James, Marie, Elizabeth, and Walter.

I

The Imagery of Greek

Ekkehard IV, a monastic chronicler fond of telling stories, once told this one about a schoolboy and a duchess. Toward the end of the tenth century Burkhard of St. Gall was taken by his teacher to meet the duchess Hadwig of Swabia, a woman known for her skill in Latin and Greek. Burkhard had a favor to ask of her and he put it into hexameter: "Esse velim Grecus, cum sim vix, domna, Latinus" ("I should like, my lady, to be a Greek, although I am scarcely a Latin").[1] This quotation, familiar to anyone who has glanced at the sources for the history of St. Gall, illustrates the perplexing situation of medieval people who wished to learn Greek.

In the course of the preceding centuries people had become increasingly accustomed to using their own vernacular tongues for speech and the necessities of daily life.[2] Latin—the language of religion, scholarship, and government—had to be taught in school.[3] If a knowledge of Latin could be acquired only with effort, a knowledge of Greek was all the more elusive. There were few teachers of Greek, and there were few textbooks with which to study. It is right to observe, as scholars often have, that not many people in medieval Europe were able to read Greek fluently.[4] Some

1. Ekkehard IV, *Casus S. Galli* 94, ed. Gerold Meyer von Knonau (St. Gall, 1877), p. 344. (Unless otherwise noted, all translations are my own.) A line by Rather of Verona served Ekkehard as a literary model: "Graecizando vanus, cum non sit saltem Latinus," in *Qualitatis coniectura cuiusdam* 2, PL 136:523. And in about 1032, an allusion to Ekkehard's verse found its way into a letter written by a pupil in the cathedral school of Mainz: "Eximiae iuventuti Wormatiensium, insudanti studiis et artibus Atheniensium, R. Mogontinus non Grecus, sed vix effectus Latinus," ed. Walther Bulst, *Die ältere Wormser Briefsammlung* (Weimar, 1949), p. 48.
2. The problem of linguistic change in medieval Europe is extremely complex. Philippe Wolff, *Western Languages, A.D. 100–1500*, trans. Frances Partridge (New York and Toronto, 1971), pp. 133–138, examines the relationship of Latin to the vernaculars and the question of bilingualism as it developed in the ninth century.
3. Bernhard Bischoff, "The Study of Foreign Languages in the Middle Ages," in *Mittelalterliche Studien: Ausgewählte Aufsätze zur Schriftkunde und Literaturgeschichte*, 3 vols. (Stuttgart, 1966–1981), 2:227–245.
4. Two works are fundamental to the history of the knowledge of Greek in the West, and my own study has taken its direction from them. Bernhard Bischoff prepared a catalogue of the Greek material found in a survey of western manuscripts ranging, approximately,

1

scholars might learn the alphabet and decipher the Greek words used by Isidore or Jerome, and merchants and travelers might know enough to carry on occasional conversations with Byzantines, but men who knew Greek well, who could understand difficult Greek prose, were very few. Bede, John Scottus Eriugena, Liudprand of Cremona, Robert Grosseteste, Roger Bacon—these were the exceptions. A real knowledge of the language was beyond the grasp of all but the most determined and fortunate of scholars.

Yet a fascination with Greek seems to pervade the whole of the Latin Middle Ages. Many manuscripts give evidence of an occupation with it. And it was not only in Ekkehard's sentimental account that writers indicated their admiration for the language.

The root of the medieval interest in Greek lay in Scripture. As St. John described the Passion, "Pilate wrote out a notice and had it fixed to the cross; it ran: 'Jesus the Nazarene, King of the Jews' . . . and the writing was in Hebrew, Latin, and Greek" (John 19.19–20). Prudentius commemorated the event in verse.[5] Early Christian commentators on the passage linked Hebrew, Greek, and Latin together in a special way; Hilary of Poitiers called them "tres linguae praecipuae," the "three principal languages."[6] For Isidore of Seville, they were "tres linguae sacrae," the "three sacred languages," and in this formulation the concept was transmitted through the Middle Ages:

> There are three sacred languages, Hebrew, Greek, and Latin, and they are supreme through all the world. For it was in these three languages that the charge against the Lord was written above the cross by Pilate. Wherefore, because of the obscurity of the Holy Scriptures, a knowledge of these three languages is necessary, in order that there may be recourse to a second if the expression in one of them leads to doubt of a word or its meaning. But the Greek tongue is considered most famous among the tongues of the nations. For it is more resonant than the Latin and all other tongues. . . .[7]

---

from the fifth through the twelfth centuries: "Das griechische Element in der abendländischen Bildung des Mittelalters," in *Mittelalterliche Studien* 2:246–275. This study was seminal. Walter Berschin's more recent history of the topic, *Griechisch-lateinisches Mittelalter: Von Hieronymus zu Nikolaus von Kues* (Bern and Munich, 1980), soon to appear in a revised English edition, is exemplary and indispensable.

5. Prudentius, *Apotheosis* 381–385.

6. Hilary of Poitiers, *Prologus in librum psalmorum* 15, PL 9:241. St. Augustine referred to "linguae principales": *Enarrationes in psalmos* 58.1.1 and *In Iohannis Evangelium tractatus* 117.4.

7. *Etymologiae* 9.1.3–4, trans. Ernest Brehaut, *An Encyclopedist of the Dark Ages: Isidore*

In the words of Hugh of St. Victor, in the early twelfth century, they were "tres . . . lingue . . . sacratiores," the "three more sacred languages."[8]

The tradition played an important role in scriptural exegesis, but had trivial consequences as well. Irish exegetes were particularly fond of giving Latin words their Greek and Hebrew equivalents, and they were not above supplying fictitious terms if they did not know the real ones. Exercises in Irish schoolbooks frequently asked for the names of things in the three languages. The author of the *Ars Sergii* (or *Sergilii*), probably writing in the ninth century, mocked his countrymen's habit when he asked: " 'What are the three rods [that make up the letter A] called in the three languages?' 'In Hebrew, *abst, ebst, ubst.*' 'What are they called in Greek?' '*Albs, elbs, ulbs.*' 'In Latin?' 'Two slanted lines and a straight one on top.' "[9]

Scripture in general determined the course of medieval linguistic theory. Scholars tended to approach linguistic problems in relation to certain biblical texts. Chief among them were the episode of the Tower of Babel in the Old Testament (Gen. 11.1−9) and the feast of Pentecost in the New (Acts 2.1−11). Discussion of the three sacred languages was conducted within this framework. The intellectual systems that evolved were complex and sometimes contradictory,[10] but through them all ran a feeling of respect for Greek. It was a sacred language, the language of the Septuagint and the New Testament, the historical language of the early church. These were all reasons to hold Greek in high esteem.

One need not have been a biblical scholar to have acquired an interest in Greek. Latin literature offered many opportunities for a casual encounter with the language. Priscian and Donatus, for example, often used Greek illustrations in their expositions of Latin grammar. The writing

---

of Seville (New York, 1912), pp. 208−209.

8. *De grammatica* 1 ("Tres enim, ut dictum est, lingue sunt sacratiores, hebrea, greca, et latina; que toto orbe maxime excellunt"), ed. Roger Baron, *Opera propaedeutica* (Notre Dame, 1966), p. 79.

9. The text is one of several illustrations of Irish writing on the sacred languages given by Bischoff, "Das griechische Element," pp. 248−251. Its manuscript tradition is discussed by Vivien Law, *The Insular Latin Grammarians*, Studies in Celtic History 3 (Woodbridge, Eng., 1982), pp. 51−52. See also R. E. McNally, "The 'Tres Linguae Sacrae' in Early Irish Bible Exegesis," *Theological Studies* 19 (1958), 395−403.

10. Arno Borst, *Der Turmbau von Babel: Geschichte der Meinungen über Ursprung und Vielfalt der Sprachen und Völker*, 4 vols. (Stuttgart, 1957−1963), 1:6, stresses the diversity of medieval thinking on language and cautions against the assumption that it was based on a single and unitary system. *Der Turmbau*, 2.1:483−541, surveys the attitudes of Carolingian scholars toward the texts on Babel and Pentecost.

of St. Jerome, a favorite author of the monks, was full of Greek words and phrases, and bilingual glossaries were prepared to assist his readers. The encyclopedias of Cassiodorus contained numerous references to Greek. Bede and Isidore discussed the alphabet and provided specimens of the letters. If one did not read Greek, one might hear it. Creeds, doxologies, and other prayers were chanted in Greek in some liturgies, and Greek alphabets were recited in ceremonies for the dedication of churches.

Yet the study of Greek was difficult in the medieval West. The major impediment was a shortage of reference materials. Until the time of Roger Bacon Europeans had no textbook that explained the principles of Greek grammar in terms comprehensible to Latins. Scholars who wished to learn the language had to make do with rough or fragmentary sketches or with the handbook of Dositheus—a work composed, originally, to explain Latin grammar to Greeks. One might hope for assistance from a visiting Byzantine or Italo-Greek, but there was no guarantee that a native speaker understood the structure of his own language, or that he had the skills with which to communicate it.[11]

In learning Greek Europe relied for the most part upon its own meager resources.[12] It should not be surprising that many persons dabbled in the language. Nor should it be surprising that only a small number mastered it. Among the Greek texts they composed or circulated among themselves, many must simply be described as mediocre. Others reveal an almost eccentric virtuosity. They have in common, however, a reverence for a language few people could hope to understand. For this reason, for the fragility of their hopes, the preoccupation with Greek is one of the most moving features of the Latin Middle Ages.

11. For an excellent demonstration of the way in which one medieval scholar attempted to overcome the difficulty, see Edouard Jeauneau, "Jean Scot Erigène et le grec," *Archivum Latinitatis Medii Aevi (Bulletin du Cange)* 41 (1979), 5–50. Jeauneau catalogues the limited resources available to John Scottus Eriugena in his study of the language and discusses the effect of these limitations upon his translations and philosophical thought.
12. Italy, with its classical tradition and long history of contact with the Byzantine Empire, was an exception. See Bischoff, "Das griechische Element," p. 247.

II

The Abbey of St. Gall

There were times and places when Greek seems to have been cultivated with particular intensity. Scholars who sought to learn the language were prominent in Gothic Italy, in early medieval Ireland and Anglo-Saxon England, in the Carolingian and Ottonian Empires, in Norman south Italy, in thirteenth-century England, and in fifteenth-century Florence.[1]

During the ninth, tenth, and eleventh centuries political considerations often encouraged an interest in the language, for contemporary rulers carried on relations with the Byzantine court.[2] Thus when Charles the Great proposed to send his daughter Rothrud as a bride to Constantine VI of Byzantium, he invited Paul the Deacon to teach her Greek. On another occasion, in 827, the Byzantine emperor Michael II sent a copy of the works of Dionysius the Areopagite as a gift to Louis the Pious. Louis presented the codex to the abbey of St-Denis, where, under Abbot Hilduin, Dionysius's four theological treatises and ten letters were translated into Latin. Charles the Bald later urged John Scottus Eriugena to prepare a new Latin version of the *Corpus dionysiacum*, and this task was completed some time before 862. Eriugena, one of the most accomplished medieval Hellenists, also translated works by Maximus Confessor, Gregory of Nyssa, and Epiphanius of Salamis.

Under the direction of Martin Hiberniensis Irishmen at Laon compiled an important Greek-Latin glossary and compendium of Greek-Latin grammatical materials. In Liège Sedulius Scottus copied a bilingual Psalter together with Greek and Latin Canticles, prayers, and the *Oracula sibyllina* of Lactantius.

Bishop Liudprand of Cremona, Otto I's legate to Constantinople, had an unusual command of the language, for he knew both the literary Greek of the classical authors and church fathers and the colloquial Greek of his own day.[3] The celebrated marriage in 972 of Otto II and the Byzantine

1. Berschin, *Griechisch-lateinisches Mittelalter*, p. 38.
2. For a fuller discussion of the examples reviewed here, see Berschin, *Griechisch-lateinisches Mittelalter*, pp. 130–157 ("Das merowingische Gallien—Karolingerhöfe"), pp. 158–193 ("Karolingische Klöster"), pp. 211–243 ("Die ottonische Epoche").
3. Johannes Koder and Thomas Weber, *Liutprand von Cremona in Konstantinopel: Unter-*

Theophano furthered an interest in things Greek, and Pope Sylvester expressed the hope that the gulf between Latins and Greeks would be bridged in the person of their son Otto III.

The scholars of the time translated and quoted the works of Dionysius and a small number of other Greek Christian authors. They also copied bilingual versions of Scripture, assembled Greek prayers to be used in Latin services, prepared glossaries and sketches for grammars, and sometimes ornamented original Latin compositions with Greek titles and quotations.

For the most part, they worked in courts, in monasteries, and in cathedrals scattered about a vast territory. The Carolingian Empire comprised most of present-day France, Germany, Switzerland, Belgium, and northern Italy. The Ottonian Empire shifted the boundaries eastward, but it too was a bulky state. Our knowledge of the cultural map of the period is incomplete. The historical records of the various centers have been unevenly preserved, and so we must be cautious in our attempts to rank them in order of importance or even to trace out their intellectual connections.[4] The great institutions, it seems, owed their positions to well-stocked libraries, learned masters, or to personal relationships they formed with other scholars or members of the court.

Some places appear to have fostered a special interest in Greek. Because of their association with prominent teachers and manuscripts St-Denis, Liège, Laon, and the court of Charles the Bald have become known as centers where Greek was studied.[5] Another of these places is the abbey

---

suchungen zum griechischen Sprachschatz und zu realienkundlichen Aussagen in seinen Werken, Byzantina Vindobonensia 13 (Vienna, 1980), p. 23.

4. For general overviews, see Emile Lesne, *Histoire de la propriété ecclésiastique en France*, vol. 4, *Les livres, "scriptoria" et bibliothèques du commencement du VIIIe à la fin du XIe siècle*, and vol. 5, *Les écoles de la fin du VIIIe siècle à la fin du XIIe siècle* (Lille, 1938–1940); Pierre Riché, *Les écoles et l'enseignement dans l'occident chrétien de la fin du Ve siècle au milieu du XIe siècle* (Paris, 1979); and *La Scuola nell'Occidente latino dell'alto Medioevo*, Settimane di Studio del Centro italiano di Studi sull'alto Medioevo 19 (Spoleto, 1972).

5. For important studies of individual centers, see John J. Contreni, *The Cathedral School of Laon from 850 to 930: Its Manuscripts and Masters*, Münchener Beiträge zur Mediävistik und Renaissance-Forschung 29 (Munich, 1978), and Edouard Jeauneau, "Les écoles de Laon et d'Auxerre au IXe siècle," in *La Scuola nell'Occidente latino*, 19.2:495–522, 555–560. Few studies have focused directly on the issue of Greek scholarship in particular monasteries: Charles Cuissard, *L'étude du grec à Orléans depuis le IXe siècle jusqu'au milieu du XVIIIe siècle*, Mémoires de la Société archéologique et historique de l'Orléannais 19 (Orléans, 1883), pp. 645–840, with a discussion of Greek at Fleury (Saint-Benoît-sur-Loire); and (on St-Denis) Roberto Weiss, "Lo Studio del greco

of St. Gall.

"In few monasteries," writes J. M. Clark, "was the study of Greek carried on with such zeal and with such success."[6] The traditional reputation of St. Gall as a center of medieval Hellenism rests upon its possession of a number of well-known manuscripts. Irish monks contributed a set of bilingual Scriptures—Gospels, Pauline Epistles, and Psalter—to the monastery library and there was also a copy of the *Ars grammatica* of Dositheus and the *Hermeneumata pseudo-dositheana*. Many of its liturgical manuscripts contain Greek prayers. Narrative sources for the history of the monastery give other indications of the monks' interest in the language. "Traces of Greek," observes Bernhard Bischoff, "appear perhaps more numerous at St. Gall than in any other place. . . . But [the quality of the occupation] remains to be critically tested."[7]

There is much to be learned from an investigation of Greek scholarship at St. Gall. To focus upon a single intellectual center is to establish a perspective for the interpretation of the mass of Greek material current in medieval Europe. It is useful to know precisely what resources were available to the members of an active scholarly community. What Greek texts were copied in the scriptorium or kept in the library? Where did they come from? How were they used? St. Gall was an important institution; for two centuries it played a leading role in learning, culture, and art. And so an inquiry into its handling of Greek materials may also cast light on contemporary scholarly attitudes and practices overall.

To modern scholars St. Gall presents a precious opportunity for research. The historical records of the abbey are very nearly complete. The wars, fires, and floods that destroyed the records of so many other European monasteries have done very little harm to St. Gall, and in thirteen hundred years the abbey library has suffered few losses. The medieval collection remains the core of the present-day library. Certainly manuscripts have gone astray, but it is generally possible to obtain a balanced view of the contents of the library at the various stages in its development. The detailed medieval library catalogues and other documentary histories of the abbey aid in these reconstructions.

I have based my study on the manuscripts. My intention has been to catalogue and identify the Greek and bilingual (Greek-Latin) texts

---

all'abbazia di San Dionigi durante il Medioevo," *Rivista di storia della Chiesa in Italia* 6 (1952), 426–438 (repr. in *Medieval and Humanist Greek* [Padua, 1977], pp. 44–59).

6. *The Abbey of St. Gall as a Centre of Literature and Art* (Cambridge, Eng., 1926), p. 289.

7. "Das griechische Element," p. 268.

contained in them. I have taken into account both the manuscripts copied in the St. Gall scriptorium and a smaller number of manuscripts that, while not of local provenance, were brought there at an early date.[8] The range of texts described is broad, for in addition to their famous treasures, St. Gall monks possessed many books that were humble and obscure. Taken together, the Greek texts form a sizable collection, testifying to the conduct of Greek scholarship at St. Gall from the early ninth through the early eleventh centuries, the abbey's happiest period.

Was St. Gall in any way exceptional in its pursuit of Greek? Were there more books, better teachers, greater opportunities for study at St. Gall than elsewhere? It is difficult to say for certain, since we do not have many bases for comparison. St. Gall was exceptionally fortunate in the preservation of its records. For how many other places can we hope to find such a full set of documents?[9] This is an old problem in our field, and perhaps it is best summed up with a resigned allusion to "the accidents of preservation." Given the present state of scholarship, we cannot directly compare the set of Greek texts known from St. Gall with a full set from any other contemporary center. To some extent the problem can be resolved in a piecemeal fashion. I have sometimes been able to compare groups of texts from St. Gall with similar texts copied elsewhere. There are specimens, for instance, of grammatical and lexicographical texts from Laon and of liturgical texts from St-Amand that should be brought into connection with texts from St. Gall. Some biblical manuscripts, like the three Irish bilinguals, belonged to scholarly networks that included the monastery but also extended beyond it. I have offered some comparisons, then, but they are limited to specific groups of texts. Other kinds of comparisons do not seem to be justified on the basis of the evidence. I have refrained from claiming any rank for St. Gall beyond what one might normally expect

8. Dates and provenance of the St. Gall manuscripts are based on the paleographical study by Albert Bruckner, *Scriptoria medii aevi helvetica: Denkmäler schweizerischer Schreibkunst des Mittelalters*, vols. 2 and 3 (Geneva, 1936–1938). Differences of opinion and more recent findings are noted in Appendices 1–5 below. Gustav Scherrer, *Verzeichnis der Handschriften der Stiftsbibliothek von St. Gallen* (Halle, 1875; repr. Hildesheim, 1975), remains an excellent guide to the holdings of the library. Readers wishing full paleographical descriptions of the manuscripts, however, are advised to consult Bruckner. In general, I have not thought it necessary to repeat such information here, since the Greek texts often take up only one or two pages of a single manuscript. Perhaps it should be noted, finally, that St. Gall manuscripts are numbered by page rather than by folio.

9. Contreni, *The Cathedral School*, p. 4, has drawn attention to the difficulty of investigating single schools in isolation. What is needed in the long run, he suggests, is "a study of all ninth-century intellectual centers."

from a distinguished center of learning.

It is perhaps helpful to begin with a brief review of the history of the abbey, its library and manuscripts, and its scholars. It was originally an Irish foundation. Early in the seventh century, Columban and twelve disciples—a certain Gall among them—left Ireland for the Continent, where they preached and founded missionary centers. Most of the group traveled with Columban to Bobbio, near the northern end of the Apennines. Gall, however, chose to stay behind in the mountains of northeastern Switzerland, where he preached to the heathen and in 612 established a hermitage for himself. After his death in the middle of the century, his grave became a place of pilgrimage for Irish travelers, and Irish and Frankish holy men began to settle on the site.[10]

The area in which they lived was known as Alemannia, and in later years it became a powerful duchy of the Frankish Empire. It comprised, initially, the (modern) German-speaking cantons of Switzerland, Württemberg, and parts of Alsace, Baden, and Bavaria. In early medieval usage, the names Alemannia and Swabia seem to have been interchangeable,[11] but the name Swabia eventually became the more usual one. When Notker Balbulus described the reputation of his countrymen, he wrote that "at that time, because of the fame and glory of Charlemagne, the Gauls, the Aquitanians, the Aedui, the Spaniards, the Germans, and the Bavarians all prided themselves on being paid a great compliment if they earned the right to be called Swabian Franks."[12]

The site Gall had chosen for his hermitage was very remote. It was in a valley high in the Alps, surrounded by mountains and forests. Yet when the abbey became established and rather more populous, the monks did not find themselves isolated. For it was near a road frequently used by travelers from the north who were crossing the Alps on the way to Rome. They followed one of the great trade routes of the Roman Empire, leading

10. *Vita Galli confessoris triplex*, ed. Bruno Krusch (1902), MGH SSrerMerov 4:229–337, 778, and (1920), MGH SSrerMerov 7:834–835. The texts of the Gallus lives are compared by Wilhelm Wattenbach and Wilhelm Levison, *Deutschlands Geschichtsquellen im Mittelalter bis zur Mitte des dreizehnten Jahrhunderts* (Weimar, 1952), 1:140–142. On the date of the foundation, see Johannes Duft and Peter Meyer, *The Irish Miniatures in the Abbey Library of St. Gall* (Olten, Switzerland, 1954), p. 21.

11. Gregory of Tours referred to "Suebi, id est Alamanni"; and Walahfrid Strabo wrote, "Alamanni vel Suebi . . . nam cum duo sint vocabula unam gentem significantia." Both are quoted by Georg Thürer, *St. Galler Geschichte: Kultur, Staatsleben und Wirtschaft in Kanton und Stadt St. Gallen von der Urzeit bis zur Gegenwart* (St. Gall, 1953), 1:571.

12. *Gesta Karoli* 1.10. Lewis Thorpe, trans., *Einhard and Notker the Stammerer: Two Lives of Charlemagne* (Harmondsworth, 1969), p. 103.

by way of Bregenz and Chur over the Julier and Septimer Passes to Italy. The route passed directly through the old Roman town of Arbor Felix and the flourishing market of Rohrschach, each within an eight-mile radius of St. Gall, and some portion of the traffic was diverted to the monastery.[13] Throughout its history, St. Gall was a favorite stopping-place for travelers, and even royal visitors were entertained.[14]

The evolution from hermitage to monastery was gradual. The pious individuals who assembled there were not gathered into a formal community until the early eighth century. Under Abbot Otmar (720–759), buildings were erected to house a growing number of monks, and a home for the poor and a hospital for lepers were constructed. Otmar may have introduced the Benedictine Rule. The rule was certainly observed by the time of his successor Abbot John (760–782).

The social composition of the monastery changed as well. Increasing numbers of monks came from the local region. The impetus given by the first Irish pilgrims had spent itself. Nearly a century would pass before the next wave of Irish immigration, and the Irish arrivals of the early ninth century were not so much missionaries as exiles. "St. Gall," concluded Samuel Berger, "was in reality an Alemannic abbey and not in any way an Irish one. Its true founder was not St. Gall, but St. Otmar."[15] And it was under the guidance of a series of Frankish abbots that the organization, economy, and intellectual life of the abbey were to be consolidated.

The abbey's immediate problem was political, for it was subject to the authority of the bishop of Constance.[16] The struggle to free itself from what it believed to be episcopal oppression was arduous, and little strength remained for intellectual activity. Charles the Great sent his bastard son

13. See Hektor Ammann and Karl Schib, eds., *Historischer Atlas der Schweiz*, 2nd ed. (Aarau, 1958), No. 19 ("Die grossen Verkehrsstrassen des Mittelalters"), and Hermann Bikel, *Die Wirtschaftsverhältnisse des Klosters St. Gallen von der Gründung bis zum Ende des XIII. Jahrhunderts* (Freiburg im Breisgau, 1914), pp. 22–23.

14. The monks were not shy of royalty. Ekkehard IV, *Casus* 16, observed that when Otto II failed to return books he had borrowed from the library, he was administered a sharp reprimand. For an indication of the provisions that might be made for such visitors, see Walter Horn and Ernest Born, *The Plan of St. Gall: A Study of the Architecture and Economy of, and Life in a Paradigmatic Carolingian Monastery*, 3 vols. (Berkeley and Los Angeles, 1979), 2:155–165 ("House for Distinguished Guests").

15. *Histoire de la Vulgate pendant les premiers siècles du moyen âge* (Nancy, 1893), p. 137. See also Clark, *The Abbey*, p. 292: "After 760, Irish influence no longer predominated at St. Gall."

16. See Theodor Mayer, "Konstanz und St. Gallen in der Frühzeit," *Schweizerische Zeitschrift für Geschichte* 2 (1952), 516.

Pippin to temporary exile there, and Notker Balbulus explained the choice by saying that it was at the time "among the poorest and most austere of all places in the far-flung empire."[17] St. Gall developed more slowly than some other monasteries—more slowly, for example, than its nearest neighbor and natural competitor, the island monastery of Reichenau.

On 3 June 818 Louis the Pious granted the abbey a privilege of immunity, thereby releasing it from the bishopric. Additional concessions followed. On 19 October 833 Louis the German gave it the right to select its own abbot.[18] St. Gall was now free of the bishop and confident that it would be supported by the monarchy.

The abbacy of Gozbert (816–837) inaugurated a flowering of monastic culture. Led by such noted abbots as Gozbert, Grimald (841–872), Hartmut (872–883), and Solomon III (890–919), St. Gall advanced quickly. By 830 a major reorganization of buildings and grounds was under way. In the scriptorium books were copied and illuminated at a brisk pace.[19] The stock of the library burgeoned. St. Gall acquired considerable holdings of land, and its economic presence was felt throughout a large area.[20] The list of monasteries in Switzerland, Germany, France, and Italy with which it entered into prayer confraternities testifies to its wide-ranging influence.[21]

In the spring of 926, when the Hungarians invaded Bavaria and Swabia and threatened the monastery, Abbot Engelbert (925–933) sent the library to Reichenau for safekeeping. When the books were returned, some at St. Gall claimed that inferior volumes had been substituted for those originally sent.[22] On 25 April 937 an angry student set fire to the library, and more books were lost. A measure of order was restored by Abbot Burkhard II (1001–1022), whose enthusiasm for scholarly pursuits dated back to his youthful days on the Hohentwiel with Duchess Hadwig. Burkhard added many volumes to the library. Under his patronage, various

---

17. *Gesta Karoli* 2.12. Thorpe, *Einhard and Notker the Stammerer*, p. 155.

18. Rudolf Pfister, *Kirchengeschichte der Schweiz* (Zurich, 1964), 1:77–78.

19. Lesne reviews the history of the scriptorium in *Les livres*, pp. 300–317, and the history of the library in *Les livres*, pp. 736–760.

20. See Ammann and Schib, *Historischer Atlas der Schweiz*, No. 15 ("Der Grundbesitz des Klosters St. Gallen um 920").

21. St. Gall was affiliated with some twenty-seven institutions: *Coenobia cum monasterio sangallensi fraternitate coniuncta*, ed. P. Piper (1884), MGH Libri confraternitatum S. Galli, Augienses, Fabarienses, p. 144. See also F. Perret, "Von der vornehmen Bedeutung des Stiftsarchivs St. Gallen," in *Gallus-Stadt 1971: Jahrbuch der Stadt St. Gallen* (St. Gall, 1971), p. 86.

22. Ekkehard IV, *Casus* 3.

texts, including the Bible and the Latin Aristotle, were translated into German. Burkhard's death, however, brought an end to the flourishing of St. Gall.

The incidents of its later history make up a sad chronicle. The plague that killed Burkhard killed many other monks. The Cluniac reforms led to conflict. The St. Gall monks resisted the changes and were compelled to accept an outsider as abbot, whose task it was to impose them. The abbacy of Norbert (1034–1072) was stressful and difficult. Political affairs also impinged upon the brothers. Rival parties in the Investiture Contest fought for the abbatial office, seizing the monastery's property and reducing the inmates to penury. The thirteenth, fourteenth, and fifteenth centuries were especially bleak: Abbot Rumo of Ramstein (1274–1281), it is often observed, could not even write.[23] There were brighter periods in the centuries that followed, but the monastery never regained its early brilliance. The abbey of St. Gall survived until 1805, when it was dissolved by the order of Napoleon.

The abbacies from Gozbert to Burkhard II (816–1022) mark the years of St. Gall's flowering and form the boundaries of my study. For some two hundred years the monks created and enjoyed a brilliant culture. Their abbey was "the first seat of humane culture in Switzerland."[24] St. Gall, along with Fulda, Tours, and Fleury, was instrumental in the transmission of classical learning north of the Alps.[25] Even its schoolboys contributed to its reputation. It was a matter of pride at the school that the children were fluent in Latin. Under the regime of one especially effective teacher, commented Ekkehard IV, all but the feeblest boys preferred to converse in Latin rather than in the Frankish tongue.[26]

The library was the essential resource of the monastery's scholars. In the early years, a chronicler complained, there was "a great scarcity of books in our place."[27] But during the ninth century the library grew rapidly. It was well ordered and well administered, acquiring books on a regular basis from the monastery's own scriptorium and from its patrons. A series of medieval catalogues gives evidence of its development and

23. Ildefons von Arx, *Geschichten des Kantons St. Gallen*, 3 vols. (St. Gall, 1810–1813), 1:471.
24. Clark, *The Abbey*, p. 291.
25. Ibid., p. 289.
26. *Casus* 89. The statement is probably an exaggeration; see Lesne, *Les écoles*, pp. 525–526. Ekkehard gives other references to the knowledge of Latin at St. Gall in *Casus* 36 and 80.
27. Ratpert, *Casus S. Galli* 6, ed. Ildefons von Arx (1829), MGH SS 2:66.

composition.[28]

The first catalogue, drawn up in the mid-ninth century, listed about four hundred volumes. Thirty were identified as *LIBRI SCOTTICE SCRIPTI* ("books written in Irish hands") and constituted a separate category. The greater part of the catalogue was entitled *BREVIARIUM LIBRORUM DE COENOBIO SANCTI GALLI* . . . ("summary of books from the monastery of St. Gall . . ."). The texts listed here were varied. There were the customary biblical, exegetical, and theological writings, as well as lives of the saints and collections of laws, Christian poetry, and some Latin classics and grammars. A second catalogue contained books specifically acquired under Abbot Grimald, and a third, books commissioned by Hartmut. The private libraries of the two abbots, which entered the main library after their deaths, were registered in a fourth and fifth. The contents of the five oldest catalogues therefore overlapped.

A calendar of hagiographical texts extending from the ninth through the fifteenth centuries offers no information on the subject of Greek. The revised catalogue of 1461, however, reported that the Carolingian library was nearly intact, and this conclusion is significant. The books described by the medieval librarians can in many cases be identified with manuscripts in the Stiftsbibliothek today. Taken together, catalogues and extant manuscripts furnish a rare instance of what German scholars call "bibliotheksgeschichtliche Kontinuität," "continuity in library history." Although the library suffered losses, they seem to have been slight.[29]

Some damage was incurred in the early fifteenth century. The Councils of Constance and Basel brought many churchmen to the area. The prelates, it appears, fetched the books they needed from monasteries in the neighborhood rather than bringing them from home. Local chroniclers claimed that wagonloads and shiploads of books were removed from St. Gall, Reichenau, and other institutions around Lake Constance. Regional patriotism surely inflated the figures, but it is likely that some plundering did take place.[30]

---

28. The catalogues are edited by Paul Lehmann, *Mittelalterliche Bibliothekskataloge Deutschlands und der Schweiz* (Munich, 1918), 1:55 – 148. For their history, see Johannes Duft, "Die Handschriften-Katalogisierung in der Stiftsbibliothek St. Gallen vom 9. bis zum 19. Jahrhundert," in Beat Matthias von Scarpatetti, *Die Handschriften der Stiftsbibliothek St. Gallen: Codices 1726 – 1984 (14. – 19. Jahrhundert)* (St. Gall, 1983), pp. 9* – 26*.

29. Bruckner, *Scriptoria*, 3:43.

30. Lehmann, *Mittelalterliche Bibliothekskataloge*, 1:277, 400; and Lehmann, "Konstanz und Basel als Büchermärkte während der grossen Kirchenversammlungen," in *Erforschung des Mittelalters* (Stuttgart, 1959), 1:256.

Three Italians who visited St. Gall in 1416 and 1417 were responsible for more serious losses. Poggio Bracciolini, Cincius de Rusticis, and Bartholomeus de Montepolitiano came to search for classical manuscripts. They found (and removed) several priceless texts, including a complete copy of Quintilian's *De institutione oratoria*, of which they had previously known only fragments. The men portrayed themselves as liberators. "Countless books," wrote Cincius in his florid humanistic way, were kept in a tower "like captives." The library was "neglected and infested with dust, worms, soot, and all the things associated with the destruction of books." At the sight, "we all burst into tears, thinking that this was the way in which the Latin language had lost its greatest glory and distinction. Truly, if this library could speak for itself, it would cry loudly: 'You men who love the Latin tongue, let me not be utterly destroyed by this woeful neglect. Snatch me from this prison in whose gloom even the bright light of the books within cannot be seen.' There were in that monastery an abbot and monks totally devoid of any knowledge of literature. What barbarous hostility to the Latin tongue! What damned dregs of humanity!"[31]

The issue of the lost manuscripts is important, because it has consequences for the question of Greek at St. Gall. Local historians have sometimes suggested that the events of the fifteenth century did particular harm to the Greek collection of the library.[32] They reason that the prelates attending the church councils would have taken books that they could use in their deliberations, such as Greek Scriptures, acts of earlier councils, and works of the Eastern Fathers. In the same way, the Italian humanists, with their fondness for the classics, would have selected works of profane Greek literature. These scholars believe, therefore, that the medieval library contained many more Greek texts than is currently the case. Some of the older scholars imply also that the monks may have had copies of Homer, or Plato, or Aristotle.

There is little reason to accept the hypothesis. The Council of Constance lasted from 1414 to 1418; the Council of Basel, from 1431 through

31. "Cincius Romanus to his most learned teacher Franciscus de Fiana," in *Two Renaissance Book Hunters: The Letters of Poggius Bracciolini to Nicolaus de Niccolis*, trans. Phyllis W. G. Gordan (New York and London, 1974), pp. 188–189. See also Remigio Sabbadini, *Le Scoperte dei codici latini e greci ne' secoli XIV e XV*, 2 vols. (Florence, 1905–1914; new ed. Florence, 1967), 1:77–80.
32. Franz Weidmann, *Geschichte der Bibliothek von St. Gallen* (St. Gall, 1841), pp. 9, 37–38; J. B. Näf, "Die Bibliothek des ehemaligen Benediktinerstiftes St. Gallen," *Studien und Mitteilungen zur Geschichte des Benediktinerordens*, N.F. 1 (1911), 219–220; Clark, *The Abbey*, pp. 111, 277.

1449. Yet in 1461, a library catalogue reported that the ninth-century collection of books was nearly intact. Either the books taken by the members of the councils had formed a peripheral part of the Carolingian library and had not been catalogued, or they had been acquired some time after the copying of the last Carolingian catalogue—and after the end of our period. It is not likely that the bookhunters of the fifteenth century effected a massive removal of Greek books. I do not think that Greek texts have been lost in disproportionate numbers, or that the present library leaves us with a seriously imbalanced view of the range of medieval texts.

Who was it, in the medieval abbey, who might have read Greek books? St. Gall tradition informs us of several individuals whose names have been brought into connection with the study of Greek. Perhaps Notker Balbulus referred to them collectively when, in a letter to a monk named Lantpert, he extended greetings from his "Hellenic brothers": "Salutant te ellinici fratres."[33] Notker's teasing words have given modern scholars merry chase. The identity of the *ellinici fratres* seems to be the sort of puzzle to which everyone wishes to find a solution. Some scholars have seen in the "ellinici fratres" monks of Greek origin, either Byzantines or Italo-Greeks, visiting or living in St. Gall. Other scholars think that the *fratres* were simply resident Latin monks with an interest in Greek. Still others distinguish between two groups of Latins, the local Alemannic brothers and the Irish.[34]

33. St. Gall, Stiftsbibliothek MS 381, p. 9. The text of the letter, which contains an explanation of forms of musical notation, has been printed often. See Anselm Schubiger, *Die Sängerschule St. Gallens vom 8. bis ins 12. Jahrhundert* (Einsiedeln and New York, 1858), p. 10, and, most recently, Rombaut van Doren, *Etude sur l'influence musicale de l'abbaye de Saint-Gall* (Brussels, 1925), pp. 105–113. Van Doren believes that both the attribution of the letter to Notker and the final greeting with its reference to the "ellinici fratres" were gratuitous additions of St. Gall scribes. But Notker's authorship of the entire text is upheld by Wolfram von den Steinen, *Notker der Dichter und seine geistige Welt* (Bern, 1948), 1:495. M. L. W. Laistner, *Thought and Letters in Western Europe, A.D. 500 to 900*, 2nd ed. (London, 1957), p. 243, n. 3, agrees with von den Steinen. MS 381, "das sanktgallische Dichterbuch," is one of the most important of the St. Gall manuscripts containing Greek liturgical material. See H. Husmann, *Tropen- und Sequenzenhandschriften* (Munich and Duisburg, 1964), pp. 42–44, and my discussion in Chapter 8 below for a fuller evaluation.

34. The authors surveyed in the following sample have for the most part couched their opinions in terms of probability, as befits the slender nature of the evidence. Monks of Greek origin: Peter Wagner, *Einführung in die gregorianischen Melodien* (Leipzig, 1912), 2:234; Maïeul Cappuyns, *Jean Scot Erigène: Sa vie, son oeuvre, sa pensée* (Paris, 1933), p. 131, n. 2. Italo-Greeks: C. P. Caspari, *Ungedruckte, unbeachtete und wenig beachtete Quellen zur Geschichte des Taufsymbols und der Glaubensregel* (Kristianstad, 1875; repr.

What is the evidence for Greek monks? St. Gall lay on a route frequently used by legates traveling between Constantinople and the western courts.[35] But Byzantine visitors have left only faint traces in the manuscripts. Indirect testimony to the presence of a Byzantine may be found in the bilingual Greek-Latin litany of the Bamberg Psalter copied at St. Gall in A.D. 909. The litany describes the emperor Louis the Child (d. 911) as "ΤΟΝ ΚΥΡΙΝ ΛΟΥΔΟΒΙΚΟ ΡΙΓΑ, domnum hludouuicum rege[m]," or as King Louis, not as βασιλέα, or Emperor Louis. In the withholding of the imperial title from Louis, Richard Drögereit sees the hand of a Byzantine or of some other person insisting upon the prerogative of the East Roman ruler.[36] Another Byzantine may have transcribed the pair of Greek alphabets, majuscule and minuscule, contained in a twelfth-century codex.[37] A greater number of Greeks came to nearby Reichenau, and among them Methodius, apostle to the Slavs, but they do not appear to have fostered the study of Greek.[38]

There is more to be learned about the Frankish monks. The chroniclers

Brussels, 1964), 3:214, 275; Agostino Pertusi, "Bisanzio e l'irradiazione della sua civiltà in Occidente nell'alto medioevo," in *Centri e vie di irradiazione della civiltà nell'alto medioevo*, Settimane di Studio del Centro italiano di Studi sull'alto Medioevo 11 (Spoleto, 1964), p. 130. Byzantines: Etienne Delaruelle, "La connaissance du grec en occident du Ve au IXe siècle," *Mélanges de la Société toulousaine d'études classiques* 1 (1946), 221; Paul Lemerle, *Le premier humanisme byzantin: Notes et remarques sur enseignement et culture à Byzance des origines au Xe siècle* (Paris, 1971), p. 16, n. 22. Latin monks: Von Arx, *Geschichten*, 1:284; Näf, "Die Bibliothek," p. 210 (whose comment, however, that the *fratres* constituted an independent association intended to promote the study of Greek, is a bit ponderous); Otto Ursprung, "Alte griechische Einflüsse und neuer gräzistischer Einschlag in der mittelalterlichen Musik," *Zeitschrift für Musikwissenschaft* 12 (1930), 205; Paul Cagin, *L'euchologie latine, étudiée dans la tradition de ses formules et de ses formulaires, 1: Te Deum ou Illatio? Contribution à l'histoire de l'euchologie latine à propos des origines du Te Deum*, Scriptorium Solesmense 1.1 (Solesmes, 1906), pp. 159, 566. Clark, *The Abbey*, p. 111: They were "the Irish monks of St. Gall and their Swabian pupils." Hermann Josef Frede, *Altlateinische Paulus-Handschriften*, Vetus Latina: Aus der Geschichte der lateinischen Bibel 4 (Freiburg, 1964), p. 78, conversely, refers the phrase to the Alemannic monks.

35. Werner Ohnsorge, "Byzanz und das Abendland im neunten und zehnten Jahrhundert: Zur Entwicklung des Kaiserbegriffes und der Staatsideologie," *Saeculum* 5 (1954), 212–213.

36. Bamberg, Staatsbibliothek Msc. Bibl. 44 (A.I.14), fol. 166v, in ed. Cagin, *L'euchologie latine*, 1:545. See R. Drögereit, "Griechisch-Byzantinisches aus Essen," *Byzantinische Zeitschrift* 46 (1953), 114, n. 2. The manuscript is discussed more fully in Chapter 7 below.

37. St. Gall, Stiftsbibliothek MS 18, p. 4. See Appendix 1, below, p. 117, for a description of the manuscript.

38. On the Greeks at Reichenau, see Berschin, *Griechisch-lateinisches Mittelalter*, p. 182.

described the teachers and pupils of the monastery school in fond and attentive detail. Iso (d. 871), whom Ekkehard IV called "the most learned monk of St. Gall," taught the friends Notker Balbulus, Tuotilo, and Ratpert. Iso's mother, in the course of her pregnancy, dreamed that she had given birth to a hedgehog, whose quills were plucked off by little boys and used to scribble on the walls.[39] Her son became a celebrated teacher. There is a suggestion that he may have occupied himself with Greek. Iso's name is written in Greek letters in the margins of a bilingual Bible. The name appears twice on a single page: "ΓΥϹѠ" and "ΓΙϹѠ."[40] It is written alongside a text of the Pauline Epistles. The first quotation is 1 Cor. 12.28, "In the Church, God has given ... the third [place] to teachers ... helpers, good leaders, those with many languages ..."; the second, 1 Cor. 12.30, "Do all speak strange languages, and all interpret them?" Iso is not likely to have placed his own name alongside such verses. The gesture is more likely to have come from a former pupil. As real evidence for a knowledge of Greek, of course, it is inconclusive.

While a guest at St. Gall, Ermenrich of Ellwangen (ca. 814–874) wrote a learned epistle in honor of Abbot Grimald. He treated grammatical and theological questions at length, and he also displayed a bit of Greek. If anyone criticized his work, he told Grimald, the abbot was to set this Greek puzzle before him:

> Hoc ipse exponat posco problema tibi:
>
> *vinum   butyrum   bibe   lac   oleum*
> Oenon paleon   pimelin gallan   eleon,
>
> Et non miraris dulcia nosse tua.
>
> *Novum   vide   loquor   verbum   move   sorbeo   prandium*
> Neon   ide   lalo   rema   sison   ripho   ariston,
>
> Vescere quis poteris tuque poeta tuis.
>
> *curator   sapiens   sufflat   studium   mortuus*
> Phrontistes phronimos phisa   philoponia nechros,
>
> Hoc fecit Christus primus in orbe deus.

---

39. This is at least the story told about her: Ekkehard IV, *Casus* 31.

40. Dresden, Sächsische Landesbibliothek, MS A.145b, fol. 34v. The name also appears in the margin of the "Bern Horace" (Bern, Burgerbibliothek MS 363); see Frede, *Paulus-Handschriften*, pp. 66, 78. Frede thinks it possible that Iso was responsible for the bilingual text of St. Gall, Stiftsbibliothek MS 17. On both St. Gall manuscripts see my discussion in Chapter 7.

In the manuscript, the Latin solutions (here italicized) were written in the margin.[41] They were terms, one suspects, that had been skillfully transposed from bilingual word lists.

Notker Balbulus (ca. 840–912) is famed as a religious poet and especially as the author of some forty liturgical poems known as sequences. Greek words appear in them, for example, "hypodiaconissa," "cenodoxia," "theotocon," "theophania," and "spermologos." The Greek vocabulary does not necessarily indicate a mastery of the language, for Notker could have found the words in glossaries. Only one of them, "spermologos," was not a conventional glossary term, and Notker probably took it from Bede's commentary on the Acts of the Apostles.[42]

Notker's fabulous history of Charles the Great, the *Gesta Karoli*, reports on some diplomatic exchanges with the Byzantine Empire. Like Liudprand of Cremona, Notker is concerned to point out examples of Byzantine fatuity and duplicity. In the famous incident of the turned fish, Charles's ambassador converts a breach of etiquette at an imperial dinner party into a moral triumph. "The empty-headed sons of Hellas," comments Notker, "were beaten in their own land, and the clever Frank who had worsted them came back home safe and sound."[43]

His attitude toward Greek Scripture was more respectful. According to Ekkehard IV, Notker copied the seven Catholic Epistles in Greek, only to have them destroyed by a malicious prankster:

> In the end an unfortunate incident occurred, which touched with pain his innermost heart. With a great deal of difficulty [*multis sudoribus*], he had copied the Greek canonical Epistles that had been requested from Liutward, the bishop of Vercelli. And see, Sindolf, who, as we have said, had already grown great and powerful in the monastery, by chance came upon the delicately written volume and stole it. He cut out the single gatherings with a knife, as can be seen today, and tore them up and disfigured them. Then he folded them back up and put them back in the place from which he had stolen them.[44]

41. St. Gall, Stiftsbibliothek MS 265, p. 72. Ermenrich, *Epistola ad Grimaldum abbatem*, ed. Ernst Dümmler (1899) MGH Epp 5:569, and see MGH Poet 3:701.
42. Laistner, *Thought and Letters*, p. 243, corrects some of the earlier exaggerated estimations of the Greek vocabulary in Notker's religious verse and identifies the source of *spermologos*.
43. *Gesta Karoli* 2.6. Trans. Thorpe, *Einhard and Notker the Stammerer*, pp. 139–140. And see J. Schneider, "Die Geschichte vom gewendeten Fisch," in *Festschrift Bernhard Bischoff* (Stuttgart, 1971), pp. 218–225.
44. *Casus* 46. The canonical, or Catholic, Epistles to which Ekkehard refers are seven New Testament letters not written by Paul.

In the same serious vein, Notker wrote to Solomon III, bishop of Constance, asking him to order someone proficient in both Latin and Greek to translate Origen's commentary on the Song of Songs. While some historians have concluded from this that Notker did not know the language, others observe that the aging Notker added simply that "morte praeventus" he would not be able to complete the translation himself.[45] Once again, the references given by the literary records of St. Gall are inconclusive. Certainly, Notker Balbulus had an active interest in the subject.

The manuscript that contains Notker's letter to Lantpert also has five poems by Hartmann of St. Gall (fl. 883). Like Notker, Hartmann made use of Greek in his liturgical verse, as in the conclusion of the fifth poem in the series:

> Agne dei patris qui mundi crimina tollis
> Optatae pacis munera dona tuis
> KYPPIE pantocrator ysos sodisse te pantes
> Su basyleos ymon XPICTE eleyson ymas.[46]

In the eleventh century, Ekkehard IV imitated the lines in his *Liber benedictionum*.[47]

Notker's friend Tuotilo was a man of many gifts—a poet, musician, sculptor, architect, and (something that particularly impressed his fellow monks) a formidable athlete. Ekkehard IV described another achievement: "concinnandi in utraque lingua potens" ("he could make verses in both languages").[48] Does this mean that Tuotilo composed in Latin and Greek, or that he composed in Latin and German?

In classical usage, the phrase *utriusque linguae peritus* (and its near variants) had signified a knowledge of Latin and Greek. It was used in precisely the same way that writers employed other doublets: *uterque parens*, *uterque sexus*, or (in a Christian context) *utrumque Testamentum*. Such medieval authors as Cassiodorus, Bede, John Scottus, and Anastasius Bibliothecarius continued to use the phrase in this exclusive sense.

---

45. *Notatio*, ed. E. Dümmler, *Das Formelbuch des Bischofs Salomo III von Konstanz* (Leipzig, 1857; repr. Osnabrück, 1964), p. 66. See also Clark, *The Abbey*, p. 109.

46. St. Gall, Stiftsbibliothek MS 381, p. 35. The text is printed by P. von Winterfeld, MGH Poet 4:321, and M. Dreves, *Analecta hymnica medii aevi* 50 (Leipzig, 1907), p. 255. The poet Hartmann should not be confused with the abbot of the same name (ca. 920–924); see von den Steinen, *Notker der Dichter*, 1:526.

47. *Liber benedictionum* 32.52; see Bischoff, "Das griechische Element," p. 269, and Berschin, *Griechisch-lateinisches Mittelalter*, p. 191, n. 93.

48. *Casus* 34.

By Ekkehard's time, it had become an almost formulaic description of proficiency in the literary languages. Writers who wished to indicate a fluency in Latin and the local idiom were careful to specify the vernacular, as *theodisca, celtica,* or *romanica.*[49] It is possible, then, that Tuotilo's verses "in utraque lingua" were in Latin and Greek.

Notker's former pupil, Solomon III, bishop of Constance (890–920), is sometimes credited with a knowledge of Greek. He commissioned the Bamberg Psalter from St. Gall. The manuscript represents one of the monastery's most original contributions to scholarship in the Middle Ages, for it was the first quadripartite Psalter. The tripartite Psalters of Carolingian times presented the three versions of St. Jerome (*Psalterium gallicanum, Psalterium romanum,* and *Psalterium iuxta Hebraeos*) in adjacent columns. To these three texts Solomon added a fourth, the Greek Septuagint (given in Latin letters). The new arrangement was influential, and copies and imitations of the Bamberg Psalter soon were made elsewhere.[50]

The unfortunately named Notker Labeo (ca. 950–1022) is chiefly known for his translations from Latin into Old High German, but he dabbled in Greek as well. In translating Boethius's *De consolatione philosophiae,* he encountered a quotation from Homer (*Il.* 12.176): "ἀργαλέον δέ με ταῦτα θεὸν ὣς πάντ' ἀγορεῦσαι" ("and it is difficult for me, as though I were a god, to tell of all these things"). He transcribed it into Latin: "Argalthon deme tauta theonos pant agopun" and translated it into Old High German: "Ter máhtigo gót téta îo in uuerlte, al daz er uuolta" ("Almighty God ever did in the world everything that He would").[51]

Two Ekkehards left traces of Greek in their work. Ekkehard I (ca. 910–973) composed a small body of hymns and sequences. One of the

49. Maurice Coens, "'Utriusque linguae peritus': En marge d'un prologue de Thierry de Saint-Trond," *Analecta bollandiana* 76 (1958), 118–150. In the *Notatio,* however, Notker Balbulus specified Latin and Greek: "alicuius hominis latina et greca lingua eruditi." D. A. Bullough, "The Educational Tradition in England from Alfred to Aelfric: Teaching *Utriusque Linguae,*" in *La Scuola nell'Occidente latino,* 19.2:453–494, points to English examples in which the phrase *utriusque linguae* signifies "the two languages Latin and 'Saxon' (Old English)."

50. On the plan and influence of the Psalter, see below, Chapter 7. On Solomon's knowledge of Greek, Clark, *The Abbey,* p. 111, and Frede, *Paulus-Handschriften,* p. 78, give generous appraisals.

51. The example is cited by Clark, *The Abbey,* p. 113. For a reinterpretation of Notker's treatment of his sources, see Jerold C. Frakes, "Griechisches im frühmittelalterlichen St. Gallen: Ein methodologischer Beitrag zu Notker Labeos Griechischkenntnissen," *Zeitschrift für deutsche Philologie* 106 (1987), 25–34.

characteristic features of his style is the attempt to weave Greek words in among the Latin and decline them so that they fit in syntactically with the rest, for example, "agio pneumati se vas exhibuit"; "physin per fidem superans"; "partenu casta genitum"; "Odon ad antropon/corda parat deo"; "pneumati to agio/nitidum vas exhibet et electum."[52]

Ekkehard IV (ca. 980–1060) also introduced Greek words into his verses. His use of them was derivative. He imitated the conclusion of Hartmann's processional hymn or he relied upon a conventional liturgical vocabulary, as in the lines,

> *omnicreator   noster   tu rex   miserere.*
> Pantocrator   imon   su basileos eleison.

Elsewhere he gave words in the three sacred languages, according to the Irish custom:

> *grece neutrum.Ebraice femininum.latine masculinum.in uirtute pari uiget.*[53]
> Pneuma Ruha Flatus. Viget omnigenis vocitatus.

In the *Casus S. Galli* Ekkehard told the story of Duchess Hadwig and the Greek lessons she gave to Burkhard when he was a pupil in the monastery school. According to Ekkehard Hadwig had been engaged to a "Greek King Constantine," who had sent eunuchs to Germany to prepare her for life in Constantinople. One of them taught her excellent Greek. Another had been asked to paint her portrait for the king. The painter had little success, for Hadwig, displeased by the marriage, so contorted her face that a revolting likeness was produced, and Constantine refused to accept her as his bride.

Some years later Burkhard's teacher took him to visit Hadwig in her residence on the Hohentwiel. She was charmed by the boy's pretty manners and his flair for making extempore verse ("Esse velim Grecus, cum sim vix, domna, Latinus"). She taught him to sing an antiphon, *Maria et flumina*, which, in her own fashion, she had translated into Greek: "Thalassi ke potami, eulogi ton kyrion;/Ymnite pigon ton kyrion

---

52. Ed. von den Steinen, *Notker der Dichter*, 2:115–118, 130, 134. See Berschin, *Griechisch-lateinisches Mittelalter*, pp. 179, 212.

53. The two examples cited above are *Liber benedictionum* 5.9 and 26.26. For a full discussion of Ekkehard IV's Greek vocabulary, see J. Egli, *Der Liber Benedictionum Ekkehards IV. nebst den kleineren Dichtungen aus dem Codex Sangallensis 393* (St. Gall, 1909), pp. xxxvi ff.

alleluja" ("Ye oceans and rivers, praise the Lord/Extol the Lord, ye waters. Alleluia"). Thereafter, said Ekkehard, Hadwig often invited Burkhard "to hear his extempore verses, to teach him to speak Greek, and to lock him in her heart."[54]

In fact, Hadwig (d. 994) was the daughter of Henry, duke of Bavaria, and niece of Otto I. A marriage to a "Greek King Constantine" was not a realistic prospect, for Constantine VII had been married to Helena, the daughter of Romanus Lecapenus, from 920 until his death in 959. Perhaps she was meant to become the second western wife of Constantine's son, the young emperor Romanus II. Or perhaps Ekkehard was simply inspired by the example of the Byzantine marriage of Otto II. In any case, Hadwig eventually married Burkhard III, duke of Swabia.

She figured in the history of the region as a learned woman, "a brilliant Minerva." Hadwig was devoted to Latin learning and the reading of Latin poetry. But what of Greek? We have only Ekkehard's story. He tells us that Hadwig herself had translated *Maria et flumina*, but the Greek-Latin text could be found in more than one book in the monastery library. Bilingual Psalters commonly included the Canticles, and "ΕΥΛΟΓΕΙΤΕ ΘΑΛΑCCΑΙ ΚΑΙ ΠΟΤΑΜΟΙ" appears in the "Hymn of the Three Youths" (Dan. 3.77–78).[55]

The Frankish monks and their friends, seen in the reflection of their chronicles, poems, and letters, are attractive figures. Notker's *Gesta Karoli* and Ekkehard IV's *Casus S. Galli* are replete with references to things Greek, whether ancient or contemporary. The verses of Notker, Hartmann, and the Ekkehards—like much religious poetry of the tenth and eleventh centuries—suggest a taste for the foreignness, the strangeness of a Greek vocabulary. Solomon III's quadripartite Psalter and, perhaps, Notker's copying of the Catholic Epistles demonstrate a more scholarly approach to the language. There is no sign, however, that any of them did any significant or independent translation from the Greek.

---

54. Ekkehard IV, *Casus* 90 (on the Byzantine betrothal) and 94 (on Burkhard's Greek lessons). For helpful notes to these passages, see Bruno Helbling, trans., *Die Geschichten des Klosters St. Gallen* (Graz, 1958), pp. 162–163, 170ff. Hadwig's translation was defective. The antiphon *Maria et flumina* is printed by René Jean Hesbert, *Corpus antiphonalium officii*, 6 vols. (Rome, 1963–1979), 3:No. 3700: "Θάλασσαι καὶ ποταμοὶ, εὐλογεῖτε τὸν Κύριον, ὑμνεῖτε πηγαὶ τὸν Κύριον. Ἀλληλούϊα."

55. On Hadwig, see Marie-Louise Portmann, *Die Darstellung der Frau in der Geschichtsschreibung des früheren Mittelalters*, Basler Beiträge zur Geschichtswissenschaft 69 (Basel and Stuttgart, 1958), pp. 128–130. Joseph Viktor von Scheffel's historical novel *Ekkehard* (Berlin, 1855) gives a romanticized account of her life.

Irish scholars also worked at St. Gall, and the two whose names have been most inextricably linked with the study of Greek are Marcus and Moengal-Marcellus. In about the year 850 a bishop Marcus, his nephew Moengal, and a company of fellow Irishmen embarked upon a pilgrimage to Rome. On their return journey they stopped to visit the grave of St. Gall. Ekkehard IV described their arrival in the monastery and reported that the monks urged them to stay. The men agreed, though the decision was not easily reached, for most of the party wished to continue. Marcus, Moengal, and a few servants remained behind. To those who traveled on Marcus gave his money and his mules; he kept "for himself and for St. Gall" his books, gold, and vestments.[56]

Moengal became known locally as Marcellus, the diminutive of his uncle's name. (The Celtic original may have been difficult for the monks to pronounce.) From 853 to 865 he directed the abbey's inner school, and, like Iso, he taught Notker Balbulus, Tuotilo, and Ratpert.[57] Moengal-Marcellus died in 871.

Ekkehard did not say that the Irishmen knew Greek or that they possessed Greek books. Nevertheless, they were responsible for planning and copying a set of three bilingual Scriptures: Gospels, Pauline Epistles, and Psalter.[58] Many details of their composition remain unclear, but it is certain that the manuscripts were written at St. Gall or brought to St. Gall by Marcus, Moengal-Marcellus, or by members of their immediate circle.

Was it the Irish, then, who were the "ellinici fratres"? Since the time of Ludwig Traube, Irishmen on the Continent have been regarded as the preeminent Greek scholars.[59] Although Traube's "Irish hypothesis" has in some respects been modified, it continues to be generally accepted: "In the ninth century," observes Bernhard Bischoff, "it was Irish scholars in the Frankish Empire who devoted themselves most eagerly to genuine studies of Greek, and who collected the resources for it."[60]

---

56. Ekkehard IV, *Casus* 2.

57. Ekkehard IV, *Casus* 33, 34.

58. The St. Gall Interlinear Gospels (St. Gall, Stiftsbibliothek MS 48), the *Codex boernerianus* (Dresden, Sächsische Landesbibliothek A.145b), and the Basel Psalter (Basel, Universitätsbibliothek A.VII.3). For a full discussion, see Chapter 7.

59. Ludwig Traube, "*O Roma nobilis*: Philologische Untersuchungen aus dem Mittelalter," *Abhandlungen der philosophisch-philologischen Classe der königlichen bayerischen Akademie der Wissenschaften* 19.2 (1892), 354: "Wer in den Tagen Karl's des Kahlen Griechisch auf dem Kontinent kann, ist ein Ire, oder zuversichtlich: es ist ihm die Kenntnis durch einen Iren vermittelt worden, oder das Gerücht, das ihm mit diesem Ruhm umgibt, ist Schwindel." For a review of the issue, see Berschin, *Griechisch-lateinisches Mittelalter*, pp. 121–124, 163.

60. "Das griechische Element," p. 251.

The case of Greek scholarship at St. Gall, however, calls for some circumspection. Because the monastery was founded by an Irish saint, the tendency to ascribe many of its later achievements to other Irishmen is very great. Yet when Johannes Duft examined the role of the Irish monks in the intellectual life of the monastery generally, he came to a conclusion that surprised him. The expectations that had been raised by favorable assessments of Irish activity in the early Middle Ages overall were not matched by the corresponding sources at St. Gall. "[The sources themselves], paradoxically . . . have scarcely been examined. Therefore entire 'genealogical trees' of errors and inaccuracies sprang up, copied from one scholar by the next . . . without even a single glance cast at the original sources. . . . Questions concerning the early medieval Irish missions have been approached, not objectively, but on the basis of preconceived opinions. . . ." In fact, he continued, "the general overestimation of the Irish influence seems to have completely suppressed the basic question of whether this influence—despite the relatively scanty evidence for it— really was so intense and widespread."[61]

Duft investigated, for example, the issue of the Irish books. In the middle of the ninth century, the library catalogue had tallied thirty "libri scottice scripti," but the books appear to have been either lost or ignored. When the catalogue was transcribed at the end of the century, their titles were omitted. From the first, the "libri scottice scripti" had represented an essentially alien deposit within the main collection of the library. The books were of no practical use to the Frankish monks. They found the insular writing hard to read, and the texts of Scriptures and liturgies were not the same as those in current use. "The influence of these books," concluded Duft, "was very small. They neither acted upon the indigenous script and illumination in any significant way, nor did their contents shape the culture of St. Gall."[62]

The abbey library today possesses fifteen volumes and fragments of Irish origin.[63] Few of the texts can be identified with the "libri scottice scripti." Indeed, most of them appear to have been simply left behind by various visitors of the ninth through the twelfth centuries.

---

61. "Iromanie—Irophobie," *Zeitschrift für schweizerische Kirchengeschichte* 50 (1956), 241–242, 245. Duft reviews the evidence from another perspective in "Irische Handschriftenüberlieferung in St. Gallen," in *Die Iren und Europa im früheren Mittelalter*, ed. Heinz Löwe (Stuttgart, 1982), 2:916–937.

62. "Iromanie—Irophobie," p. 261, and see Duft and Meyer, *The Irish Miniatures*, pp. 40–43.

63. Listed in Duft and Meyer, *The Irish Miniatures*, p. 66, and see pp. 13, 43.

Of course, Irish scribes might learn to copy books in continental hands, and Irishmen taught in the school. They contributed to the intellectual well-being of the monastery. But the surprisingly limited influence of the "libri scottice scripti" suggests that in other areas as well it might be advisable to exercise restraint before assuming the importance of Irish influence at St. Gall.

It is undeniable that Irishmen such as John Scottus Eriugena and Martin Hiberniensis were among the leading authorities on Greek in the Frankish Empire. But continental scholars also participated actively in the study of the language, and it would not do to neglect their efforts.

Who, then, were the *"ellinici fratres"*? Notker's greeting to Lantpert offers little information, for he extended it in a playful spirit. The *fratres* may have included his teachers Iso and Moengal-Marcellus, friends and colleagues such as Hartmann and Tuotilo, and pupils like Solomon III. The phrase probably referred, casually, to all who were interested in Greek and dabbled in it. The study of Greek at St. Gall was a collective enterprise. It was not dominated by a single brilliant figure in the way that John Scottus presided over the court of Charles the Bald. Nor were Greek studies directed by a prominent teacher, as was the case with Martin Hiberniensis in the cathedral school of Laon. There were many at St. Gall who cared for Greek and occupied themselves with it. They found there a climate hospitable to their interest. For evidence of their accomplishments, we must turn to the manuscripts themselves.

III

Transcription and Orthography

The Greek texts surveyed in the following pages are distinctive in both form and content. Indeed, as paleographical and philological documents, they are quite unusual. Few western scribes were accustomed to write in Greek. They were not trained in the conventions of the Byzantine scriptoria, and their own scribal traditions did little to prepare them for the copying of an unfamiliar language. They wrote, as it were, within the interstices of two cultures, and it is no wonder that to many modern readers the medieval Greek hands appear somewhat peculiar.

The St. Gall texts were copied over a span of two centuries, and many scribes took part. In some cases, as with the Irish Scriptures, they were copied skillfully and reveal an individual and pleasing aesthetic. In other cases, as in some of the briefer glossaries, the transcription was less fluent. The texts present a number of variations, and their relevant features will be summarized in later chapters. I wish to offer here some general observations on the script and language of the collection as a whole.

The western scribes of Antiquity were often as skilled in the copying of Greek as they were in Latin. It is sometimes difficult to distinguish between Greek texts copied in Italy and those copied in Constantinople. As late as the sixth and seventh centuries Greek characters used for Latin words in texts from Ravenna and Naples show no sign of their western origin.[1] With the spread of Frankish rule north of the Alps, however, this facility was lost. Gregory of Tours provides an illustration of the break in continuity. King Chilperic (d. 584), he reports, attempted to reform the Latin alphabet through the addition of several Greek characters. He equated the Greek letter "Θ" with the Latin phoneme "w"; the letter "Ψ" with the phoneme "ae"; "Z" with "the"; and "Δ" with "uui."[2] When, in the ninth century, western scribes were once again called upon to copy Greek, they had few points of reference. And so they began anew.

---

1. Viktor Gardthausen, *Griechische Palaeographie*, 2nd ed. (Leipzig, 1913; repr. Leiden, 1979), 2:257–258.
2. Gregory of Tours, *Historia Francorum* 5.45, ed. B. Krusch (1937), MGH SSrerMer 1:237–238.

In St. Gall manuscripts of the ninth through the eleventh centuries, the Greek material is rendered in three ways. There are, in the first place, manuscripts in which the Greek text is written in Greek script, most often in a hand termed the "western majuscule." Texts written entirely in Greek script are usually accompanied by Latin translations, placed either between the lines of the Greek or in columns parallel to it. The bilingual Scriptures are the finest specimens of this kind.

Greek letters are used, in the second place, for Greek words contained in predominantly Latin texts. Such writers as Priscian, Donatus, and Jerome frequently employed Greek terminology, and their works give numerous examples of this use of Greek.[3] Scribes who copied such texts did not necessarily have prior experience with the language. If a scribe did not know the alphabet, he could hope only to reproduce the shapes of the letters from sight. As might be expected, in the course of repeated copying, Greek words often became distorted and lost their original sense.[4]

For many scribes, the attempt to achieve a graphic representation of the Greek words of the prototype was futile. What they produced was a kind of imitation Greek, in which the forms of the Greek letters approximated those of the Latin. Or they contrived a hybrid script, in which some Latin letters appeared among the Greek. At times the imitation Greek seems to have been valued for its decorative qualities. Walter Berschin refers to a "hypergraecizing" tendency among scribes who sought a foreign or exotic effect: Greek words might be made to look even "more Greek" by avoiding letters that were too much like the Latin.[5] St. Gall MS 7, p. 309, provides a good illustration: "Nolite tangere ΧΠΥСΘΥС" (for "Christus"). The imitation Greek script sometimes appears at St. Gall in the superscriptions of prayers or religious verses, and in incipits and explicits of Latin texts.

Greek material is presented, finally, in Latin transliteration. Latin letters were used in place of the Greek when it was the sound of the

---

3. The phenomenon is familiar to Latin paleographers. See Louis Havet, *Manuel de critique verbale appliquée aux textes latins* (Paris, 1911; repr. Rome, 1967), pp. 873–875, 1073–1076, 1138, 1379, and, for a special instance, Augustin Mansion, "Disparition graduelle des mots grecs dans des traductions médiévales d'Aristote," in *Mélanges Joseph de Ghellinck* (Louvain, 1951), 2:631–645.
4. Bischoff, "Das griechische Element," pp. 274–275, cites an amusing example of the progressive deterioration of the Delphic maxim "ΓΝΩΘΙ ΣΕΑΥΤΟΝ" in a series of Juvenal manuscripts.
5. *Griechisch-lateinisches Mittelalter*, p. 42. They preferred the "more Greek" letters Θ, H, Y, and ω to T, E, I, and O. The same impulse led to the substitution of Π for the Greek P: see Bischoff, "Das griechische Element," p. 256, n. 50.

words, rather than the sight of them, that was considered important. Transliterations are often found in texts intended for public performance. The bilingual liturgical books of the eleventh century regularly contained Greek prayers in Latin transliteration, for they were to be chanted or recited during the mass. Bilingual Scriptures might also include texts in Latin transliteration.[6]

The "western majuscule" was the hand characteristically used for Greek in the West throughout the Middle Ages. In Byzantium, majuscules had been replaced by minuscules toward the end of the eighth century,[7] but there is little reflection of this development in western sources.[8] And when western scribes copied passages containing both languages, they gave the Latin in minuscules and the Greek in majuscules. (This accounts for the mixed appearance of *Graecolatina* in medieval manuscripts.) Not until the Italian Renaissance did it become customary to use minuscules when transcribing Greek.

With certain exceptions, the letters have the usual majuscule forms. Medieval scribes did not know the forms "Σ" and "Ω," which had been out of use since the Augustan period; instead they wrote "C" and "ω." They usually wrote the letters "E" and "Ξ" as uncials: "Є" and "Ξ." They found a special form "Ͻ-C" for "M" and, less frequently, "Ͻ-" or "-C" for "N." Bernhard Bischoff refers to the letter as the characteristic "western M," while Walter Berschin prefers the name "siglum M."[9]

In texts copied in the western majuscule, divisions between the words are not always indicated, or not always correctly indicated; accentuation and aspiration are inconsistent or absent; and punctuation is erratic. There are few abbreviations and contractions. The *nomina sacra*, or "sacred

6. Alfred Rahlfs, *Septuaginta-Studien, 2: Der Text des Septuaginta-Psalters* (Göttingen, 1907), pp. 38–39, attempts a classification of the bilingual Psalters according to the type of script in which they were written.

7. According to Jean Irigoin, "Survie et renouveau de la littérature antique à Constantinople (IXe siècle)," *Cahiers de civilisation médiévale* 5 (1962), 288, minuscules had come into use at least by 790. See also Lemerle, *Le premier humanisme byzantin*, pp. 68–108, 121.

8. Occurrences of Greek minuscules in western manuscripts have been collected by Traube, MGH Poet 3:822; Bischoff, "Das griechische Element," pp. 254–255; and Berschin, "Drei griechische Majestas-Tituli in der Trier-Echternacher Buchmalerei," *Frühmittelalterliche Studien* 14 (1980), 307 (a splendid example). To these I add the Greek minuscule equivalents given to the Hebrew alphabet in Zurich, Zentralbibliothek Z XIV 17, fol. 2 (twelfth century).

9. Bischoff, "Das griechische Element," pp. 253–254, n. 36. Berschin, "Griechisches bei den Iren," in *Die Iren und Europa im früheren Mittelalter*, ed. Heinz Löwe (Stuttgart, 1982), 1:504–505.

names," receive the abbreviations found in Greek Bibles, for example, "Θ͞C" for "Θεός," "K͞C" for "Κύριος," "I͞C" for "Ἰησοῦς," "X͞C" for "Χριστός," "Π͞NA" for "Πνεῦμα." Sometimes the endings of nouns and adjectives are contracted, as are the more common conjunctions. New abbreviations are not attempted, although the forms of the *nomina sacra* are sometimes adapted to fit the requirements of Latin syntax, for example, "X͞PI" for "Christi," "X͞PM" for "Christum."[10] It seems likely that the scribes, unused to writing in Greek and unsure of their skill in the language, were reluctant to take liberties with the prototypes.

Scribal errors hold considerable interest for modern scholars concerned with the pronunciation and evolution of the language. Since scribes copied from dictation as well as from written exemplars, it is possible to classify the errors accordingly. Some letters might be confused with one another because they seemed to sound alike, or because they were, in fact, pronounced alike:

Γ and Κ
Δ and Τ
Ι, ΕΙ, Η, ΟΙ, and Υ
Θ and Τ
Κ and Χ
Ξ and C
Ο and ⲱ
Π and Φ

Other letters might be confused because they seemed to look alike:

Α, Δ, and Λ
Γ and Τ
Ε and Η
Η and Ν
Θ, Ο, and C
Κ, ΙC, and C
ΛΛ, Μ, and Ν
Ο and ΟΥ
ΟC and ΟΥC
Π, Τ, ΤΙ, and ΤΤ

10. A. Cappelli, *Dizionario di abbreviature latine ed italiane*, 6th ed. from the 3rd ed. of 1929 (Milan, 1961), p. 402. See also Bischoff, *Paläographie des römischen Altertums und des abendländischen Mittelalters* (Berlin, 1979), pp. 194–195.

Misunderstandings like these are at the root of much of the poor spelling in western texts.

The explanation for many of the problems we have in reading these texts is simply that they were written by inexperienced scribes. In their hands the Greek letters took shape slowly and cautiously, with the result that a page of western majuscules seldom presents a graceful appearance. We see in each letter, remarked Viktor Gardthausen, "too much of its making."[11]

The language of the texts is interesting, for it reflects the changes Greek had undergone in the Hellenistic period and, to a lesser degree, in the Byzantine period. The influence of the Hellenistic Koine, or Common Greek, is most pronounced. Here a radical simplification of the vowel system, known as iotacization, took place. Briefly stated, the Greek vowel "η," or "eta," originally pronounced as a long "e" (in the "Erasmian," or etacistic, fashion), was given the sound value "i" (in the "Reuchlinian," or itacistic, manner). It was, in other words, pronounced as though it were identical to the letter "ι," or "iota." The process of iotacization extended the simplified pronunciation to other vowels and diphthongs. The sound values of "ει," "οι," "υ," and "υι" were, in effect, reduced to that of "ι." A similar reduction in pronunciation occurred when the diphthong "αι" received the sound value of the letter "ε"; and the long letter "ω" that of the short "o." The pronunciation of some consonants was also modified; the equation of "θ" with "τ" is perhaps the commonest example. It is not known precisely when these changes occurred, but most appear to have been complete by the end of the Hellenistic period.[12] Itacism is a marked feature of the St. Gall texts.

Reflections of later changes in the language are more difficult to determine. The manuscripts give occasional evidence of familiarity with contemporary Byzantine speech patterns. But much remains to be learned about the phonology and morphology of Byzantine Greek.[13] Scholars have

---

11. *Griechische Palaeographie*, 2:261.

12. On the phonology of Hellenistic Greek, see Friedrich Blass and Albert Debrunner, *Grammatik des neutestamentlichen Griechisch*, 15th ed. rev. by Friedrich Rehkopf (Göttingen, 1979), pp. 19–29. For a demonstration of orthographic variations in the papyrus texts (with further evidence for dating), see Sven-Tage Teodorsson, *The Phonology of Ptolemaic Koine* (Göteborg, Sweden, 1977), pp. 274–278.

13. See André Mirambel, "Pour une grammaire historique du grec médiéval: Problèmes et méthodes," in *Actes du XIIe congrès international des études byzantines* (Ochride, 1961), 2:391–403. A review of scholarship on the language is given by S. G. Kapsomenos, "Die griechische Sprache zwischen Koine und Neugriechisch," *Berichte zum XI. Internationalen Byzantinisten-Kongress* (Munich, 1958), pp. 1–39. For spelling in Byzantine

suggested that evidence for the pronunciation of Byzantine Greek may come from transliterations of Greek words into other languages—Latin, Hebrew, Arabic, Slavonic, and so on—as well as from Greek loan-words in these languages.[14] Perhaps the St. Gall sources will offer additional material for investigations of this kind.

Some degree of itacism seems to have suffused most Greek texts copied in medieval Europe, and idioms and orthographic variations associated with more recent developments in Byzantine Greek are also occasionally to be found. We should not, however, too readily attribute such features to direct influences from Byzantium. It would be rash to conclude, for instance, that Byzantine visitors were necessarily responsible for the appearance of itacistic variants in any particular text. Indirect transmission seems to have been more common. At St. Gall the Greek material transcribed by the monks was, for the most part, drawn from Scripture or from the school texts of late Antiquity, and very little of it came directly from the Eastern Empire.

manuscripts, see Stamatios B. Psaltes, *Grammatik der Byzantinischen Chroniken* (Göttingen, 1913), pp. 109–137.

14. See Robert Browning, *Medieval and Modern Greek* (London, 1969), p. 62. W. B. Stanford, *The Sound of Greek: Studies in the Greek Theory and Practice of Euphony,* Sather Classical Lectures 38 (Berkeley, 1967), pp. 122–135, makes a similar point with regard to the pronunciation of classical Greek. For exercises in the method, see Koder and Weber, *Liutprand von Cremona,* pp. 52–57, and Ilona Opelt, "Die Essener 'Missa Greca' der liturgischen Handschrift Düsseldorf D 2," *Jahrbuch der Österreichischen Byzantinischen Gesellschaft* 23 (1974), 84–87.

IV

Alphabets

The Greek alphabet was known throughout the Middle Ages, and, at least from the ninth to the eleventh or twelfth centuries, it was the common property of educated persons. When a scholar of the late tenth century wrote to a colleague saying that the search for a Greek alphabet had cost him great effort, he betrayed either a shamefully inadequate library or a touching incompetence.[1] The alphabet ought to have been easy to find.

Several popular Latin works contained Greek alphabets. Isidore (*Etymologiae* 1.3) gave a historical account of the development of the Greek alphabet. He began with a list of the seventeen letters Cadmus brought from Phoenicia to Greece and described the letters contributed by Palamedes, Simonides, and Pythagoras. Five of the letters, he added, were "litterae mysticae": "Y" was the Pythagorean sign for life; "Θ" a sign for death; "T" symbolized the cross of the Lord; and "A" and "Ω," the beginning and end of the alphabet, together stood for the cycle of history. Bede (*De temporum ratione* 1) presented the alphabet and gave an explanation of the numerical values of the letters.

The Greek letters, when supplemented by three other signs, also serve as numerals. A knowledge of the numerical values of the letters was required for the calculation of the ecclesiastical computus.[2] It was also required for the composition of *epistolae formatae*. In the latter case, *cautelae*, or sureties in Greek script, were added to ecclesiastical passes and letters of recommendation in order to guarantee their authenticity. It was generally believed that the system had been invented at the Council of Nicaea. Notker Balbulus explained it in the formulary he compiled for Bishop Solomon III:

> Anyone who knows the Greek language even slightly recognizes that the Greek symbols for the letters also represent numbers. In order, therefore, to forestall

---

1. Letter of A. Scholasticus to Marinus Philosophus (Vatican City, Bibl. Vat., Vat. lat. 4929, fol. 1r–v), cited by Bischoff, "Das griechische Element," p. 251, n. 25.
2. On the role of Bede's *De temporum ratione* in the treatises on the ecclesiastical computus, see Dáibhí Ó Cróinín, "Mo-Sinnu moccu Min and the Computus of Bangor," *Peritia* 1 (1982), 290.

some heedless deception in the drawing up of canonical letters, which Latin custom calls *formatae*, the 318 fathers gathered in Nicaea found it very salutary and established that the *epistolae formatae* should be computed or added in the following manner: Let the addition include the Greek first letters of [the names of] the Father, the Son, and the Holy Spirit, which are Π, Υ, and Α, representing the numbers 80, 400, and 1. To this should be added the first letter of [the name of] the apostle Peter, Π, representing 80; the first letter of the writer of the *epistola*; the second letter of the addressee; the third letter of the bearer; the fourth of the city in which it is written; and the number of the current indiction. And so when all of these Greek letters, which, as we have said, represent numbers, have been added, the sum should be recorded on the letter. The recipient should examine it with great care. He should also add separately in the letter the number 99, which according to the Greek symbols represents "AMHN."[3]

The instructions for the composition of the *epistolae formatae* sometimes provided helpful tables of the Greek letters and their numerical values. In the Carolingian period, the text of the *regula formatarum* was often transmitted in collections of canons and formularies, and *epistolae formatae* were indeed composed. But the complexity of the system and the numerous errors made in its execution raise some doubt as to its practicality.[4]

There were other places in which one might ordinarily expect to see Greek letters. Biblical exegetes sought in them a key to the numerical symbolism of the Apocalypse. *Ordines romani* prescribed the tracing out of the alphabet in ceremonies for the consecration of churches. Greek characters were used in cryptography, and sometimes they were used to count pages and quires in manuscripts.[5]

More interesting from the point of view of the Greek language, however, were the occasions when the alphabet was transcribed independently. From the eighth century onward, a growing curiosity about foreign scripts led to the collection of alphabetical specimens of all kinds—invented as well as real. In some manuscripts, Greek and Hebrew alphabets appeared alongside such imaginative fictions as the alphabet of the kingdom of Prester John, or the "Scythian" alphabet of the pseudonymous Aethicus Ister.[6] They might be introduced by texts containing

---

3. *Qualiter debeat epistola formata fieri exemplar*, ed. E. Dümmler, *Das Formelbuch*, pp. 26–27, No. 24.
4. For a review of the topic, see Berschin, *Griechisch-lateinisches Mittelalter*, pp. 91–93.
5. For a general review of the uses of the alphabet, see Bischoff, "Das griechische Element," pp. 251 259.
6. The "Scythian" alphabet appears with Greek and other alphabets in St. Gall MSS 237,

various kinds of alphabet lore, such as verses on the meaning of the letters, or excerpts from Isidore's account. Excerpts from Isidore were used in the composition of the *De inventione litterarum,* an early-ninth-century treatise on the history of the alphabet. The treatise was transmitted in two or three versions, usually presenting five alphabets (Hebrew, Greek, Latin, "Scythian," and runic), together with brief introductory texts on their origins.[7]

The copyist of an eleventh-century manuscript from Tegernsee explained that he was including the Greek alphabet because Latin writers were sometimes compelled to mix in Greek words with the Latin: "And [the Greek words] cannot be read or understood by us if we do not first obtain some little knowledge of their letters."[8]

The alphabets themselves were presented in various forms, ranging from simple lists of letters to elaborate charts and tables. The charts gave, as a rule, some combination of the following: the Greek letters (usually in majuscules), their numerical values (in Roman numerals), the names of

---

p. 327, and 876, pp. 278–280. For an edition of the text in which the alphabet first appeared, see Heinrich Wuttke, *Die Kosmographie des Istriers Aithikos* (Leipzig, 1853), with a facsimile on p. 85. For the alphabet, see Heinz Löwe, "Aethicus Ister und das alttürkische Runenalphabet," *Deutsches Archiv* 32 (1976), 1–22. On the controversial identity of "Aethicus Ister," see Franz Brunhölzl, *Geschichte der lateinischen Literatur des Mittelalters* (Munich, 1975), 1:63–64, 517–518, and H. L. C. Tristram, "Ohthere, Wulfstan und der Aethicus Ister," *Zeitschrift für deutsches Altertum und deutsche Literatur* 111 (1982), 157–158.

7. Both the text and the manuscript tradition are puzzling: see R. Derolez, *Runica Manuscripta: The English Tradition* (Bruges, 1954), pp. 279–354. Melchior Goldast mistakenly attributed the text to Hrabanus Maurus and published it under the title *De inventione linguarum ab Hebraea usque ad Theodiscam, et notis antiquis,* in *Rerum Alemannicarum Scriptores* (Frankfurt, 1661), 2:66–68. This edition was reprinted with minor changes by Migne, PL 112:1579–1584. Since, as Derolez points out (p. 283), Goldast seems to have used only one manuscript, "a new edition is badly needed indeed." Derolez (pp. 376–378) believes that the material that appears in St. Gall MS 878, pp. 320–321, represents a "preliminary state" of the *De inventione* text, and that the version of St. Gall MS 876, pp. 278–280, represents an important early stage. For references, see the entries in Appendix 1, below.

8. Munich, Bayerische Staatsbibliothek Clm 19129, fol. 1v: "Istas suprascriptas graecas literulas ideo usitatas oportet haberi, quia expositores librorum latinae linguae graecorum verba cum suis characteribus mixtis ob quandam necessitatem habent inserta. Et non possunt illa a nobis legi vel intellegi nisi prius eorum apicum aliquantulam scientiam habeamus." Fol. 1r–v presents an excerpt from Isidore, *Etymologiae* 1.3, a large Greek majuscule alphabet with the numerical values of the letters and the names of the letters and numbers, the text given above, and a brief coded statement employing the numerical values of the letters.

the Greek letters and numbers (in phonetic Latin transcription), and the corresponding Latin letters.[9]

The Greek alphabets and numerals in the St. Gall manuscripts are described in Appendix 1 (below, pp. 117–120). Seven ninth-century manuscripts (MSS 184, 251, 459, 671, 751, 878, and 902) and one tenth-century manuscript (Zurich, Zentralbibliothek C 62) furnish examples of majuscule alphabets used in such conventional sources as Isidore's *Etymologiae*, Bede's *De temporum ratione*, the computus, and the *epistolae formatae*.

Charts and tables reflecting a more independent interest in the alphabet are found in one manuscript of the late eighth or early ninth century (MS 876) and six manuscripts of the ninth century (MSS 17, 237, 397, 459, 877, and 878). Of them, three are especially noteworthy. MS 237, p. 327, gives the Hebrew, Greek, and "Scythian" alphabet of the pseudonymous Aethicus Ister. The information supplied for the Greek alphabet is somewhat confused. The alphabet omits the letter "epsilon" and adds an extra "psi" in place of "upsilon." The corresponding Latin letters and the names of the letters, set above and below the Greek characters, are often incorrect. (The Latin value "r" is assigned to "psi" and "ps" to "chi.") MS 459, p. 111, presents a fine specimen of an alphabetical chart. See Plate 1 for an illustration. Each alphabetical entry is in four parts: first (beginning from the bottom line and reading up), the Greek character; second, the name of the letter (in Latin transliteration); third, the numerical value (in Roman numerals); and fourth, the name of the number. Seven specifically numerical entries are included. MS 876, pp. 278–280, presents the Greek alphabet and four other alphabets (Hebrew, Latin, "Scythian," and Anglo-Saxon runes), together with a Latin commentary on writing. A thirteenth-century manuscript (MS 1026) also contains a majuscule alphabet. MS 18, p. 4, finally, contains two alphabets, majuscule and minuscule, apparently written in a Byzantine hand.

Greek letters are used to order the quires in the Basel Psalter (Basel, Universitätsbibliothek A.VII.3). The first page of each quire is marked on the upper right margin with a Greek letter and, on the upper left, with the equivalent Latin letter. (The Latin letters were probably intended for the bookbinder, who could not be expected to follow the Greek.)[10]

---

9. A facsimile of one such chart from the year 799 (Vienna, Österreichische Nationalbibliothek MS 795, fol. 19r) appears in Berschin, *Griechisch-lateinisches Mittelalter*, plate 2 ("Formae litterarum secundum Grecos").

10. Other examples of the practice are collected by Berschin, *Griechisch-lateinisches Mittelalter*, p. 54, n. 38.

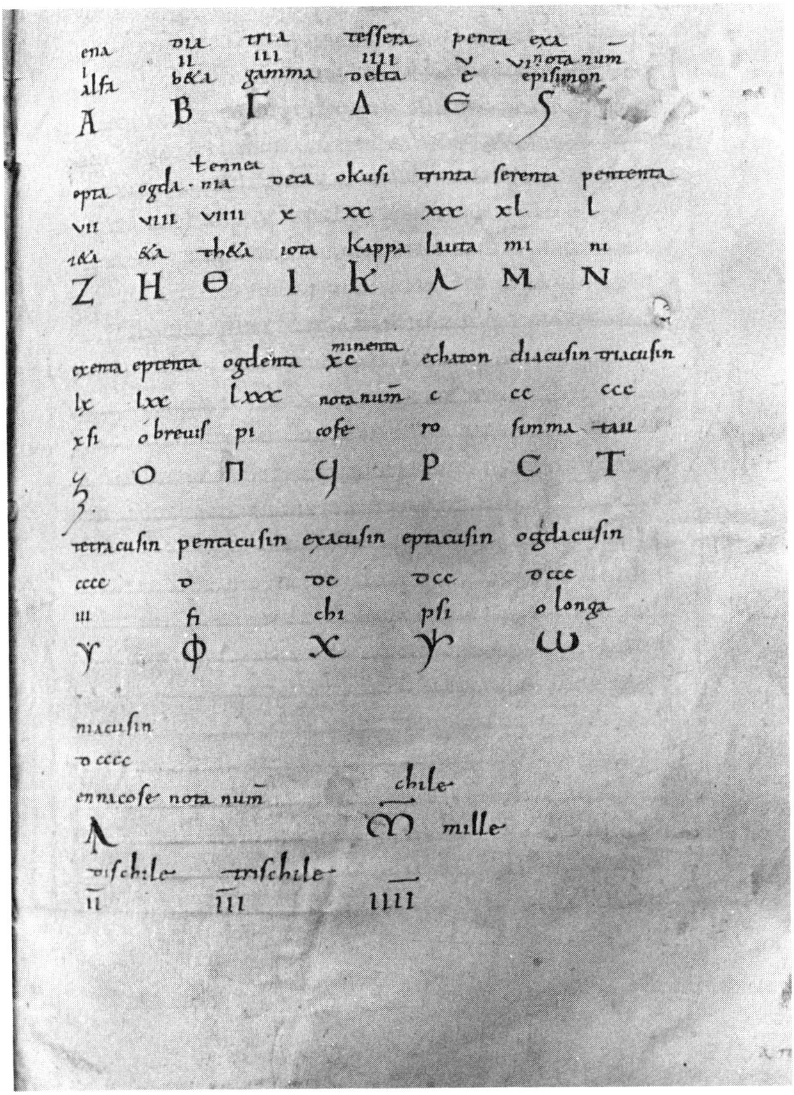

Plate 1. Alphabetical Chart.
St. Gall, Stiftsbibliothek, MS 459, p. 111.
(All plates reproduced by permission of the Stiftsbibliothek.)

It is instructive to look more closely at the tables in which the scribes spelled out the names of letters and numbers. Bischoff has observed that such tables are linguistic curiosities, for they tend to transmit the contemporary Byzantine names of the numbers rather than the classical names.[11] A glance at MS 459 bears out the statement. If we compare the names given in the manuscript with the classical names, we see a preference for the vulgar forms, e.g., "penta" (for "πέντε"); "ogda" (for "ὀκτώ"); "nia vel ennea," where the reader is given a choice of the vulgar and classical ("ἐννέα") forms; "trinta" (for "τριάκοντα"); "serenta" (for "τετταρά-κοντα"); and "chile" (for "χίλιοι"). The same preference exists in other tables containing the series of the names of the numbers in MSS 671 and 877.

While only a few of the tables give the names of the numbers, nearly all of them give the letter names. And these names provide a small bit of evidence for the pronunciation of Greek in the late ninth and early tenth centuries. The pronunciation was in general itacistic, although there is some variability in the manuscripts. MS 459 suggests a confusion between the probable etacistic pronunciation of Antiquity and the itacism of modern Greek. It represents the letter "eta" by "epsilon" ("beta," "zeta," "eta," "theta," for "βῆτα," "ζῆτα," "ῆτα," "θῆτα"). But it presents the itacistic "mi" and "ni" for "μῦ" and "νῦ." Other phonological changes are evident in the treatment of the consonants: "lauta" for "λά(μ)βδα," and "simma" for "σῖγμα."

The many vulgar forms used for the numbers raise the possibility of contemporary sources of information. Perhaps the lists were originally contributed by Byzantine merchants or travelers. For this reason, the alphabetical charts and tables are unusual among western Greek documents, which more often derived from literary exemplars.

These charts and tables seem to have been viewed as collector's items in medieval libraries. The superficial knowledge gleaned from them sometimes found an immediate outlet in word games or transliteration exercises. Around the peripheries of Latin texts, for example, in superscriptions, incipits, autographs, and explicits, scribes and scholars displayed

---

11. "Das griechische Element," p. 264. (It is because medieval writers relied upon these lists, he explains, that the Greek numbers used in Latin literary works of the period appear in the vulgar forms.) Byzantine names are found in a computus in Brussels, Bibliothèque Royale, MS 5413–22, fol. 79r (late ninth or early tenth century). The computus derives from a seventh-century archetype; see Dáibhí Ó Cróinín, "A Seventh-Century Irish Computus from the Circle of Cummianus," *Proceedings of the Royal Irish Academy*, sect. C, vol. 82, C, no. 11 (1982), 405–430.

their skills.

At St. Gall, a hypergraecizing technique was especially favored by copyists of liturgical and biblical texts. Scribes in search of exotic effects commonly introduced Latin prayers with titles written in Greek and concluded them with a Greek "AƆCYN" (intended to represent "ἀμήν"). A ninth-century book of Pericopes combined Greek with Latin letters in several headings: "ΘΕΟΡΗΑΝΙΑΕ," "IN ΤΗΕΟΦΑΝΙΑ," "ΤΗΕΟΦΑΝΙΑΕ," "AD S. STEΦΑΝUΜ," "LECTIO HIEREMIAE PROΦETAE," "AD ΤΙΜΟΘ.," "AD ΦΙΛΙΠ."[12] Liturgical chants in an eleventh-century manuscript are entitled "CYƆCΠΦWNIA" and "CYƆCΠHWNIA" (for "symphonia"), and similar titles occur in other service books.[13]

In a late-ninth-century Gospel book now in Einsiedeln, the Gospel of Matthew is headed "ΚΑΤΑΜΑΘΕWN," and not "secundum Mattheum."[14] Two early-tenth-century manuscripts containing glosses to the New Testament occasionally give headings using Greek, or imitation Greek, letters. In MS 294, p. 186, we find "AD ΦΙΛΕΜ."; in MS 295, pp. 39, 41, "AD EΦESIOS," "AD ΦΙΛΙΠ.," "AD ΘΕCCΑΛΟΝ.," "AD ΦΙΛΕΜΟΝΕΜ."

Greek titles also ornament the pages of secular literature. In MS 557, p. 2 (ninth century), Severus's *Apologia* is introduced as "INCIPIT ΑΠΟ-ΛΟΓΙΑ SEVERI RHETORIS. . . ." The superscription to a poem by Walahfrid Strabo in MS 869, p. 258 (end of the ninth century), includes the Greek phrase "ΟΙCΤΙΧΟΙΠΡΟCΤΟΝΑΡΧΟΝΤWNΑΓΑΘWN." In MS 899, p. 57 (tenth century), verses are headed "ΕΡΙΤΑΦΙΟΝ" and "ΕΠΙ-ΤΑΦΙΟΝ." East Berlin, Deutsche Staatsbibliothek, Hamilton 542, fol. 147v (end of the ninth century), gives in the explicit of a volume of Prudentius: "DE ΨΙΧΟΜΑΧΙΑ."[15] Zurich, Zentralbibliothek C 129, fols. 101v – 102r (end of the ninth century), presents a dialogue entitled "En carissime ΑΔΗΛΦΟC," which makes use of the Greek letters "M" and "Δ" to indicate the speeches of teacher and pupil.[16]

---

12. Zurich, Zentralbibliothek C 60, fols. 6r, 6v, 9v, 78r, 78v, 174r, 212v. On the date, see Bruckner, *Scriptoria*, 3:125.

13. St. Gall, Stiftsbibliothek MS 381, pp. 373, 379. In the Folchart Psalter (MS 23, pp. 7, 14) the title of the Kyrie Eleison is given in Greek letters.

14. Einsiedeln, Stiftsbibliothek MS 17; see Adolf Merton, *Die Buchmalerei in St. Gallen vom neunten bis zum elften Jahrhundert*, 2nd ed. (Leipzig, 1923), plate 34, fig. 1.

15. On the manuscript, see Bruckner, *Scriptoria*, 3:51; and Helmut Boese, *Die lateinischen Handschriften der Sammlung Hamilton zu Berlin* (Wiesbaden, 1966), pp. 261 – 262.

16. This is a reversal of the traditional procedure, for here "M" stands for teacher ("magister") and "Δ" for pupil ("discipulus"). In the Greek system, however, "M" stands for "μαθητής" and "Δ" for "διδάσκαλος." This curious reversal seems to have been introduced to the West by Aldhelm; see Berschin, "Griechisches bei den Iren," pp. 504 – 505.

Even illustrations and diagrams make use of Greek terms. In the illuminated initial of a late-ninth-century Psalter, a spring, drawn alongside a stag, is given the caption "ΦѠNC."[17] In an early-ninth-century text describing the months and seasons, Greek letters are arranged in four segments around a circular diagram: "ѠPѠ — ΛѠ — ΓΙ — OYM" (for "ὡρολόγιον" or "horologium").[18] In a table in a tenth-century mathematical text, Greek words indicate the positions of the moon: "YΠEP ΓEIA I O-P-OI-Z-ON I YΠO ΓEIA."[19]

People wrote their names in Greek letters—in much the same spirit, one supposes, as beginning students today play with the letters when they first learn them. In MS 560, p. 374 (eleventh century), the scribe Herimannus, who normally signs his name in Latin letters (as on p. 6), chooses to write it in a hybrid script: "HEPIϽCANNI."[20] A simple transliteration exercise figures prominently among the pen trials of MS 44, p. 185 (flyleaf of the second of two codices bound in the volume, eighth century): "ROSILI/PѠCYΛY." The term is of Germanic origin. Is "Rosili" a little horse, a little rose, or a little girl?[21] Writing autographs in Greek letters was not an unusual practice at the time, and scholars have collected numerous examples from elsewhere in medieval Europe.[22]

Three ninth-century St. Gall manuscripts contain Greek-lettered explicits. The scribe of MS 94, p. 112, ended his work with a flourish: "HXΠΛICIT ΦHΛIKITHP" (for "explicit feliciter"). The termination of MS 123, p. 151, is rather more esoteric:

The text from the Zurich manuscript is printed by Paul von Winterfeld and J. Schwalm, *Neues Archiv* 27 (1902), 742–743.

17. Göttweig, Stiftsbibliothek MS 30, fol. 71; see Merton, *Die Buchmalerei*, p. 32.

18. Zurich, Zentralbibliothek C 12, fol. 167v. On the date, see Bruckner, *Scriptoria*, 2:82.

19. Zurich, Zentralbibliothek C 62, fol. 211v. On the date, see Bruckner, *Scriptoria*, 3:125.

20. See Bischoff, "Das griechische Element," pp. 253–254, n. 36. In the seventeenth century, the autograph was misunderstood by Melchior Goldast, who read the letters as Latin and attributed the *Annales sangallenses maiores* to a certain "Hepidannus." Ludwig Traube, "*O Roma nobilis*," p. 399, charged Goldast with having wholly fabricated the character of "Hepidannus." The incident is amusing, for Goldast, who certainly was a notorious counterfeiter, had been misled himself this time.

21. The possibilities were suggested to me by Professor Konstantin Reichardt, then in the Department of Germanic Languages and Literatures, Yale University. The term is not noted in Heinrich Hattemer's catalogue of Old High German at St. Gall, *St. Gallens altdeutsche Sprachschätze*, 3 vols. (St. Gall, 1844–1848).

22. For a selection, see A. Salmon, "Notice sur l'abbaye de Saint-Loup, près Tours," *Bibliothèque de l'Ecole des Chartes* 6 (1844), 444–445; Bischoff, "Das griechische Element," p. 255, n. 46; Berschin, *Griechisch-lateinisches Mittelalter*, p. 54, n. 36.

FINIT EXPLANATIO IN NAUM PROPHETAM

ΦΗ   ΚΙ

ΤΗΡ   ΛΙ

(Read the Greek letters diagonally, from top left to bottom right, and from top right to bottom left.) The explicit of MS 876, p. 32, is poorly done: "ΗΞΠΛΕΚΕΘ. ΔϽCΗ + ΦΕΔΘ" (for "explicit. d<o>m<in>e + fiat"). (The scribe has written "Η" for the Latin "e"; "E" for "i"; "Θ" for "t"; and has once confused "Δ" with "A.")

A fourth specimen appears in another manuscript of the same period, but one whose St. Gall provenance is doubtful.[23] Montpellier Univ. H 409, fol. 331v, concludes a Latin commentary on the Psalms with the following:

ΗΧΠΛΚΕΟΝΤ

ΛΕΒΡΕΔΛШΕΔ

ΝΟΜΗΡШξ

ΟΕΝΟΟΗ

Hoc est ex

pliciunt li

bri david

numero

quinque

Medieval scribes, finally, favored a number of paleographical devices which made use of Greek letters. The name of Jesus Christ was often written in Greek, and in contracted form it appeared in majuscule hands as "I͞HC" and "X͞PC." When these terms came to be written in minuscules, the scribes treated them as though they were Latin terms written in Latin letters and transcribed them as "i͞hc" and "x͞pc." The final letter "c" (for "s") was extended by analogy to other terms, as "e͞pc" (for "episcopus"), "s͞pc" (for "spiritus"), "t͞pc" (for "tempus"). It was chiefly from St. Gall, remarks Bischoff, that the practice spread throughout Europe.[24] Greek formulae such as "xƀ" (for "Χριστὲ βοήθησον," or "Christe benedic") were also popular. In the second half of the ninth

---

23. On the provenance, see Bruckner, *Scriptoria*, 2:14. The explicit is printed by Arthur Allgeier, "Exegetische Beiträge zur Geschichte des Griechischen vor dem Humanismus," *Biblica* 24 (1943), 276–277, who comments: "So unbeholfen bewegt sich kein St. Gallener Schreiber."

24. "Das griechische Element," p. 256.

century, the formula "x'b" became a virtual stamp of the St. Gall scriptorium.[25]

Another St. Gall manuscript of the second half of the ninth century bears the mark of a familiarity with Byzantine sources. Zurich, Zentralbibliothek C 78, fol. 157r, displays in a margin an alphabetical cross surrounded by a legend:

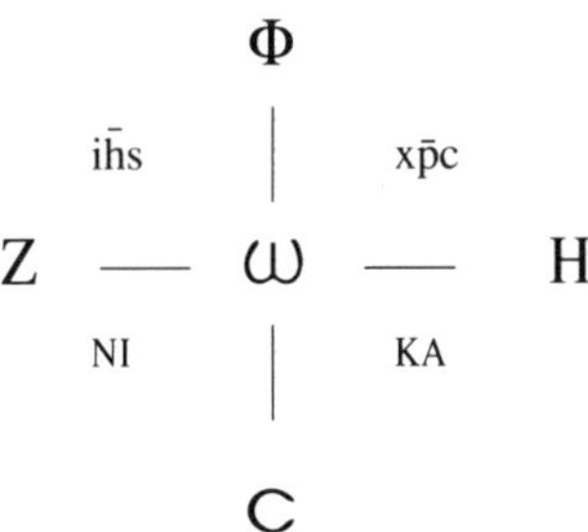

Perhaps the scribe imitated a symbol found on Byzantine coin faces.[26]

The significance of the various employments of the Greek alphabet is not difficult to assess. When used in liturgical and biblical titles and in paleographical devices, Greek letters were thought to create an impression of mystery and formality. But very often their primary purpose was simply to amuse the writer, and the Greek letters in autographs and explicits are examples of these facile entertainments.

25. Bischoff, "Das griechische Element," p. 257, n. 60, cites MSS 102, 130, 132, 157, 158, 173, 208, 566, 670. To these we can add the Basel Psalter, fols. 36r, 57r, 58v, 71r, and Zurich, Zentralbibliothek C 78, fol. 94v.
26. Bischoff, "Das griechische Element," p. 257 and n. 61. On the provenance, see Bruckner, *Scriptoria*, 3:126. The manuscript also contains a partial Latin translation of the *Akathistos Hymnos*; see Appendix 5, below, p. 135.

V

Grammars

The fundamental problem for medieval students who wished to learn Greek was that they had no proper grammar of the language. There was no authoritative textbook that presented, in terms familiar to users of Latin, an analysis of the structure of Greek. Medieval students were for the most part denied a systematic consideration of the features of the language—of its sounds, its words, its syntax. Without an elementary grammar, they were obliged to turn to a varied and in the end unsatisfactory collection of materials.[1]

Some knowledge of Greek might be obtained from conventional Latin grammars. In his exposition of the rules of the Latin language, Donatus in the *Ars maior* repeatedly cited Greek forms.[2] Resourceful students might learn a few rules for the formation of Greek nouns, the translation of various prepositions, and the meaning of roots in composition. They would find little concerning the Greek verb. Priscian's *Institutiones grammaticae* supplied additional instruction.[3] It was based on a comparison of Greek and Latin forms and usage and gave attention to the terms, rules, and exceptions in both languages. From it students might derive most of the Greek rules for noun declension, a notion of the treatment of verb stems, and some sense of syntax. Indeed, Carolingian teachers collected Priscian's *Graeca* and included them in a handbook for the study of Greek.[4] Macrobius's *De differentiis et societatibus graeci latinique verbi epitome*, a difficult work that compared the Greek and Latin verb, served ninth-century students in the same limited way.[5]

1. The problem is reviewed in Bischoff, "Das griechische Element," pp. 259–260, and Berschin, *Griechisch-lateinisches Mittelalter*, pp. 46–47.
2. H. Keil, ed., *Grammatici latini*, 7 vols. (Leipzig, 1857–1880; repr. Hildesheim, 1961), 4:367–402.
3. Keil, *Grammatici latini*, vols. 2 and 3.
4. Laon, Bibliothèque Municipale MS 444; see n. 18 below.
5. Keil, *Grammatici latini*, 5:599–655. The text is known chiefly through the excerpts made in the ninth century by a certain John. "Explicuit defloratio," read his subscription, "de libro Ambrosii Macrobii Theodosii, quam Ioannes carpserat ad discendas graecorum verborum regulas."

Possibly the most effective of the late antique texts in circulation in medieval Europe were the *Ars grammatica* of Dositheus and the bilingual schoolbooks known as *Hermeneumata*, both of which were known at St. Gall.

The *Ars grammatica* had originally been composed, probably in the late fourth century, to assist Greeks in learning Latin.[6] It comprised an outline of Latin grammar together with a Greek translation. The Latin text was based on the same authorities used by Charisius, Diomedes, and the author of the *Excerpta bobiensia*.[7] It surveyed such topics as accentuation, punctuation, and phonology, as well as the eight parts of speech. The survey of Latin grammar was followed by exercises for translation from Latin into Greek and by a Latin-Greek index of 122 verbs.

Because the *Ars* had a long history of use as a schoolbook, its text underwent many changes. It is likely that Dositheus wrote his Greek translation between the lines of the Latin text, or perhaps set it in a parallel column. But a later copyist interspersed the Greek with the Latin, so that Latin words were followed immediately by their Greek equivalents ("Ars Τέχνη grammatica γραμματική est ἐστιν scientia γνῶσις," etc.). Toward the end of the work the Greek translation was omitted entirely. Other alterations further damaged the text.[8]

Dositheus translated the Latin into the Greek of his own time, and the translation reflected contemporary vocabulary and idiom.[9] The Greek text of the *Ars* was a translation of the Latin—and a literal one at that. The *Ars grammatica* was intended to be a practical handbook for studying Latin. In this capacity it served Byzantine pupils well. They could easily make use of a Latin grammar with a Greek translation, for the presentation of Latin grammar had traditionally depended upon a comparison with the Greek. But the *Ars* was not well suited for Latin pupils hoping to study Greek. There was no exposition of Greek grammar. And although the comparison

6. The standard edition, *Dosithei Ars grammatica*, ed. Iohannes Tolkiehn (Leipzig, 1913), is sometimes difficult to find. There is an older edition in Keil, *Grammatici latini*, 7:365–436.

7. On the relationship of Dositheus's *Ars* to other late antique grammars, see Louis Holtz, *Donat et la tradition de l'enseignement grammatical* (Paris, 1981), pp. 81, 427–428.

8. See M. von Schanz, *Geschichte der römischen Literatur bis zum Gesetzgebungswerk des Kaisers Justinian*, 2nd ed. rev. by C. Hosius and G. Krüger (Munich, 1914; repr. Munich, 1959), 4.1:177, and W. S. Teuffel, *Geschichte der römischen Literatur*, 6th ed. rev. by W. Kroll and F. Skutsch (Leipzig, 1913; repr. Aalen, 1965), 3:310.

9. Viktor Reichmann, *Römische Literatur in griechischer Uebersetzung* (Leipzig, 1943), pp. 88–100, with examples. See Tolkiehn, *Dosithei Ars*, pp. 106–108, for a list of Greek words of popular origin.

of Latin and Greek texts might prove instructive, there was little to be learned about the grammatical system of the Greek language. The rules of inflection were not explained, and even a motivated pupil would learn nothing about the declension of nouns and almost nothing about the conjugation of verbs. Nevertheless, despite its limitations, the *Ars grammatica* was sometimes used for studying Greek in the West. It survives only in three St. Gall manuscripts of the ninth and tenth centuries.

Also used for the study of Greek were collections of *Hermeneumata*, bilingual school manuals commonly dated to the third century A.D. As a rule, they contained one or more of four different elements: an alphabetical dictionary (with an emphasis on verbs); a topical dictionary (word lists under such headings as "De officiis," "De diebus festis," or "De natura"); *colloquia*, or conversations from everyday life; and texts for reading practice (such as some of Aesop's fables, extracts from the mythological handbook transmitted under the name of Hyginus, or gnomic texts). The *Hermeneumata* were designed to teach language, probably to teach Latin to Greek children, but they also served to teach Greek to Latins.[10] In medieval Europe, they seem to have been used by solitary adults interested in Greek. At least eight recensions of *Hermeneumata* were in circulation.[11]

Hermeneumata were transcribed alongside the *Ars* in the St. Gall Dositheus manuscripts, a circumstance that led scholars from the sixteenth to the nineteenth century to attribute them to Dositheus as well.[12] In fact, we do not know who compiled the *Hermeneumata*, and it is unlikely that a single author will be found. Such schoolbooks were continually revised and brought up-to-date, and many people probably tinkered with them. The *Hermeneumata pseudo-dositheana* are of great importance in the

---

10. As historical sources on the school life of late Antiquity, they promise to be of some value to modern scholars. They have not been very much studied and they merit further investigation. For a general treatment, see Henri Marrou, *Histoire de l'éducation dans l'antiquité*, 6th ed. (Paris, 1965), pp. 386–388. Some texts are published in Georg Goetz, ed., *Corpus glossariorum latinorum*, 3 (1892; repr. Amsterdam, 1965), hereafter cited as *CGL*. Goetz's methodology is critically examined by A. C. Dionisotti, "From Ausonius' Schooldays? A Schoolbook and Its Relatives," *Journal of Roman Studies* 72 (1982), 85–86. For a demonstration of their use in the history of education, see Alan D. Booth, "Elementary and Secondary Education in the Roman Empire," *Florilegium* 1 (1979), 8–9.

11. For a table listing texts and manuscripts, see Dionisotti, "From Ausonius' Schooldays?" p. 87.

12. Schanz-Hosius, *Geschichte der römischen Literatur*, 4.1:178, and Teuffel, *Geschichte der römischen Literatur*, 3:310–311, review the problem.

history of Greek scholarship at St. Gall. Before discussing the St. Gall manuscripts, however, it may be helpful to describe the collection as a whole.

The *Hermeneumata* transmitted in the St. Gall manuscripts belong to a recension known as the *Leidensia*, after their chief manuscript source (Leiden, Universiteits-Bibliotheek, Voss.gr.Q.7, fols. 3r–39v, early tenth century). Georg Goetz, who published the text,[13] believed that the recension originally comprised twelve books: (1) *Glossae*, a dictionary only partially alphabetized; (2) *Capitula*, a topical dictionary ("De diis," "De caelo," "De aedibus," "De diebus festis," etc.); (3) *Divi Hadriani sententiae et epistolae*, anecdotes, letters, and rescripts of the emperor Hadrian; (4) *Fabulae Aesopiae*; (5) *Quae pertinent ad forum aut in curiam*, a tract on manumission recently ascribed to Gaius; (6) *Hygini genealogia*, extracts from the mythological handbook of Hyginus; (7) *Niciarii interrogationes et responsiones*; (8) *Carfilidis interrogationes et responsa*; (9) *Responsa sapientum*; (10) *Praecepta in Delphis ab Apolline in columna scripta*; (11) *Narratio de bello troiano*, a history of the Trojan War, abridged from the *Iliad*; (12) *De conversatione cotidiana*, an account of a day in the life of a schoolboy presented in dramatized form.

But the Leiden manuscript has only eight of the books. Goetz found the four gnomic texts (Niciarius, Carphilides, *Responsa sapientum*, *Praecepta delphica*) in another set of *Hermeneumata*. There no longer seems to be any reason to accept his interpolation of them.[14] The *Leidensia* recension simply comprises the eight books found in the manuscript.

In only one of the books is there any indication of the possible time of composition. The author of the preface to the Hyginus text comments, "In the consulship of Maximus and Aper [A.D. 207] on the eleventh of September I translated Hyginus's *Genealogy* which is known to all." Scholars once thought that an early-third-century date could be assigned to all of the books, but more recent inquiry has cast doubt on this assumption.[15]

Whatever the problems of their origin, it is clear that in the Middle Ages the *Hermeneumata* were viewed as aids to the study of Greek. And

---

13. Printed in *CGL* 3:1–72, 384–387. There is an earlier edition by Eduard Böcking, *Dosithei Magistri Interpretamentorum Liber Tertius* (Bonn, 1832). (Böcking believed that Dositheus was the author.)

14. Dionisotti, "From Ausonius' Schooldays?" p. 90, rightly observes that the source of the difficulty lies in Goetz's reliance upon a genealogical model: "As for the Leiden corpus, I suspect we should turn the theory upside down: not a grand archetype, but rather a late (and remarkable) gathering of originally separate material of this kind."

15. Dionisotti, "From Ausonius' Schooldays?" p. 89.

they were useful in a way. The texts contained in these serviceable hand-books afforded an opportunity for practice in reading simple Greek prose. They did not make explicit any rules of grammar and they did not present impressive specimens of literary language (the highest literary level in the *Hermeneumata* was reached by some Babrius fables included in the Aesop), but the bilingual texts in them did give students beneficial exercise.[16]

Carolingian scholars naturally sought to add to the pool of resources. A brief bilingual fragment, "TI ECTIN doctus," was composed early in the ninth century.[17] The text, in the form of a dialogue, reviewed the technical grammatical vocabularies of Latin and Greek. The fragment survives in only one manuscript and does not seem to have been very influential.

The most important of the Carolingian contributions was prepared at Laon under the direction of Martin Hiberniensis (819–875). Laon, Bibliothèque Municipale MS 444 is a collection of materials for the study of Greek.[18] The manuscript is divided into three parts: (1) preliminary matter, including a table of contents, (2) Greek-Latin glosses deriving primarily from the so-called Cyrillus glossary (represented by the eighth-century London, British Library MS Harley 5792), along with *Idiomata generum*, lists of nouns whose genders are different in Greek and Latin, and (3) a compendium of grammatical materials put together by Martin Hiberniensis and copied largely in his own hand. The grammatical notes, not all of which have been precisely identified, were drawn from a wide variety of sources.[19] Martin employed, directly or indirectly, works of Macrobius, Priscian, Theophrastus, and Martianus Capella. He copied into the manuscript poems by John Scottus as well as some of his own verse,

16. *Hermeneumata* were used in other ways as well. For an illustration of the possible use of their Aesopic material in a Latin verse, see Bernice M. Kaczynski and Haijo Jan Westra, "Aesop in the Middle Ages: The Transmission of the Sick Lion Fable and the Authorship of the St. Gall Version," *Mittellateinisches Jahrbuch* 17 (1982), 31–38.

17. Paris, BN lat. 528, fols. 134v–135r; H. Omont, ed., "Grammaire grecque du IXe siècle," *Bibliothèque de l'Ecole des Chartes* 42 (1881), 126–127. On the debate over provenance, see Berschin, *Griechisch-lateinisches Mittelalter*, p. 55, n. 55.

18. Portions of the text were printed by Friedrich A. Eckstein, "Ein griechisches Elementarbuch aus dem Mittelalter," in *Programm der Lateinischen Hauptschule in Halle* (Halle, 1861), pp. 1–11, and by M. E. Miller, "Glossaire grec-latin de la bibliothèque de Laon," *Notices et extraits des manuscrits de la Bibliothèque Nationale* 29.2 (1880), 1–230. On the manuscript, see Contreni, *The Cathedral School*, pp. 55–58, 67–70, and Jeauneau, "Les écoles de Laon et d'Auxerre," pp. 501–502.

19. See Contreni, *The Cathedral School*, p. 70, who emphasizes the need for further study of the individual texts.

Greek prayers with Latin interlinear translations, a brief bilingual phrase book, some *Declinationes Graecorum*, and numerous assorted notes on Greek grammar and vocabulary. Bischoff has called the book "a veritable *Thesaurus linguae Graecae* in its century."[20]

Some of the grammatical material merits a more detailed description, for it came to be included in other Carolingian manuals. In the *Declinationes Graecorum*, occupying seven leaves of the manuscript,[21] paradigms are given for the declension of nouns and adjectives, along with examples of other words from the same class. For instance, the declension of "Κύριος, dominus," is followed by the instruction "Δὸς ὁμοῖα, i.e. da similia," and the reader is presented with a list of appropriate nouns and adjectives ("μακάριος, beatus," etc.). The Greek articles and personal pronouns are simply declined, without the addition of exercises. The paradigms for nouns, adjectives, articles, and pronouns were most likely obtained from classical texts, although there are signs of familiarity with more recent sources. The irregular feminine noun "ἡ γυνή," for instance, is declined as though it were a regular noun of the first declension: "τῆς γυνῆς, τῇ γυνῇ, τὴν γυνήν," etc.—a tendency found in colloquial Greek.[22]

The presentation of the remaining parts of speech is less organized. Verbs are not conjugated, and they are arranged without reference to person, tense, or mood. They are listed, presumably, as they occur in the scriptural texts from which most of them are derived (a bilingual Psalter with Canticles, a bilingual text of Deuteronomy). Finally, there are indices of adverbs, participles, conjunctions, prepositions, and interjections. There is no discussion of syntax.

The text seems to have circulated among Irish scholars on the Continent. It appears, with some variation, in two St. Gall manuscripts of the late ninth or early tenth century: St. Gall, Stiftsbibliothek MS 902, pp. 61–68, and London, British Library MS Harley 5642, fols. 4r–8v. (Both manuscripts will be examined below.) An Irish hand transcribed a portion of the *Declinationes* in the middle of the ninth century in the so-called *Reichenauer Schulheft* (St. Paul im Lavanttal, Stiftsbibliothek MS 86b/1 [25.2.31b], fols. 3r–4v).[23] Another fragment appears in the tenth-century

---

20. "Das griechische Element," p. 266.
21. MS, fols. 300r–306r; printed by Eckstein, "Ein griechisches Elementarbuch," pp. 3–11, and Miller, "Glossaire," pp. 202–205 (excerpts).
22. MS, fol. 300v, in Miller, "Glossaire," pp. 203–204. On Byzantine sources for the regular forms, see Psaltes, *Grammatik der Byzantinischen Chroniken*, p. 153.
23. The shelfmark of the manuscript has been changed so often that publications on it can be

Glossarium andegavense, or Angers Glossary (Angers, Bibliothèque Municipale MS 477, fols. 7v – 8v).[24] More specimens may well be found embedded in the pages of other medieval glossaries.[25]

What, then, was there at St. Gall in the way of grammatical resources for teaching and learning Greek? As was to be expected of a serious scholarly institution the monastery possessed a full complement of traditional Latin grammars. Library catalogues from the mid-ninth century onward referred to numerous copies of works by Donatus, Priscian, Isidore, and other grammarians.[26] Some of the grammars appeared in collectanea manuscripts that contained incidental Greek material.[27]

One of the Priscian texts, the so-called "Irish Priscian" (MS 904), has been brought into connection with bilingual manuscripts copied on the Continent by Irish scholars with a knowledge of Greek.[28] In three of the biblical manuscripts belonging to this group there are marginal notations

difficult to trace; they are reviewed by Berschin, *Griechisch-lateinisches Mittelalter*, pp. 192 – 193, n. 104. Contreni, *The Cathedral School*, pp. 88 – 89, compares the glossary items of the St. Paul codex with those of Laon MS 444. Wilhelm Krause, "Das Fragment einer griechischen Grammatik des Cod. Vindob. 114 und das griech.-lat. Glossar der St. Pauler Handschrift XXV D/65," *Jahrbuch der Österreichischen Byzantinischen Gesellschaft* 5 (1956), 7 – 25, compares the text with the notes on Greek grammar made by Froumund of Tegernsee in the late tenth century (Vienna, Österreichische Nationalbibliothek Cod. 114, fols. 13r – 15v). See also Hans Oskamp, "The Irish Material in the St. Paul Irish Codex," *Eigse* 17.3 (1978), 385 – 391.

24. H. Omont, ed., "Glossarium Andegavense. MS. 477 (461) de la bibliothèque municipale d'Angers," *Bibliothèque de l'Ecole des Chartes* 59 (1898), 686 – 687.

25. Professor David Ganz, of the Department of Classics, the University of North Carolina at Chapel Hill, has recently drawn my attention to material from the *Declinationes Graecorum* in London, BL Harley 2735. He has found additional texts on Greek grammar in London, BL Harley 2688, which he identifies as a detached quire, hitherto unrecognized, of BL Harley 3095, copied during the last quarter of the ninth century in Lotharingia. Professor Ganz is preparing a study of the manuscript.

26. Lehmann and Ruf, *Mittelalterliche Bibliothekskataloge*, 1:75, 80 – 82, 84, 87, 101, 112, 118. See also Lesne, *Les livres*, pp. 755 – 756.

27. MS 877 includes Donatus, the Greek alphabet, and a bilingual glossary; MS 878, Donatus, Priscian, and the Greek alphabet. MS 237 includes Isidore's *Etymologiae* and, on its last folio, a Greek Lord's Prayer, brief bilingual glossary, and a Greek alphabet. Perhaps this is the manuscript meant in a catalogue entry printed by Lehmann and Ruf, *Mittelalterliche Bibliothekskataloge*, 1:75: "Aethimologiarum libri XX [Ysydori episcopi] et ratio horologii et glosa Grecorum verborum in volumine I."

28. For an edition of the glosses in this important manuscript, see Whitley Stokes and John Strachan, *Thesaurus Palaeohibernicus: A Collection of Old-Irish Glosses, Scholia, Prose and Verse* (Cambridge, Eng., 1903), 2:xviii – xxiii, 49 – 224. On the position of the manuscript in the St. Gall transmission, see Berschin, *Griechisch-lateinisches Mittelalter*, pp. 23, 173, and Duft, "Irische Handschriftenüberlieferung," p. 928.

on the grammatical and stylistic peculiarities of the Greek text.[29] In the Basel Psalter, fol. 51v, for example, a St. Gall teacher explains a conditional clause: "ΙΠΟΘΕΤΙΚΥC CΥΛΟΓΙCΜΟC id est suppositiuus silogismus. ut si ambulat mouetur thesis. positio. ΙΠΟΘΕCΙC suppositio. inde ΥΠΟΘΕΤΙΚΥC ut si primum. secundum et reliqua."[30]

Traces of a more casual activity are found in MS 270, p. 52. Someone practicing his Greek lesson tries to conjugate a verb: "ΓΡΑΦΟ. ΓΡΑΦΗC. ΓΡΑΦΗ. ΓΡΑΦΟΜΗ. ΓΡΑΦΗΤΕ. ΓΡΑΦΟΥCΗΝ." Perhaps the influence of Byzantine Greek is to be detected in the form "ΓΡΑΦΟΜΗ": the modern form also lacks the final "nu." The Greek lines are in the same hand that, earlier on the page, transcribed and commented upon a runic alphabet.

The reputation of the monastery as a center of Greek scholarship is based chiefly on its role in the transmission of the *Ars grammatica* of Dositheus and the *Hermeneumata pseudo-dositheana*. Three manuscripts are involved. MS 902, the most significant single manuscript for the study of Greek at St. Gall, was copied there in the second half of the ninth century.[31] Its contents include the *Ars grammatica* of Dositheus, portions of the *Hermeneumata pseudo-dositheana* (books 2 and 3 and a fragment of book 4), and a new recension of the *Declinationes Graecorum* of Laon MS 444. Plate 2 gives a specimen of the *Declinationes Graecorum* from MS 902.

Two other manuscripts (London, BL Harley 5642 and Munich, BSB Clm 601) were probably also copied in St. Gall at the end of the ninth or the beginning of the tenth century.[32] Neither is so extensive as MS 902.

29. The St. Gall Interlinear Gospels (St. Gall, Stiftsbibliothek MS 48), the *Codex boernerianus* (Dresden, Sächsische Landesbibliothek A.145b), and the Basel Psalter (Basel, Universitätsbibliothek A.VII.3).

30. Some of the notations in the Basel Psalter were taken from Cassiodorus; others were composed by the St. Gall writer. See Arthur Allgeier, "Exegetische Beiträge zur Geschichte des Griechischen vor dem Humanismus," *Biblica* 24 (1943), 265–267.

31. Although the provenance of the manuscript was disputed in the past, it is now known to have been copied at St. Gall; see Bruckner, *Scriptoria*, 3:122. Four codices are bound in the volume, and this is the first of the four (MS 902, pp. 7–68). An entry in the ninth-century library catalogue refers to the three other codices in the volume: "LIBER AStrologiae et compotus Rabani et alius compotus in volumine I" (Lehmann and Ruf, *Mittelalterliche Bibliothekskataloge*, 1:80). But it is not unusual for medieval catalogues to omit one of several titles in a collectanea volume. MS 902 is certainly the book described in the catalogue of the year 1461: "Gramatica Dosithei; astrologia; computi quidam" (Lehmann and Ruf, *Mittelalterliche Bibliothekskataloge*, 1:118).

32. Karl Krumbacher, "Ein neuer Codex der Grammatik des Dositheus," *Rheinisches Museum für Philologie* 39 (1884), 349, proposed a St. Gall provenance for the London and Munich manuscripts on the basis of their textual relationship to MS 902 as well as on

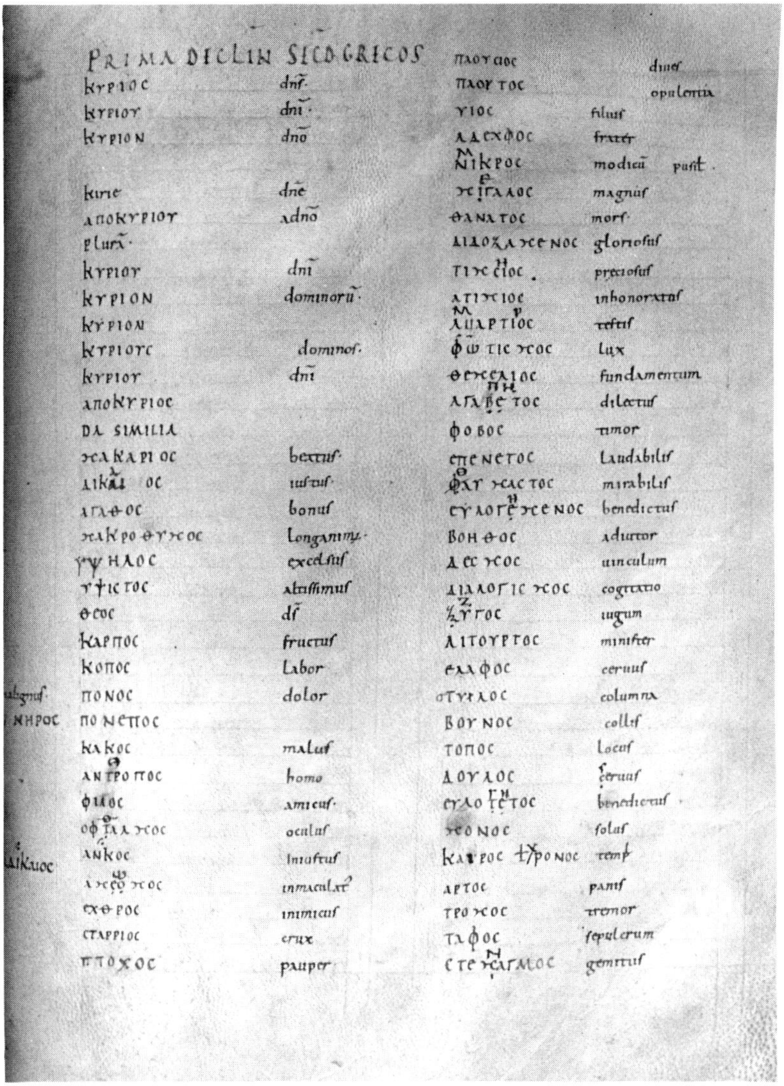

Plate 2. *Declinationes Graecorum.*
St. Gall, Stiftsbibliothek, MS 902, p. 61.

The London manuscript comprises a bilingual glossary, the new recension of the *Declinationes Graecorum*, parts of the *Ars grammatica*, portions of the *Hermeneumata pseudo-dositheana* (books 2 and 3 and a fragment of book 4), and a bilingual conversation entitled by its modern editor *Colloquium harleianum*. The Munich manuscript includes portions of the *Hermeneumata pseudo-dositheana* (fragments of books 2 and 3) and parts of the *Ars grammatica*. More detailed descriptions of the three manuscripts are given in Appendix 2 (below, pp. 121–122).

The *Ars grammatica* is known to us only through these St. Gall manuscripts. The role of the monastery was crucial in the preservation and transmission of the work. The monks did in fact make use of the book. It was certainly familiar to Notker Balbulus, who commented that the grammarians Dositheus, Donatus, Nicomachus, and Priscian were vastly inferior to his own favorite, Alcuin.[33] The monks were also instrumental in the transmission of the *Hermeneumata*. But their contribution here was not so exceptional, since the *Hermeneumata pseudo-dositheana* of the St. Gall manuscripts represented only one of at least eight recensions of *Hermeneumata* in circulation at the time.

Karl Krumbacher proposed the following stemma for the manuscripts on the basis of their transmission of the *Ars grammatica*:[34]

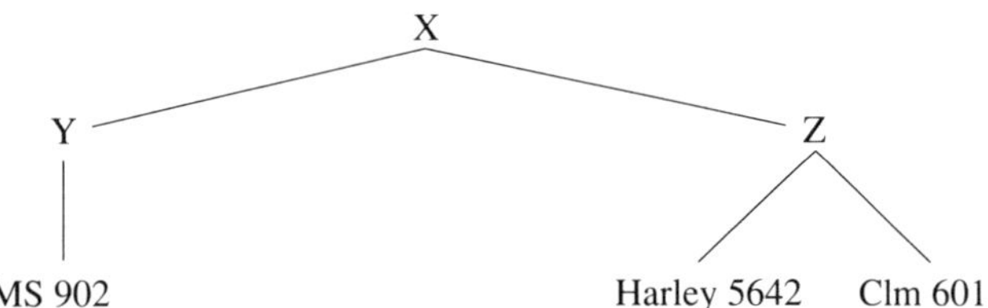

---

their external similarities with regard to format, parchment, and script. Perhaps the two volumes were removed from the library during the Councils of Constance or Basel, since they are not listed in the 1461 catalogue. On the contents of Harley 5642, see Krumbacher, "Eine neue Handschrift der Grammatik des Dositheus und der Interpretamenta Leidensia (Codex Harleianus 5642)," in *Sitzungsberichte der Akademie der Wissenschaften, phil.-hist. Klasse* (Munich, 1883), 3:193–203.

33. *Notatio*, ed. Dümmler, *Das Formelbuch*, p. 72: "Ille (sc. Albinus) talem grammaticam condidit ut Donatus Nicomachus Dositheus et noster Priscianus in eius comparatione nihil esse videantur."

34. "Ein neuer Codex," p. 348. Tolkiehn, *Dosithei Ars*, pp. viii–ix, followed this stemma in the preparation of his edition.

Of the extant manuscripts, MS 902 is the most nearly complete. The London and Munich manuscripts are closer to each other than either is to MS 902: the correspondence between them extends at times to the distribution of lines on a page. They share much of the same text, but each manuscript also contains material not found in the other. In MS 902, the bilingual text of the *Ars* is written continuously, each Latin term followed immediately by its Greek translation ("Ars Τέχνη," etc.). The same technique is used for the beginning portion of the *Hermeneumata*, but part way through the scribe changes his method and copies the Greek and Latin texts in parallel columns. Here the scribe seems to be reverting to the style of his prototype, for the columnar arrangement is the earlier of the two methods. It is used in the London and Munich manuscripts. In both of these, every page is divided into four (sometimes six) columns, of which the first, third (and fifth) contain the Greek text; the second, fourth (and sixth), the Latin. All three of the manuscripts have many readings, lacunae, and scribal errors in common.

As if to underline the importance of St. Gall in the transmission of the text, Krumbacher adds that manuscripts "Y" and "Z" were probably also copied there during the course of the ninth century.[35] And where did St. Gall obtain archetype "X"? One possibility is the northern Italian monastery of Bobbio. Of the published medieval catalogues I have seen, only that of Bobbio makes explicit reference to the work: "librum I. Dosithei de grammatica."[36]

In addition to the grammatical texts, MS 902 contains other material testifying to an interest in Greek. The awkward hand that transcribed the *Declinationes* on pp. 61–68 also scrawled a note across the top of p.7 (the first page of the codex): "ICTO ΛIBPO. YCYC. ΦYIOMAΠCEIP <IOAN-NEC?>CΠOPEP." The ink is far too faded to be fully decipherable even with the aid of an ultraviolet lamp. But the line is a transliteration into Greek of a Latin clue to the identity of its puerile author: "Isto libro usus fui . . ." (followed by some unintelligible terms that are probably proper names).

On the same page of the manuscript, a more expert hand has transcribed, in small uncial letters, a Greek fragment of seventeen lines. (See

---

35. "Ein neuer Codex," p. 353.

36. Gustav Becker, *Catalogi bibliothecarum antiqui* (Bonn, 1885; repr. Hildesheim, 1973), p. 69. According to James Westfall Thompson, *The Medieval Library* (Chicago, 1939), p. 159, the text is a tenth-century copy of an index drawn up in the second half of the ninth century. For references to Dositheus in some humanistic book lists, see Dionisotti, "From Ausonius' Schooldays?" pp. 84–85.

Plate 3.) This intriguing text is part of a Byzantine letter, and the circumstances of its composition are unknown.[37] The letter was written by a certain Lazaros to an anonymous "spiritual lord" ("Πνευματικῷ μου / δεσπότη," 11. 2–3), possibly a bishop.[38] In it, Lazaros explains what has happened to him since he left his lord on January 4. It is now January 21. Lazaros has encountered some sort of hostility on the part of the "king," and he attributes the problem to a certain evil George, "whom all the barbarians and even I myself, if I may say so, call a 'Jew'":

10   . . . γέγονα ἐν μικροτάτῃ λύπῃ διὰ
11 τὸ μεγάλ᾽ ἔχθραν θῆναι ὁ ἐκτὸς παντὸς ἀγαθο(ῦ) κ(αὶ) ὁ παρὰ πᾶσι
12 τοῖς βαρβάροις κ(αί) γε ἠπεῖν κ(αὶ) παρ᾽ ἐμοὶ καλούμενος Ἑβραῖος
13 Γεώργιος ἀναμέσον ἐμο(ῦ) κ(αὶ) τοῦ ῥίγος . . .

He goes on to describe himself sitting expectantly in the night by the fireside, and here, abruptly and in mid-sentence, the fragment breaks off.

The document is difficult to interpret, for its language is sometimes puzzling and we know little of its history. It is likely that the letter was copied at St. Gall in the second half of the ninth century in order to provide students with an example of Greek prose. Perhaps the scribe found the letter in a manuscript from Italy. In any case, he worked from the original text of the letter or from a text not far removed from the original.

The letter was copied in MS 902 together with other materials assembled for the study of Greek. How well did it serve this purpose? It was probably not much used as a reading exercise. Too many words are strange or, at least, unattested in the bilingual glossaries in use at the monastery. And unlike the other Greek texts in the codex, the letter of Lazaros was not supplied with a Latin translation. It may simply have been too hard for them to read.

St. Gall scholars who relied on manuals such as MS 902 for their knowledge of Greek grammar were not well equipped for reading

---

37. Jørgen Raasted, "A Byzantine Letter in Sankt Gallen and Lazarus the Painter," *Cahiers de l'Institut du moyen âge grec et latin* 37 (1981), 124–138, attempts to identify the author and date the letter to 869–871. But Raasted's line of reasoning is highly circumstantial, and, as he himself remarks (p. 135), "it rests on so many assumptions that it can hardly be termed more than a qualified guess." The edition Raasted presents is serviceable, although it should be compared with Plate 3. (Surely Raasted's "πικροτάτη" on line 10 is a misprint.) There is more work to be done on the text from the point of view of language and stylistics.

38. Lucilla Dinneen, *Titles of Address in Christian Greek Epistolography to 527 A.D.* (Washington, D.C., 1929), pp. 56–57 (for δεσπότης).

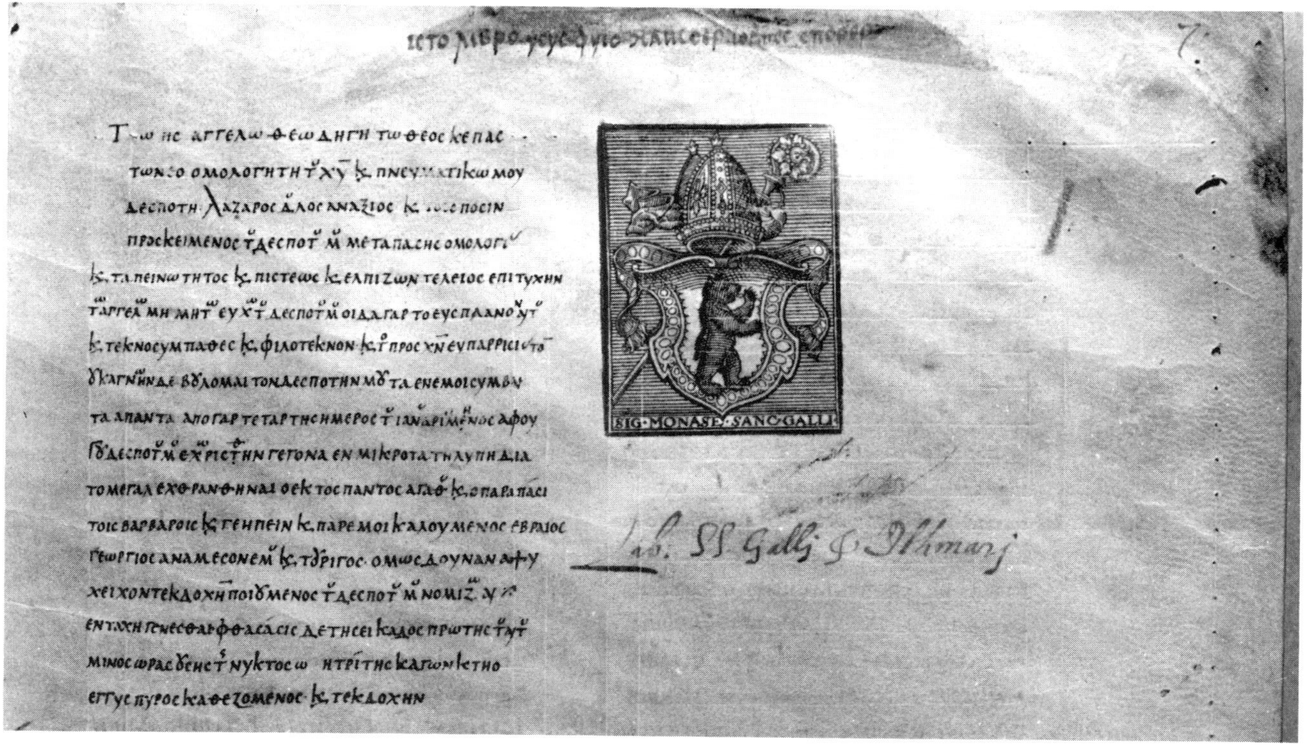

Plate 3. Fragment of Byzantine Letter.
St. Gall, Stiftsbibliothek, MS 902, p. 7 (top).

unfamiliar prose. What instruction did the book provide? The *Ars grammatica* of Dositheus, written to prepare Greeks for reading Latin, gave no explanation of the rules for Greek. The simple prose texts of the bilingual *Hermeneumata*, while serving to illustrate vocabulary and syntax, gave no analysis of the structure of the language. Only the *Declinationes Graecorum* attempted to come to terms with the language in a systematic way. Indeed, the *Declinationes* represented an attempt on the part of Carolingians to remedy the deficiencies of their sources and to present a practical outline of Greek grammar for those in need of an introduction. But the *Declinationes*, at least in the form in which they appear in the surviving manuscripts, seem hardly adequate to the task.

That Carolingian scholars themselves recognized the problem is suggested by the frequency with which they emended the texts. The different recensions of *Declinationes*—from Laon, St. Gall, and elsewhere—show that local teachers routinely corrected the texts, adding or subtracting material as they saw fit. These editorial interventions, of course, were not always for the best. And despite the vigilance of editors, new errors crept in. A confusion between the letters "A" and "Δ," a characteristic mistake of western scribes, yielded this declension in MS 902, p. 65: "ANIP, ANAPOC, ANAPI, ANAPA," etc. (for "ἀνήρ, ἀνδρός, ἀνδρί, ἄνδρα," etc.). It was a conspicuous error in a conspicuous paradigm, but later readers of the text do not seem to have noticed.

When ninth-century scholars like John Scottus succeeded in learning Greek, they did so despite many obstacles. They depended upon a motley collection of reference materials including inadequate grammars and fragments of dictionaries. The more fortunate among them might turn to a visiting Byzantine or Italo-Greek who had some knowledge of grammar. Not until the thirteenth century, when Roger Bacon composed his elementary grammar, did medieval people have an orderly and effective introduction to the language.[39]

---

39. *The Greek Grammar of Roger Bacon and a Fragment of His Hebrew Grammar*, ed. E. Nolan and S. A. Hirsch (Cambridge, Eng., 1902), pp. 1 – 182.

Glossaries and Word Lists

Information about Greek words was easier to come by than information about grammar. The school texts of late Antiquity included a range of bilingual materials—lexica, *Idiomata*, *Hermeneumata*—which, during the course of the Middle Ages, came to be prized for their lexicographical content. The principal bilingual lexica were the Greek-Latin glossary of pseudo-Cyrillus (mistakenly attributed to the fifth-century patriarch of Alexandria) and the Latin-Greek glossary of pseudo-Philoxenus (mistakenly attributed to a consul of A.D. 525). Collections of idioms, such as those attributed to Charisius and to Servius, were designed to illustrate points of grammar, but they also served as sources of new words. And as we have seen, the *Hermeneumata* normally contained some books of glossaries. In later years the *colloquia* and other books in them came to be treated as glossaries as well. By the ninth century *colloquia* were frequently transcribed as though they were running lists of vocabulary words rather than conversational exercises. Reduced to sets of words, Greek terms paired with Latin, the texts of the *Hermeneumata* were taken apart, and the lexical fragments used in the composition of new medieval dictionaries.[1]

When Carolingian scholars assembled bilingual glossaries, they turned, predictably, to these late antique schoolbooks. The glossaries of pseudo-Cyrillus and pseudo-Philoxenus were among the many texts used by Martin Hiberniensis in the composition of Laon, Bibliothèque Municipale MS 444. The *Scholica graecarum glossarum*, another important Carolingian work, comprised about 450 terms, mostly Greek in origin, together with Latin definitions.[2] Its sources included Isidore, Fulgentius, Martianus

---

1. The various texts are briefly reviewed by Bischoff, "Das griechische Element," pp. 260–261, and Berschin, *Griechisch-lateinisches Mittelalter*, pp. 43–46. Fragments of late antique *Idiomata* and *Hermeneumata* are edited by Johannes Kramer, *Glossaria bilinguia in papyris et membranis reperta*, Papyrologische Texte und Abhandlungen 30 (Bonn, 1983).

2. The text was edited by M. L. W. Laistner, "Notes on Greek from the Lectures of a Ninth-Century Monastery Teacher," *Bulletin of the John Rylands Library* 7 (1923), 421–456. Laistner believed that it was the work of Martin Hiberniensis. On the basis of

Capella, and commentaries to Martianus Capella, as well as several earlier bilingual glossaries. The alphabetical arrangement of the glossary lent a spurious order to the text, for in reality it was a hodgepodge of miscellaneous information. The author seems not always to have chosen his sources wisely. "The good monk," observes his modern editor, "had a passion for labelling any word, which was unfamiliar, Greek, and derivations are at times exceptionally quaint. *Mechanica ars* is derived from *moechus*, an adulterer, apparently because both pursuits require exceptional *ingeniositas*."[3]

In addition to these works, which represent collections of bilingual material drawn from several sources and put more or less successfully into some new shape, Carolingian scholars transcribed large numbers of incidental glosses. They gathered together the Greek words and phrases used by Latin authors and supplied them with Latin translations—or perhaps simply copied translations that already existed in the margins of their manuscripts. The writings of Quintilian, Lactantius, Jerome, Boethius, Cassiodorus, Macrobius, and Priscian were replete with Greek vocabulary. The lists that resulted, based on the vocabulary of a single author or text, are known as *Graeca collecta*. They vary considerably in length. At St. Gall, a set derived from Boethius consists of only four terms, while sets derived from the works of St. Jerome (of whom the monks were very fond) take up as many as four manuscript pages.

Of course the *Graeca collecta* of any particular author might be used in later collections of glossaries, and such collections might then be excerpted themselves. Laon MS 444 contained a glossary of Greek words used in the verses of John Scottus, and Martin Hiberniensis used Greek glossary words when he put together his own forgettable verse. It is impossible to draw clear boundaries between groups of glossaries in the Carolingian period and we cannot assume that their development followed any sort of logical sequence.

Nineteenth-century scholars adopted a genealogical model for the study of glossaries: tracing for various recensions of *Hermeneumata*, for instance, an orderly descent from an early-third-century parent glossary.[4] But the genealogical model is misleading, for their composition was not

---

more recently discovered manuscripts, however, this attribution has been called into question. See John J. Contreni, "Three Carolingian Texts Attributed to Laon: Reconsiderations," *Studi medievali* 17 (1976), 802–808.

3. M. L. W. Laistner, "The Revival of Greek in Western Europe in the Carolingian Age," *History* 9 (1924), 183.

4. Goetz, *CGL* 1:17–23.

linear; it was haphazard. Glossaries were often assembled very casually: "We must banish from our minds the notion that each glossary is an isolated work, the result of the learned labour of a life-time, the slowly amassed collectanea of some wide reader like Bede or Lupus. . . . Glossaries are much more hasty make-shifts, the mere result of massing the word-collections that were available at this or that monastery and then re-arranging the mass. In fact, there was often no 'compiler' properly so called. The original glossary was not *made* (by mental effort); it *grew* (by the mechanical fusion of the different parts of a volume which had been made a receptacle for 'glossae collectae' of various authors). . . ."[5] Glossaries were infinitely plastic: material could be added, subtracted, and conflated at will.

This process of composition means that identical copies of a glossary are rare. The texts are different because they were copied at specific times and places in order to accomplish specific aims. The relationship of one text to another is often a puzzle. How do we decide, in the case of two glossaries with similar words, whether one was copied from the other, whether they are two separate glossaries, or whether both were copied from a third? The decision is surprisingly difficult. Despite the considerable efforts of such scholars as Goetz and Lindsay, the question of how best to edit glossaries continues to trouble the modern scholars who deal with them.[6]

In the ninth and early tenth centuries, Carolingian thinkers gave serious attention to Greek-Latin glossaries, and bilingual word lists of one sort or another appeared in a number of contemporary manuscripts. The usual form taken by such texts was that of a formal arrangement of Greek words together with Latin translations or explanations. The glossaries might represent sets of coordinated lexical units (Greek terms paired with Latin terms equivalent in their lexical meaning) or, as was frequently the case, Greek terms with detailed explanatory or descriptive notes in Latin. Most of the bilingual glossaries survive in a single exemplar, and it is likely that Carolingians possessed far more of them than we have today.[7]

5. W. M. Lindsay and H. J. Thomson, *Ancient Lore in Medieval Latin Glossaries*, St. Andrews University Publications 13 (Oxford, 1921), p. viii.

6. In "The Biblical Glosses of Haimo of Auxerre and John Scottus Eriugena," *Speculum* 51 (1976), 412, John Contreni observes that glossaries pose complex problems: "Indeed, studies of early medieval glossaries in general—which seem to have tapered off since the days of Goetz, Lindsay, Steinmeyer, Sievers, and others—are inherently obscure, with their still unresolved problems of dating, origin, and influences."

7. On the large numbers of glossaries transcribed during the ninth century, see Bischoff,

The St. Gall glossaries demonstrate the variety available at one Carolingian monastery. Some of them are texts one would expect to find at other monasteries as well, such as glossaries taken from *Hermeneumata*. Others more probably reflect local concerns or personal idiosyncrasies of St. Gall monks. Several texts are surely works of impulse, quickly copied and used, not intended to be presented as the most polished accomplishments of their authors. There are more of these occasional glossaries in the manuscripts than one might gather from reading the generally admirable nineteenth-century library catalogue. The glossaries are easy to overlook, especially when they are short and written in messy script on flyleaves or are copied so closely to other texts that they seem to be a part of them.

Glossaries and word lists in the St. Gall manuscripts are described in Appendix 3 (below, pp. 123–125). In general, I have not included such conventional treatments of Greek and Latin words as Isidore's *Etymologiae*. Now and then, however, excerpts from Isidore that give definitions of Greek words are arranged as glossaries and combined with other glossaries in a way that suggests a particular interest in their Greek vocabulary. These texts are noted in the Appendix. It has seemed sensible to record this material when it is evidently being used as a source of information about Greek words. More often, of course, the antiquarian texts present a Greek vocabulary that has in fact been domiciled in Latin and is no longer recognized as foreign. I have omitted from consideration one other group of texts, *Onomastica sacra*, or interpretations of Greek and Hebrew biblical names. These are specialized glossaries that tend to be transmitted in a separate stream and they belong less to the realm of lexicography than to that of biblical scholarship and exegesis.

The texts described in Appendix 3 were written during the ninth century; one, perhaps, during the early tenth. The form of all of them is Greek-to-Latin, which probably reflects the predisposition of their sources. As a rule, then, the "lemma," or subject for consideration, is in Greek, and the "interpretamentum" or the "hermeneuma," the interpretation or translation, is in Latin. Greek lemmata are written in western Greek majuscules, in Latin letters, or in combinations of the two. Occasionally scribes give titles to the glossaries or some other indication of their sources, but more often they do not, and it is left to the hapless reader to make the identification. I have not been able to identify every source.

MSS 196, front flyleaf recto, 299, pp. 292–293, and 397, p. 38, contain

---

"Das griechische Element," p. 261, and Goetz, "Glossographie," Pauly-Wissowa *RE* 7:1449–1450.

a brief bilingual glossary whose history illustrates the sometimes surprising routes by which information about Greek words made its way into the Carolingian world. The text comprises six Greek terms and their Latin definitions. The Greek terms are names of charitable institutions in Byzantium: "xenodochium," a public building for the reception of strangers; "ptochotrophium," a poor-house; "nosochomium," a hospital or infirmary; "orphanotrophium," an orphanage; "gerontochomium," a public hospital or alms-house for poor old people; "brephotrophium," a foundling hospital.

Two of the terms had long been known in the West. Jerome and Isidore used "xenodochium" and "nosochomium," and Jerome employed the former as though it were a Latin word that did not require explanation. They are not the sources of the St. Gall text.

The Greek names first appeared as a group in the *Novellae* of the emperor Justinian, promulgated between A.D. 534 and 556. They were first defined, in Latin, by Julian Antecessor, a sixth-century Constantinopolitan jurist who composed an *Epitome*, or summary, of the *Novellae*. Julian gave the definitions in his comment on novel 7, in which the emperor forbade the alienation of property belonging to hospitals and charitable institutions. It is Julian's definitions that appear in the Carolingian glossary.

Where did the monks find them? They very likely saw them in a collection of capitularies made in 827 by Ansegisus, abbot of St. Wandrille. Ansegisus reproduced Julian's discussion of the inalienability of church property in Byzantium in an attempt to safeguard church property in the realm of Louis the Pious. The monks recognized in this text a source of information about Greek words, and they recast it in the form of a bilingual glossary.

The material was taken up by the compilers of a few other Greek-Latin glossaries, and in later centuries it entered the general fund of Latin lexicography. The names and descriptions of the Greek charitable institutions survived in lexicography long after Justinian's novel had lost its force. In about 1286, John of Genoa (Giovanni Balbi or Johannes Balbus Januensis) brought them into the *Catholicon*, the preeminent dictionary of the Latin Middle Ages.[8]

The flyleaf of MS 196 contains, beneath the glossary of charitable institutions, a list of the Greek names of the twelve signs of the zodiac. There are no Latin translations, but each Greek name is preceded by the initial

---

8. I edited the text and gave a detailed account of its history in "Some St. Gall Glosses on Greek Philanthropic Nomenclature," *Speculum* 58 (1983), 1008–1017.

letter of the corresponding Latin sign. The spelling of the Greek is corrupt, and the apparatus entitled *Graeca* indicates the Greek terms as they are normally written:

> A. ΚΡΙΟϹ
> T. ΤΑΥΡΟϹ
> G. ΔΥΔΙΜΙ
> C. ΚΑΝΚΡΟϹ
> L. ΛΕΟΝ
> V. ΠΑΡΘΙΝΟϹ
> L. ΖΙΧΟϹ
> S. ϹΚΟΡΠΕΙΟϹ
> S. ΤΟϵΑΤΙϹ
> C. ΕΓΕΑΚΕΡΟϹ
> A. ΙΔΡϹΧΟϹ
> P. ΙΧΤΙϹ

> *Graeca*: 1. κριός 2. ταῦρος 3. δίδυμοι
> 4. καρκίνος 5. λέων 6. παρθένος
> 7. ζυγός 8. σκορπίος 9. τοξότης
> 10. αἰγόκερως 11. ὑδροχόος 12. ἰχθύς

The Greek names of the signs of the zodiac were available in several places. One occasionally finds them listed in the Greek computus and—perhaps more to the point—in *Hermeneumata* of the *Leidensia* recension. At St. Gall, they appear with Latin translations in MS 902, p. 51, and Munich, Clm 601, fol. 61r.[9]

MS 237, p. 326, contains a glossary of twenty-six metrical and grammatical terms. The spelling of the Greek words (transliterated into Latin) is poor. The text begins, "Poesis, opus multorum librorum," and ends, "Cletike, vocativus. Afrettretike, ablativus." The metrical vocabulary is derived from Isidore, *Etymologiae* 1.39.21, while the grammatical vocabulary is conventional (parts of speech, names of the cases, and the like) and therefore available in several sources, including the *Ars grammatica* of Dositheus.[10] Some of the lemmata also appear in the *Scholica graecarum glossarum*.

Two marginal glosses in MS 249 are interesting because they contain Greek words written in Greek minuscules. The glosses refer to the text of Bede's *De orthographia*. (The ink is very faded and some words are

---

9. See also *CGL* 3:30.
10. See Keil, *Grammatici latini*, 7:389, 391, 392.

illegible even under ultraviolet light.) On p. 5, alongside Bede's comment, "... coenon enim graece commune est, unde coenobium a communi vita nomen accepit ... ," someone has written: "κοῖνον † · cte επι κοῖνον commune genus οἱ † ... diphthongon."

On p. 11 Bede explains the use of the diastole, an editorial notation that serves to separate words combined improperly: "Diastole graece, latine interdictum. est autem nota ad pedem litterae posita, quae male coniuncta separet, ne puer legens erret. ... " His explanation is soon followed in the manuscript by an inadvertent example of the error. A scribe who ought to have transcribed "in o videlicet" has written instead "inovi delicet." The error is remarked by a later reader or corrector of the manuscript, who underlines the improperly divided words, draws the sign for the diastole under them, and adds the note: "Dυαζολε <G>r<ece> etiam subdistinctio † ..."

MS 270, pp. 55–68, contains a series of glossaries, some of which are bilingual. On p. 57 there is a glossary of twenty-nine mostly biblical terms. The text begins, "Prathema id est interrogatio, Ψychen id est anima," and ends, "Astipulatus id est fideiussor, Atoron id est voratus hominum." Many of the lemmata (e.g., "Ypnus id est somnus," "Carpos id est fructus," "ΟΦis id est serpens") appear to be derived from Genesis 1–3. The lemma ΦШCZOE is noteworthy.

On pp. 60–62 there are Greek-Latin glosses with many biblical and ecclesiastical terms. These manuscript pages probably reflect the conflation of at least two glossaries. Greek words on p. 60 are written in Greek majuscules. The text begins, "MYC, mus; ΤΟΥΓΡΑΤΗΡ, filia," and ends, "Εξ, sex; ΕΠΤΑ, septem." Greek words on pp. 61–62 are written in Latin letters. The text begins, "Epistimi, id est disciplina; Epistatis, id est magister," and ends, "Philacas, id est vigilias vel excubias vel custodias."

The final bilingual glossary in the series brings us to one of the most characteristic groups of St. Gall texts—glosses made up of Greek words used by St. Jerome. *Graeca collecta ex Hieronymo* appear in three manuscripts. In MS 270, pp. 62–64, they are Greek terms derived from Jerome's *De viris illustribus*, together with Latin translations. The glossary begins, "De catalogo ieronimi. ΥΠΟΕ; ΥΠΟΕΕCΕΟΝ, dispositionum," and ends, "Commaticos, compendiosos." The Greek words are, for the most part, the titles of books written by the illustrious men. A glossary derived from *De viris illustribus* also appears in MS 902, p. 68, where it is inserted between the lists of adverbs and conjunctions in the *Declinationes Graecorum*. The source of the glossary is not identified in the manuscript. The text begins, "ΑΡΧΙΑ, principatus; ΔΙΑΛΟΓΟC, conflictus; ΔΙΑ, duo; ΛΟΓΟC, verbum," and ends, "ΔΕΙΤΕΡΕCΗΝ, iterationem." The third glossary derived from the *De viris* is in MS 299, pp. 288–292. Plate 4 presents a page of this glossary. The text begins, "De catalogo virorum inlustrium Hieronimi; ΚΑΤΑΛΟΓΟC, series sive subputatio," and ends, "ΝΕШΦΙΤΟC, nuper adveniens." On p. 292 there is a brief glossary derived from the *De viris illustribus* of Gennadius. The text begins, "De catalogo Gennadii; ШΜШΟCΙΟΝ, aequalis substantiae," and ends, "ΑΓΝΟΙΤΟΙC, castis." (It is immediately followed by the glossary of Greek charitable institutions and a few miscellaneous glosses.) The bilingual *De viris* glossaries in MSS 270, 299, and 902 are not the same: they differ in the selection of Greek terms, in their spelling, and in their Latin translations.

MS 299, pp. 281–283, has another set of *Graeca collecta ex Hieronymo* taken from selected commentaries and letters. The spelling of the Greek is poor. The glossary portion of the text begins, ". . . Strimphalidas ΓΝΗCΙΟΤΗΚΝΟ id est proprio filio," and ends, "ΤΑΑΝΟCΙΑΝ, inventa vel manifesta; Item de epistolis Hieronimi."

It is easy to imagine how these glossaries came about. Jerome used Greek words and Greek allusions freely in his writings. But Jerome's public was not the same as Cicero's, and medieval readers needed help in order to grasp them. This was the reason for the marginal or interlinear translations of *Graeca* that one frequently finds in manuscripts of his works. The St. Gall *Graeca collecta ex Hieronymo* are the result of the gathering together of vocabulary and marginalia from earlier manuscripts.

This derivative process accounts, I think, for some of the very poor spelling of Greek words in the glossaries. The transcription of *Graeca* in Latin texts was generally a problem for scribes unfamiliar with the Greek majuscule script. After repeated copying by men who did not in fact know what they were doing, *Graeca* might be rendered almost unintelligible. Marginal or interlinear transliterations sometimes helped to keep the reader on course. Here are some fairly typical specimens from a text of Jerome's biblical commentaries: "ΜΗΤροΠΟΝC" and "ΜΗΤρΤΟΟΛΙC," both with transliteration "metropolis" (for "μητρόπολις"); "ΑΝΙШΤΗΝ," "anagogen" (for "ἀναγωγήν"); and "ΕΤΟΙΜΟΛΟRΙΑΝ," "ethimologian" (for "ἐτυμολογίαν").[11]

The three *De viris* glossaries represent separate collections of marginalia, and it is instructive to compare them. In the following table the

---

11. MS 119, pp. 58, 61, 73, 138, and elsewhere. On the editorial problems created by the transcription of Jerome's Greek vocabulary, see Berschin, *Griechisch-lateinisches Mittelalter*, p. 65.

ΠΡΑΖΕΟΝ· actionū·
ΠΕΡΙΟΔΟC· contextus·
ΑΠΟΚΡΙΦΑC· ñ pscriptura occulta
CΗΥΕCΤΕΝ· amicum·
ΔΙΑΦωΝΙΑΝ· dissonantiā
ΙΕΡΕΟΝ· sacerdotale·
ΠΕΡΙΤΗΖΟΝ· de hac uita
θεωΡΙΚΑ· ctēplatiua·
ΗΟΠΛΑΤΟΝ· hic plato·
ΤΟΝΦΙΛΟΝΑ· hunc philonē·
ΑΚΛΟΥθΕΙ· sequitur·
ΗΟΦΙΛΟΝ· hic philo·
ΤΟΝΠΛΑΤΟΝΑ· hunc platonē·
ΑΡΧΕΟΡΗΤΟC· ctlictus
ΠΕΡΙΤΗΚΡΑΤΟΡΙΑ· de hac potenti
ΤΟΥθΥ· huius di·
ΚΑΡΑΚΤΕΡΙ· stilo t figura·
ΔΕΥΤΕΡΟCΙΝ· nouitatē·
ΦΙΛΟΛΟΓΟC· ratioñ samatoris·
Α·Β·Γ·Α·ΖΑ·C·I·II·C·I·LX·I·CC·
ΕΛΕΧΟC· castigatio·
ΜΟΝΟC· vnū·
ΜΟΝΑΡΧΙΑ· singularis principat
ΑΡΧΙΑ· principat
ΔΙΑ· duo·
ΠΙΛΛΟΤΟC· ctlictus

ΛΟΤΟC· uerbū· tratio·
ΔΙΑΤΡΙΒΑC· dissensiones·
ΦΙΛΟ· amor·
ΦΙΛΟΖΕΝΙΑ· amor donorū·
ΖΕΝΙΑ· donum·
ΚΑΙΠΕΡΥΤΟΥ· & de hoc·
ΟΝΟΜΑΤΟΥCΤΟΥΡ· ā nomine hui di·
ΦΡΑCΙΝ· eloquentia·
ΚΑΤΑΦΡΑCΙΑC· secdm frigas·
ΤΗCΤΙΚΟΥ· sapientes·
ΕΝΚΡΑΤΙΑ· cōtinentes·
CΥΝΤΑΓΜΑΤΑ· documeta·
ΥΕΟΛΟΕΠΙΓΡΑΦΙΑ· false supscripta·
ΕΖΑΗΜΡΟΝ· sex dierū t partiū·
ΗΜΗΡΑ· pars·
ΚΑΤΑΚΕCΕΟΝ· doctrinarū
CΤΡΟΜΑ· uariātātū·
ΠΡΟCΕΦΑΝΕΝ· manifestauit·
ΚΡΟΝΟΓΡΑΦΙΑC· teporalis scripture·
ΑΡΧΟΤΟΝΙΑΝ· aquitatē·
ΤΕCΕΡΟΙC· quadris·
ΤΕCΕΡΑ· quattuor·
ΕΙΚΤΑCΕΙ· excessu· t mtus·
ΜΟΝΟΓΑΜΙΑ· de singularib, nuptiis·
ΜΟΝΟC· vnus·
ΓΑΜΟC· nuptie·
ΦΙCΚΟC· frons·

Plate 4. Greek-Latin Glossary of Terms Derived from
Jerome's *De viris illustribus.*
St. Gall, Stiftsbibliothek, MS 299, p. 289.

first three columns show the words and translations from each glossary's treatment of the Life of Clement of Alexandria. The fourth column gives the Greek words as they appear in the most recent edition of the text.[12]

MS 270, p. 63	MS 299, p. 289	MS 902, p. 68	Jerome, *De viris illustribus* 38
KATAKECEAN, eruditio vel doctrinarum	KATAKECEON, doctrinarum	KATAKECHⲰN, doctrinarum	κατηχήσεων
CTPOMACTIC, varietatis	CTPOMA, varietatum	CTOMATⲰN, varietatum CTOMA, varietas	Στρωματεῖς
ΥΠΟΕΕCΕⲰN, dispositionum		ΥΠΟΘΕCΕⲰN, dispositionum	Ὑποτυπώσεων
ΠΡΟC ΕΦΑΝΗCΕΝ, elegantem	ΠΡΟCΕΦΑΝΕΝ, manifestavit	ΠΡΟCΕΦΑΝΕΙΝ, manifestavit	προσεφώνησεν
ΚΡⲰΝΟΓΡΑΦΙΕ, temporalis scripturae vel caracteris	ΚΡΟΝΟΓΡΑΦΙΑC, temporalis scripture	ΚΡΟΝΟΓΡΑΦΙΑC, temporalis scriptum	χρονογραφίας
ΑΡΧΟΤΝΙΑΝ, antiquitatem	ΑΡΧΟΤΟΝΙΑΝ, a<nti>quitatem	ΑΡΧΟΤΟΝΙΑΝ, antiquitatem	ἀρχαιολογίαν

Here, as in other *Graeca collecta*, Greek terms are listed in the order in which they occur in the source text. They are copied in the same inflection used in the source: nouns are regularly given in oblique cases and verbs in various persons, tenses, and moods. Basic or canonical forms are rarely indicated. The compilers of MSS 299 and 902 attempt to do this with "CTPOMA" and "CTOMA" (for "στρῶμα"), but this is exceptional behavior. There is no discussion of syntax.

Only Latin translations are supplied. There are occasional errors. The compiler might simply get the wrong meaning for a word, or he might have the right meaning but be confused as to what part of speech it is. In the Life of Clement of Alexandria, Jerome uses "προσεφώνησεν" to signify "dedicavit." The compiler of MS 270 views the term as an adjective in the accusative case, "elegantem." The translation "manifestavit" of MSS 299 and 902 is better, but it is still not quite precise. Elsewhere, the verb "MANΘANOMEN" (for "μανθάνομεν") is taken for a noun: "idest doctrina vel disciplina" (MS 299, p. 283).

---

12. *Hieronymus liber de viris inlustribus. Gennadius liber de viris inlustribus*, ed. Ernest C. Richardson (Leipzig, 1896), pp. 26–27.

The quality of the bilingual glossaries is disappointing, but it is under-standable given the circumstances of their composition. The St. Gall glossaries were not assembled by methodically abstracting Greek vocabulary from promising texts and then referring to the corresponding entries in some authoritative parent glossary. As far as we know they had no such glossary. Instead, the glossaries contain material originally prepared to serve as a sort of running commentary on the source text. The marginalia were in the manuscripts in the first place in order to facilitate the reading of Jerome's *De viris illustribus*. Their use for language study in the bilingual glossaries represents a second stage in the processing of the material. A still more advanced stage was to arrange the material in alphabetical order in some new dictionary, but this did not happen at St. Gall.

Scholars elsewhere in the medieval world occupied themselves with Jerome's Greek vocabulary. There is a bilingual glossary with lemmata taken from Jerome's *Adversus Jovinianum* 1 in Valenciennes, Bibliothèque Municipale MS 81 (74), fol. 102v.[13] An important set of *Graeca collecta ex Hieronymo* appears in Paris, BN lat. 3088, fols. 116r–121v. The glossary comprises about 200 lemmata derived from forty letters in Jerome's correspondence. Unlike the St. Gall texts, which simply give literal translations of Greek words, the Paris manuscript presents relatively lengthy discussions of them. Most of the information seems to come from Isidore's *Etymologiae*. According to John Contreni, who is editing the text, the glossary may be the work of John Scottus.[14] The interest in Jerome did not end with the Carolingians. In the twelfth century Moses of Bergamo, an interpreter at the court of Constantinople, composed an *Expositio in graecas dictiones quae inveniuntur in prologis S. Hieronymi*.[15]

MS 397, p. 37, and MS 899, p. 107, contain explanations of four Greek theological terms: "OYCIA," "OYCIOCEIC," "ΥΠOCTACIC," "ΠPOCO-ΠON" (for "οὐσία," "οὐσίωσις," "ὑπόστασις," "πρόσωπον"). In MS 899 the terms serve to illustrate the "ΥΠTONGI GRECORUM: AI (e), OY (u), OI (y)." The source of the text, which is unidentified in the

---

13. Bischoff, "Das griechische Element," p. 267, n. 109.

14. John J. Contreni, "John Scottus, Martin Hiberniensis, the Liberal Arts, and Teaching," in *Insular Latin Studies: Papers on Latin Texts and Manuscripts of the British Isles: 550–1066*, ed. Michael W. Herren, Papers in Mediaeval Studies 1 (Toronto, 1981), p. 31. See also Jeauneau, "Jean Scot Erigène et le grec," pp. 31–33.

15. See G. Cremaschi, *Mosè del Brolo e la cultura a Bergamo nei secoli XI–XII* (Bergamo, 1945), pp. 163–195, for an edition.

manuscripts, is Boethius's *Contra Eutychen et Nestorium*.[16]

MS 899, p. 84, presents an interesting list of Neoplatonic formulae. The Greek vocabulary derives from a work by Marius Victorinus, a Roman rhetorician of the fourth century. The Latin translations derive from marginal notes added to a later manuscript:[17]

1	ΝΟΥϹ ΠΑΤΡΙΚΟϹ	sensus paternus
	ΛΟΓΟϹ	verbum sive ratio
	ΟΝ	quod est
	ΤΟΥ ΟΝΤΟϹ	qui sit
5	PRO ON	prae existentia
	ΤΟ ΜΗ ΟΝ	quod non est
	ΜΗ ΟΝΤΑ	quae non sunt
	ΛΟΓΟΙ	sermones
	ΤШΝΟΙ	sensui
10	ΤΟΥ ΟΝΤΟϹ	qui sit
	hyle	materia vel corpus
	ΜΗ ΟΝΤШϹ	non sit
	ΥΛΗΝ	corpus
	ΤΗ ΥΛΗ	huic corpori
15	per kerycem	praeconem
	aeones	secula
	ΟΜΟΟΥϹΙΟΝ	unius eiusdemque substantiae
	ΑΝ⟨Τ?⟩ΘΕΑ	ac si divina
	ΑΘΕΙΑ	sine divinitate

Graeca: 5. προόν 9. τῷ νῷ 11. ὕλη 15. κῆρυξ (for 'κήρυκα,' here given a Latinized accusative ending) 18. ἀντίθεα 19. ἄθεια

The terms seem to appear in the order of their occurrence in the source. They retain the original inflections (the nominative "hyle, materia vel corpus" and, later, the oblique cases "ΥΛΗΝ, corpus" and "ΤΗ ΥΛΗ, huic corpori"). The same Greek word may appear several times, each time with the Latin translation deemed most appropriate to the context ("ΛΟΓΟϹ, verbum sive ratio" and, later, "ΛΟΓΟΙ, sermones").

16. PL 64:1345–46.

17. The transcription of the glossary printed by Karl Neff, *Die Gedichte des Paulus Diaconus*, Quellen und Untersuchungen zur lateinischen Philologie des Mittelalters 3.4 (Munich, 1908), p. 60, is incomplete. There is no reason to connect the text with Paul the Deacon. For the original source, see *Marii Victorini Rhetoris Urbis Romae ad Candidum Arrianum*, in CSEL 83.1:15–48. The manuscript source is perhaps Bamberg, Staatsbibliothek Patr. 46 (Q VI 32).

The glossaries we have discussed so far have been based on literary or scholarly sources. But the St. Gall library also possessed a Greek-Latin glossary of a more informal type. MS 877, pp. 65–66, contains a glossary of fifty-seven lemmata. Some of the terms represent conventional *Hermeneumata* vocabulary (names of parts of the body and the like), others are Christian formulae, and still others give popular or colloquial expressions. This is an unusual text. There are certainly other examples of bilingual glossaries and phrase books intended for the use of travelers to Byzantium (or Greek-speaking regions), but there are few texts in which conversational material is mingled with material from the *Hermeneumata*.[18]

Some of the lemmata are repeated in the Angers Glossary, or *Glossarium andegavense*, of the tenth century.[19] In the portion of the Angers Glossary that corresponds to the St. Gall manuscript, there are seventeen lemmata. Fourteen of them are the same and three of them are new, and they are arranged in a sequence different from that in MS 877. These are words that come from some common source, and in the Angers Glossary they are given more correctly than they are in MS 877.

An edition of the text in MS 877 is given below. Both Greek and Latin words are written in Carolingian minuscules and the Greek is extremely corrupt. The edition reproduces the spellings of the manuscript. (In a small number of doubtful cases I have intervened with pointed brackets.) The capitalization is erratic, and it has been regularized. The few abbreviations used are conventional (for example, "sp̄s," "sc̄s," "dm̄," "dn̄s"), and I have expanded them. In the manuscript, the text is written continuously, Greek terms followed immediately by their Latin equivalents. Points are used to separate words, sometimes incorrectly (for example, 1.48, "mu.crus"). The edition presents the text in columns, and each pair of Greek and Latin terms is numbered consecutively.

There are two critical apparatus. The first gives the readings of the Angers Glossary and the second proposes a reconstruction of the Greek words as they might properly be written in Greek letters. (In the glossary

---

18. Bischoff, "Das griechische Element," p. 261, nn. 81 and 85. See also Bischoff, "The Study of Foreign Languages," pp. 237–239. Professor Bischoff has recently edited another glossary of colloquial Greek: *Anecdota novissima: Texte des vierten bis sechzehnten Jahrhunderts*, Quellen und Untersuchungen zur lateinischen Philologie des Mittelalters 7 (Stuttgart, 1984), pp. 248–249 (No. 37: "Vulgärgriechisch-lateinisches Glossar [Zehntes bis elftes Jahrhundert]").

19. The fragment appears on fol. 3v of the manuscript. See Omont, "Glossarium Andegavense," p. 676.

Greek words frequently appear in oblique cases, but in the apparatus it has seemed most sensible to give their basic or canonical forms.)

MS 877, pp. 65–66

(p. 65)	IN G<raeco> cyras	manus
	dactulo	digito
	pudas	pedes
	stuma	os
5	oftalmos	oculos
	<r>unas	nares
	ota	aures
	cardie	cordis
	tax	postulo
10	prosince	oratione
	equaecax	damo
	oranus	celos
	gen	terra
	italasum	mare
15	andropus	homines
	erimin	pacem
	transmascia	mirabilia
	insopia	in sapientia
	ergum	opus
20	inyrge	in ira
	pogma	spiritus
	agius	sanctus
	pisteucus	credo in deum
	quirius	domnus
25	basileus	rex
	dispantus	semper
	diceius	iustus
	permatontheon	per domnum
	aumateoteon	non per domnum
30	zuizuiri	vivis domni
	kalosatos siotheus	bene dedit tibi deus
	kacosatos	malum
	zuriccefilaxisse	domnus te custodiat
	t<roi?>dimithomo	manduca mecum
35	troizuiri	manduca domni
	piissonacapi	fac caritatem
	uti	quoniam
	pullas	multas
	soteria	salute
40	auditia	iniqualis

	nomu	lege
	quercum	tempus
	topum	locum
	sarcem	carnem
45	erga	opera
	elius	misericordia
	epi	super
	mu crus	pusillus
	amanus	inmaculatus
50	oenus	seculi
	fone	voce
	in zoe	in vita
(p. 66)	tantella	modica
	hyronia	similitudo
55	eplogison mezuuiron	g vel benedic me domni
	zuirie eplogisse	domnus te benedicat
	otheus eplogisisse	deus te benedicat

Glossarium andegavense: 12. *Ab hac glossa accedit Codex andegavensis.* uranos, caelum [*MS* uranus, *corr.* uranos] 13. gen, terram 14. talassum, mare 15. antropos, homines 16. erinen, pacem 17. taumastia, mirabilia 18. in sophia, in sapientia 19. ergum, opus 20. *Abest* 21. pneoma, spiritus [*MS* pnioma, *corr.* pneoma] 22. agius, sanctus 23. *Abest* 24. quirius, dominus 25. basilius, rex 26. dipantus, semper 27. diceus, justus *Et Codex andegavensis addidit* epistus, credendus; eleun, solem [*MS* eliun, *corr.* eleun]; selenen, lunam

Graeca: 1. χείρ 2. δάκτυλος 3. πούς 4. στόμα 5. ὀφθαλμός 6. ῥῖνες 7. οὖς 8. καρδία 9. τάσσω 10. προσευχή 11. ἐξ οἴκου, *Gr.* (?); domo, *L.* (?) 12. οὐρανός 13. γῆ 14. θάλασσα 15. ἄνθρωπος 16. εἰρήνη 17. θαυμάσια 18. ἐν σοφίᾳ 19. ἔργον 20. ἐν ὀργῇ 21. πνεῦμα 22. ἅγιος 23. πιστεύω εἰς θεόν 24. κύριος 25. βασιλεύς 26. διαπαντός 27. δίκαιος 28. per μὰ τὸν θεόν 29. οὐ μὰ τὸν θεόν 30. ζῇς κυρίῳ 31. καλῶς ἔδωσε ⟨σοι⟩ ὁ θεός 32. κακῶς ἔδωσε 33. κύριος σὲ φυλαξήσῃ 34. τρώγε δὴ (or δὲ) μετ᾽ ἐμοῦ 35. τρώγε κυρίῳ 36. ποίησον ἀγάπην 37. ὅτι 38. πολύς 39. σωτηρία 40. ἀδικία, *Gr.*; inaequalis, *L.* 41. νόμος 42. καιρός 43. τόπος 44. σάρξ 45. ἔργον 46. ἔλεος 47. ἐπί 48. μικρός 49. ἄμωμος 50. αἰών 51. φωνή 52. ἐν ζωῇ 53. tantilla, *L.* 54. εἰρωνεία 55. εὐλόγισόν με κύριε 56. κύριε, εὐλογήσῃ⟨ς⟩ 57. ὁ θεὸς εὐλογήσῃ σε

Free translations of some of the conversational phrases may indicate their flavor: 1.31, "God treated you well"; 1.33, "May the Lord protect you"; 1.34, "Eat with me"; 1.36, "Perform a kindness" (or might this phrase have the more intimate meaning it does in modern Greek?); 1.57, "May God bless you." These are all useful speeches, and they were probably assembled for some practical purpose. They may have been contributed by a Greek-speaking visitor to the place where the glossary was first compiled. The spelling of both the colloquial phrases and the hermeneutical vocabulary shows the influence of contemporary pronunciation. At some point in the transmission of the glossary—perhaps at the copying of this manuscript—the scribe copied from dictation.

What purposes were served by the bilingual glossaries compiled at St. Gall and elsewhere in the Carolingian Empire? *Graeca collecta* were used by scholars who wished to understand Greek words in the writings of Boethius, Jerome, Priscian, and other authors whose work was important to them. They were also used in the study of language. Carolingian handbooks for the study of Greek, such as St. Gall MS 902 and Laon MS 444, provided their readers with collections of glossaries as well as grammars. Of course the quality of the glossaries was uneven, and no matter how many sets of *Graeca collecta* were gathered together, the generally uncritical method of transcribing them limited their usefulness for learning Greek.

During the eleventh and twelfth centuries, lexicographers and grammarians began to seek out Greek words in order to etymologize them. The principal feature of the "schoolmen's Greek" lay in its vision of the Greek vocabulary as a collection of static and discrete particles, as words having no relation to any text or, indeed, to each other. All nouns, whether masculine, feminine, or neuter, were arbitrarily assigned an ending in "-os" or "-on"; all verbs were required to end in "-in" or "-on." Bischoff describes the process as a "mummification" of the Greek language.[20] Greek words and word fragments wandered through an endless series of Greek-Latin and Latin dictionaries, subject to alteration each time they were handled.

The Greek lemmata of one of the St. Gall glossaries underwent just such a transformation over the years. The list of names of charitable institutions, presented in the ninth century as a bilingual glossary, eventually entered the general fund of Latin lexicography. In about 1053, Papias broke up the list (or perhaps an earlier author had done so) and put the words in their appropriate alphabetical positions in the *Elementarium doctrinae rudimentum*. Other lexicographers copied them as well, and in some

---

20. "The Study of Foreign Languages," p. 235. On the Latin lexicographers and their treatment of Greek words, see Giovanna M. Gianola, *Il Greco di Dante: Ricerche sulle dottrine grammaticali del Medioevo* (Venice, 1980), as well as my review of the book in *Mittellateinisches Jahrbuch* 17 (1982), 310–311.

cases the misspellings threaten to make the terms unrecognizable. By the time John of Genoa brought them into the *Catholicon* in about 1286, both the form of the words and their definitions were considerably changed.[21]

While some people attempted to use the glossaries to further their studies, others saw in them an opportunity for display. The glossaries presented an irresistible temptation to pedants and literary dilettantes in search of unusual words. At the court of Charles the Bald it became the rather pretentious fashion to compose verses with words gleaned from glossaries. The "Carmina Scottorum Latina et Graecanica" in Ludwig Traube's edition of the Carolingian poets furnish more of these compositions than most of us today are prepared to appreciate. Traube was being kind when he observed that the verses were "touching in their ugliness."[22]

A contemporary, Hincmar of Reims, was less sympathetic. In a letter he savagely ridiculed the tastes of his nephew, Hincmar of Laon:

Even the abstruse words you have cited in your works—collected from whatever glossaries and interpolated without reason—convict you of vaingloriousness. As the Apostle says, "Shun novelty in words" [1 Tim. 6.20], and "When I am in the presence of the community I would rather say five words that mean something than ten thousand words in a tongue" [1 Cor. 14.19]. For you are not only unable to speak your native tongue, you are unable to understand it without an interpreter. There are enough Latin words you could have cited in the places where you cited Greek, and abstruse, and occasionally Irish and other barbarous words. . . . It is obvious that you have very inappropriately cited Greek words (which you yourself do not understand) not out of humility or to clarify what you wished to say, but for show. For the sake of a vain display you have very foolishly inserted them, so that all who read them may know that you wish to vomit forth things that you have not yet swallowed. . . .

"And," Hincmar continues, speaking of his contemporaries, "we ... stretch out and prolong short discourses, so that we can quote Greek or

---

21. For the texts and references, see Kaczynski, "Some St. Gall Glosses," pp. 1008–1017.

22. "Carmina Scottorum" in MGH Poet 3.3:685–701. Traube's comment in *"O Roma nobilis,"* p. 354: "Aber die alten griechischen Flicken, die man aus Glossarien und Commentaren trennte, um sein Buch damit zu zieren, und die wir heute verwünschen, waren der Purpur des damaligen Dichtergewandes und sind in ihrer Hässlichkeit doch rührend. . . ."

abstruse words taken from glossaries. . . . Scripture opposes this vanity when it says, 'Vanity of vanities. All is vanity!' [Eccles. 1.2]."[23]

---

23. *Opuscula et epistolae quae spectant ad causam Hincmari Laudunensis* 43, in PL 126:448–449. See also Berschin, *Griechisch-lateinisches Mittelalter*, pp. 167–169.

VII

Bibles

It was the need to understand Holy Scripture that prompted the most serious of the Carolingian efforts to learn Greek. Hebrew, Greek, and Latin were, according to Isidore of Seville and his successors, "three sacred languages." Greek was the original language of the New Testament and, as for the Old Testament, Greek was represented by the venerable Septuagint.

At the turn of the fifth century Jerome composed his famous letter to the Goths Sunnia and Fretela, urging them to study the biblical languages. In cases where the interpretation of the Latin text was unclear, he explained, the ambiguity might be resolved by recourse to the "fountains" of Greek and Hebrew speech. Jerome's letter on the translation of the Psalms became for the Middle Ages the prototypical formulation of the problem, and the letter was often copied as part of the preliminary matter of Psalters and Bibles.[1]

The characteristic instrument of medieval scholars who wished to study the language of Scripture was the bilingual codex. Greek-Latin and Latin-Greek books had been in widespread use in the late antique Mediterranean world, with bilingual editions of Vergil perhaps the best-known examples. But medieval scholars were interested in Christian works, and although they carried on the late antique form, they used it mostly for Greek-Latin editions of Scripture. Manuscripts that survive today give us bilingual versions of the Psalter, the Gospels, the Pauline Epistles, and the Acts of the Apostles. The survival of the bilingual Acts was quite lucky, for the transmission depended upon only two late antique manuscripts. Carolingian scholars seem not to have transcribed the Acts. They copied the Psalter, Gospels, and Epistles, sometimes in the new interlinear format especially favored by the Irish. Bilingual Epistles ceased to be copied in

---

1. *Epist.* 106.2, in CSEL 55:249. On the influence of the letter in the Middle Ages, see Allgeier, "Exegetische Beiträge," p. 282. For a new source see Bernice M. Kaczynski, "Greek Glosses on Jerome's *Ep. CVI, Ad Sunniam et Fretelam,*" in MS Berlin (East), Deutsche Staatsbibliothek, Phillipps 1674," in *The Sacred Nectar of the Greeks: The Study of Greek in the West in the Early Middle Ages,* ed. Michael W. Herren, King's College London Medieval Studies 2 (forthcoming).

the Ottonian period, and bilingual Gospels came to be copied very rarely. The transcription of Greek-Latin Psalters, however, continued without interruption on through the time of the humanists. This is surely because the Psalter, the most familiar of all books to medieval Latin readers, was uniquely suited to teach them Greek as well.[2]

When Bede studied Greek and wrote his *Retractatio in Actus Apostolorum*, he relied upon a bilingual copy of the Acts of the Apostles. The manuscript Bede used still exists.[3] Another scholar who very likely made use of a bilingual codex is Christian of Stavelot. His commentary on the Gospel of Matthew demonstrates a familiarity with both the Greek text of the Gospel and a series of Greek-Latin marginal notes that goes back to the fifth century.[4] During the ninth century in general, observes Beryl Smalley, "Greek scholarship . . . probably reached a higher point, at least in relation to exegesis, than it would do until towards the end of the thirteenth century."[5] The greatest of the Carolingian scholars, of course, was John Scottus. Although he referred several times to the text of the Septuagint, he may not have had access to a complete copy. Once, when he wished to expand a biblical allusion of pseudo-Dionysius, he was unable to do so, ". . . for we have no Septuagint at hand."[6] He did, however, have the Greek Psalter. As for the New Testament, it is possible that he had access to a Greek text of the Epistles, and it is certain that he had access to a Greek text of the Gospel according to John.[7]

The pattern of distribution suggested by John Scottus is borne out by

2. This paragraph summarizes the extremely useful discussion in Berschin, *Griechisch-lateinisches Mittelalter*, pp. 49 – 51, 251.

3. Oxford, Bodleian Library Laud. gr. 35. It was probably copied in Sardinia around A.D. 600: Lowe, *CLA* 2:No. 251. Berschin, *Griechisch-lateinisches Mittelalter*, pp. 15, 126, reviews the scholarship on the manuscript. On Bede's knowledge of Greek, see Anna Carlotta Dionisotti, "On Bede, Grammars, and Greek," *Revue bénédictine* 92 (1982), 111 – 141.

4. See Berschin, *Griechisch-lateinisches Mittelalter*, pp. 161 – 162, and Bischoff, "Das griechische Element," p. 262, n. 87. These marginal notes are also found in several St. Gall manuscripts and are examined more fully below.

5. *The Study of the Bible in the Middle Ages*, 2nd ed. (Oxford, 1952), p. 44.

6. *Expositiones in Ierarchiam caelestem* 13.374, ed. J. Barbet, in Corpus Christianorum. Continuatio mediaevalis 31 (Turnhout, 1975), p. 176: "Septuaginta enim prae manibus non habemus."

7. Jeauneau, "Jean Scot Erigène et le grec," pp. 27 – 30. On John's use of the works of the Greek Fathers, see Jeauneau, "Pseudo-Dionysius, Gregory of Nyssa, and Maximus the Confessor in the Works of John Scottus Eriugena," in *Carolingian Essays*, ed. Uta-Renate Blumenthal, Andrew W. Mellon Lectures in Early Christian Studies (Washington, D.C., 1983), pp. 137 – 149.

the body of surviving medieval manuscripts. We do not yet have a precise count of Greek and Greek-Latin Scriptures in western libraries, but some figures are available. Complete copies of the Greek Old Testament were rare north of the Alps; today only a few bilingual fragments remain. Greek-Latin Psalters, on the other hand, were copied throughout the Middle Ages. Arthur Allgeier identified thirty-two Psalters and Psalter fragments from the sixth through the thirteenth centuries. Books of the New Testament were also copied. Albert Siegmund listed nine western copies of Gospels, Epistles, and Acts.[8]

The monastery of St. Gall took a leading part in the transmission of these texts. Of the thirty-two Psalters listed by Allgeier, four were copied at St. Gall, one served as a model for later St. Gall recensions, and five derived from St. Gall prototypes. In other words, nearly one-third of surviving Greek-Latin Psalters can be connected with the monastery. Of the nine bilingual New Testament manuscripts, three were copied at St. Gall and one at the neighboring monastery of Reichenau (from a prototype shared with St. Gall). The total figures are provisional, since more bilingual texts from elsewhere in Europe are sure to be identified in the future. But there is already enough evidence to point to a considerable interest on the part of St. Gall scholars in the Greek text of the Bible.

Appendix 4 (below, pp. 127 – 130) presents an overview of the Greek-Latin Scriptures in St. Gall manuscripts. Nine manuscripts contain bilingual biblical texts or fragments of bilingual biblical texts.[9] In addition, three manuscripts containing Latin Gospels have Greek notes in the margins.

8. For a list of extant western Old Testament fragments, Psalters, and New Testaments, as well as a discussion of texts described in contemporary narrative sources, see A. Siegmund, *Die Ueberlieferung der griechischen christlichen Literatur in der lateinischen Kirche bis zum 12. Jahrhundert* (Munich, 1949), pp. 24 – 32. Bilingual Psalters are catalogued by Allgeier, "Exegetische Beiträge," pp. 263 – 264. Allgeier's catalogue is supplemented by H. Schneider, "Die biblischen Oden im Mittelalter," *Biblica* 30 (1949), 479 – 500. Many of the same manuscripts are discussed by Alfred Rahlfs, *Verzeichnis der griechischen Handschriften des Alten Testaments*, Mittheilungen des Septuaginta-Unternehmens der Königlichen Gesellschaft der Wissenschaften zu Göttingen 2 (Berlin, 1914), pp. 6 – 25. The most recent list of extant New Testaments can be found in Kurt Aland, *Kurzgefasste Liste der griechischen Handschriften des Neuen Testaments, 1: Gesamtübersicht*, Arbeiten zur neutestamentlichen Textforschung 1 (Berlin, 1963), and in its supplement, *Materialien zur neutestamentlichen Handschriftenkunde* 1, Arbeiten zur neutestamentlichen Textforschung 3 (Berlin, 1969), pp. 1 – 53.
9. According to Gustav Scherrer, *Verzeichnis*, p. 580 (index), there is also a Greek biblical text, the underlying text of a palimpsest, in MS 912, p. 25. But the reference is mistaken, for although the underlying text is indeed biblical (verses from Jeremiah), it is written in Latin, not in Greek.

There are four bilingual Psalters. Basel, Universitätsbibliothek, A.VII.3, known as the Basel Psalter, dates from the middle of the ninth ·century.[10] Two other texts are from the same century. MS 17 contains Psalms and Canticles, as well as bilingual versions of the Apostles' Creed, the Lord's Prayer, and a litany.[11] Plate 5 illustrates its treatment of Psalm 101. MS 1395, a collectanea volume, contains Psalter fragments on pp. 336–361.

The most distinctive of the Psalters is Bamberg, Staatsbibliothek, Msc. Bibl. 44 (A.I.14), known as the Bamberg Psalter. It was commissioned from the St. Gall scriptorium in A.D. 909 by Solomon III, bishop of Constance and abbot of St. Gall. In form it is quadripartite; that is, it presents, in four parallel columns, the three Latin versions of St. Jerome (*Psalterium gallicanum, Psalterium romanum*, and *Psalterium iuxta Hebraeos*) and (in Latin letters) the Greek text of the Septuagint. Its novelty lies in the addition of the Septuagint text. Carolingians had for some time been familiar with tripartite Psalters that presented Jerome's Latin versions. But Solomon's contribution of the Greek column was an innovation, and it would have lasting consequences for biblical scholarship. The Bamberg Psalter was a book for learned men. Among other texts in it are Jerome's letter on the translation of the Psalms, a dedicatory poem that explains the purpose of the quadripartite edition, and a series of bilingual prayers and a litany.[12]

The monastery's New Testament manuscripts were copied during the

---

10. Facsimile edition of the manuscript by Ludwig Bieler, *Psalterium graeco-latinum: Codex Basiliensis A.VII.3*, Umbrae Codicum Occidentalium 5 (Amsterdam, 1960). Part of the Greek text is printed by Allgeier, "Bruchstücke eines altlateinischen Psalters aus St. Gallen in Codd. 1395 St. Gallen, C 184 Zürich, und 587 Wien," *Sitzungsberichte der Heidelberger Akademie der Wissenschaften, phil.-hist. Klasse* 2 (Heidelberg, 1928–1929), especially pp. 62–141. A small part of the Latin text is printed by A. Dold and A. Allgeier, *Der Palimpsestpsalter im Codex Sangallensis 912*, Texte und Arbeiten 21–24 (Beuron, 1933), especially pp. 114–115.

11. The bilingual prayers and litany appear in MS 17, pp. 334–341. They are discussed in Chapter 8 below.

12. On the contents of the manuscript, see F. Leitschuh and H. Fischer, *Katalog der Handschriften der Königlichen Bibliothek zu Bamberg* (1895; repr. Wiesbaden, 1966), 1:36–39. For a paleographical description, see A. Chroust, *Monumenta Palaeographica: Denkmäler der Schreibkunst des Mittelalters*, Ser. 1, Lief. 16 (Munich, 1904), plates 3 and 4. On the historical background, see Allgeier, "Das Psalmenbuch des Konstanzer Bischofs Salomon III. in Bamberg. Eine Untersuchung zur Frage der mehrspaltigen Psalterien," *Jahresbericht der Görresgesellschaft 1938* (Cologne, 1939), pp. 102–121. The bilingual prayers and litany appear in the Bamberg Psalter, fols. 162r–168r. They are discussed in Chapter 8 below.

ercussus sum ut
foenum & aruit
cor meum quia
oblitus sum
comedere
panem meum
uoce gemitus mei
adhesit os meum
carni meae
imilis factus sum
pellicano
solitudinis factus
sum sicut
nicticorax in
domicilio
igilaui & factus
sum sicut passer
solitarius intecto
tota die exprobrabant
mihi inimici
mei & qui
laudabant me

ΕΠΛΗΓΗΝ · ωCΕΙ
ΧΟΡΤΟC · ΚΑΙ ΕΖΗΡΑΝΘΗ
Η ΚΑΡΔΙΑ ΜΟ ΟΤΙ
ΕΠΕ ΛΑ ΘΟΜΗΝ
ΤΟΥ ΦΑ ΓΕΙΝ
ΤΟΝ ΑΡΤΟΝ ΜΟΥ ·
ΑΠΟ ΦωΝΗC · ΤΟΣ ΤΕ ΝΑΓΜωΝ
ΕΚΟΛΛΙΘΗ · ΤΟ ΟC ΤΟΥ ΗΜΟ
ΤΗΣ ΑΡΚΙ ΜΟΥ
ΟΜΟΙ ωΘΗΝ
ΠΕΛΕ ΙΚΑ ΝΙ ω
ΕΡΗΜΗΚ ω · ΕΓΕΝΗ
ΘΗΝ · ωCΕΙ
ΝΥΚ ΤΙ ΚΟΡΑΞ · ΕΝ
ΟΙ ΚΟΠΕ Δ ω ·
ΗΓΡΥ ΠΝΙCΑ · ΚΑΙ ΕΓΕΝ
ΜΗΝ · ωCCΤΡΟΥ ΘΙΟΝ
ΜΟΝΑ ΖΟΝ · ΕΠΙ ΔωΜΑΤ
ΟΛΗΝ ΤΗ ΝΗΜΕΡΑΝ ωΝΗ
ΔΙ ΕΧΘΡΟΙ ΜΟΥ
ΚΑΙ ΟΙ
ΕΠΑΙ ΝΟΥ ΝΤΕC ΜΕ

Plate 5. Greek-Latin Psalter, Psalm 101.
St. Gall, Stiftsbibliothek, MS 17, p. 133v.

ninth century. One Greek Gospel book was dismembered early on, its leaves erased and reused in other books. Seven leaves of the original codex have been recovered. Most of them are palimpsests. They are bound in MS 18, pp. 143–146, MS 45, pp. 1–2, and Zurich, Zentralbibliothek, C 57, fols. 5r, 74r, 93r, 135r.[13] The Gospel book is considered to be of a bilingual type, although the surviving fragments have only a Greek text. This is because blank spaces for an anticipated Latin text have been left alongside the Greek columns.

MS 48, the well-known Interlinear Gospels, contains Greek Gospels with a Latin interlinear translation.[14] There is some incidental material that is also of interest. On p. 395 a scribe congratulates himself on his knowledge of Greek with the bilingual verse,

ΓΡΑΜΜΑΤΑ ΓΡΑΙΥΓΕΝΩΝ ΚΑΤΑ CΚΗΜΑΤΑ CΟΦΕ ΓΥΝΟCΚΕΙC
Cerne labore meo lingua pelasga patet . . .

There is a curious text on p. 129, immediately following the Gospel of Matthew. (See Plate 6.) It describes, in brief captions, forty-two illustrations for the Gospels of Matthew, Luke, and John. The titles of the illustrations are given in Greek, and the descriptions of the scenes to be portrayed are given in Latin. So, for instance, there is a scene of *"the sinful woman Mary,* with a jar of ointment in the dining room, wiping the feet of the Lord with her hair."* (Words originally in Greek are italicized.) And a scene from the raising of Lazaros: *"Lazaros* lies wrapped in a shroud. Or two who lament. The dead man smells. *Martha and Mary* (that is, the sisters of *Lazaros*) lie with outstretched hands at the feet of the Lord." Sometimes only names or titles of the biblical scenes are given. Both the Greek and the Latin are poorly written.[15]

The manuscript itself does not have any illustrations, although it is

13. Aland, *Materialien,* 1:8.
14. Facsimile edition of the manuscript by Hans Christian Michael Rettig, *Antiquissimus Quatuor Evangeliorum Canonicorum Codex Sangallensis Graeco-Latinus interlinearis* (Zurich, 1836). Berschin, *Griechisch-lateinisches Mittelalter,* p. 16, praises the quality of the edition.
15. Edition by Samuel Berger, "De la tradition de l'art grec dans les manuscrits latins des Evangiles," *Mémoires de la Société nationale des antiquaires de France* 52 (1891), 146–148. Berger's text was reprinted with minor changes by H. Leclercq, "Gall (Saint-)," in *Dictionnaire d'archéologie chrétienne,* 6.1:178–179. Scholars with a particular interest in the language of the text should compare the printed versions with Plate 6. Berger gives the Greek words in minuscules rather than in the majuscules used by the scribe, and he reorders some of the captions.

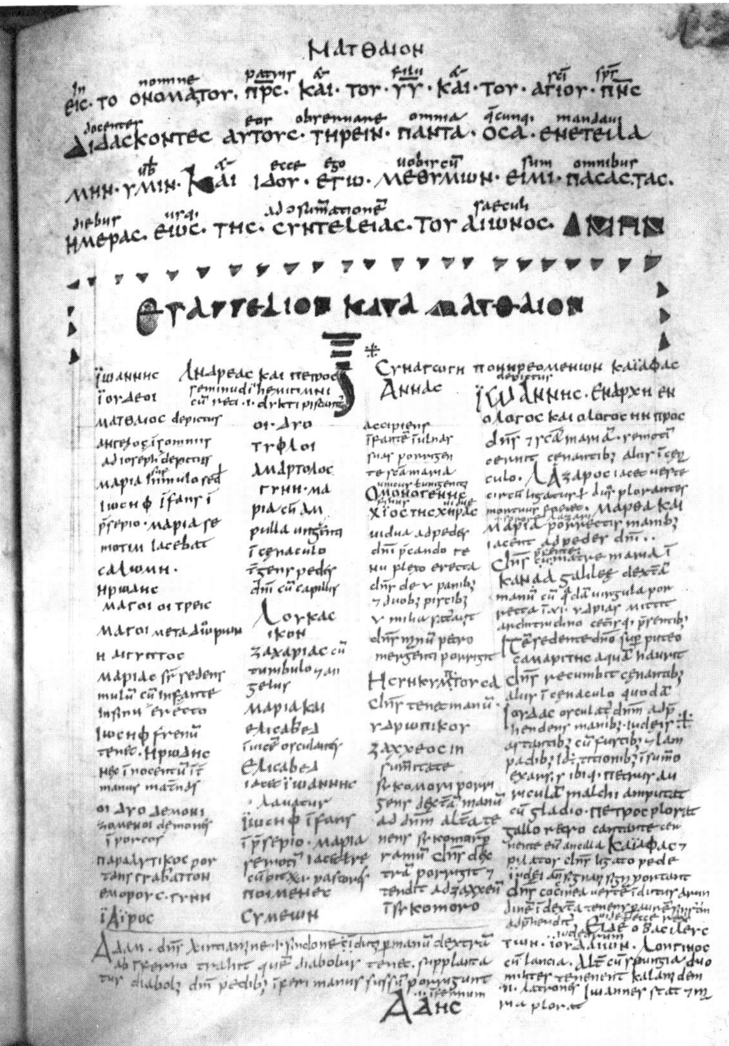

Plate 6. Catalogue of New Testament Illustrations with
Greek Titles and Latin Descriptions.
St. Gall, Stiftsbibliothek, MS 48, p. 129.

possible that illustrations formed part of some early plan. The text seems to describe the miniature cycle of a Greek Gospel book. Perhaps the scribe sat with the Greek book in front of him, copying out Greek titles inscribed near the figures and adding mnemonic Latin descriptions of his own. The result was a text that could serve as a guide for illuminators of future Gospel cycles.

The iconographical catalogue of MS 48 has long interested art historians. This portion of the manuscript was copied in northern Italy, and therefore André Grabar's observation that it corresponds in nearly all respects to the Byzantine fresco cycle at Castelseprio (near Milan) is especially intriguing.[16] But more work certainly remains to be done on the text.

Dresden, Sächsische Landesbibliothek A.145b is known as the *Codex boernerianus*, after the name of Christian Friedrich Boerner, an early owner. It contains the Epistles of St. Paul (with the exception of the Epistle to the Hebrews) in Greek, with a Latin interlinear translation.[17] On fol. 111v, there is a fragment of eighteen lines (Greek with Latin interlinear translation) attributed to a certain "Marcus Monachus." It is part of a treatise entitled Περὶ νόμου πνευματικοῦ, "On the spiritual law."[18] The Greek text of the Pauline Epistles is doubled by that of a manuscript copied at the same time in Reichenau, the *Codex paulinus augiensis* (Cambridge, Eng., Trinity College, B. 17.1).[19] The St. Gall and Reichenau

16. "Les fresques de Castelseprio et l'occident: Art du haut moyen âge," in *Actes du IIIe congrès international pour l'étude du haut moyen âge* (Olten and Lausanne, 1954), pp. 85–93. For a discussion of the themes of the iconographical catalogue and examples of possible Byzantine models and western copies, see Gérard Cames, *Byzance et la peinture romane de Germanie* (Paris, 1966), pp. 247–269. Instructions to the painter in early Christian Bible illustration are discussed by Walter Cahn, *Romanesque Bible Illumination* (Ithaca, 1982), pp. 21–22.

17. Facsimile edition of the manuscript by Alexander Reichardt, *Der Codex Boernerianus der Briefe des Apostels Paulus (Msc. Dresd. A 145b) in Lichtdruck nachgebildet* (Leipzig, 1909). There is an earlier edition of the text by C. F. von Matthaei, *XIII epistolarum Pauli codex graecus cum versione latina veteri vulgo antehieronymiana olim boernerianus nunc bibliothecae electoralis dresdensis summa fide et diligentia transcriptus et editus . . . cum tabulis aere expressis. Accessit ex eodem codice fragmentum Marci Monachi* (Meissen, 1791; editio minor Meissen, 1818). Biblical text critics have drawn attention to errors in Matthaei's edition; see Reichardt, *Der Codex Boernerianus*, pp. 21–22. The manuscript was damaged during World War II.

18. The fragment is edited by Matthaei, *XIII epistolarum Pauli*, but it does not appear in Reichardt's facsimile edition.

19. Frederick H. Scrivener, *An Exact Transcription of the Codex Augiensis, a Graeco-Latin Manuscript of St. Paul's Epistles, Deposited in the Library of Trinity College, Cambridge*

Epistles seem to have used the same prototype for their Greek texts; the Latin texts differ.

Narrative sources suggest that the monastery possessed still other Greek Scriptures. We have already mentioned Ekkehard IV's account of the Catholic Epistles copied by Notker Balbulus and destroyed in a malicious prank by the monk Sindolf. The library catalogue of 1461 describes two manuscripts that may also have formed part of the Carolingian library. One entry refers to "Matheus et psalterium grecum"; another, to a "Plenarium Latinum et Grecum."[20] (In the Middle Ages, of course, the term "plenarium" was applied to any collection of readings intended for practical use, so that this collection need not necessarily have been a biblical one. But in the catalogue it is grouped together with other Bibles under the heading "Libri textuales veteris ac novi testamentorum.")

The list of scriptural texts at St. Gall is rounded off by a series of Greek marginal notes in Latin Gospel books. These marginal notes, which appear in several Carolingian manuscripts, derive from a remarkable source: the oldest surviving exemplar of the Vulgate Gospels. This manuscript was copied in Verona at the end of the fifth century. At some early stage in its history, it was taken to St. Gall. There, in 1461, it was dismembered and used for repairing and binding a number of other manuscripts. The fragments are now widely scattered, and not more than three-fifths of them have been recovered. According to E. A. Lowe, "the number of surviving folios, based on published records, amounts to c. 110, many being mere shreds and some mere offsets; the largest portion is in St. Gall MS 1395, but exactly how many folios are in any one library is almost impossible to determine, since parts of one and the same leaf are often scattered in several places. . . ."[21]

At or near the time of composition, the codex was supplied with many marginal notes. Some of them are Latin notes in the critical style of St. Jerome. Others indicate equivalent readings in the Greek text of the

<hr>

(Cambridge, Eng., 1859). On the history of the manuscript, see Berschin, *Griechisch-lateinisches Mittelalter*, p. 15. On the relationship of the St. Gall and Reichenau texts, see Frede, *Altlateinische Paulus-Handschriften*, pp. 81–84.

20. Lehmann and Ruf, *Mittelalterliche Bibliothekskataloge* 1:103–104.

21. *CLA* 7:No. 984. Other manuscripts known to contain fragments are St. Gall, Stadtbibliothek S.N. (formerly in MS 292); St. Paul in Carinthia 25.4.21a (25d.86a or XXVd.65); Zurich, Staatsarchiv A.G.19, No. II, fols. 2–5; Zurich, Zentralbibliothek C 43 (offset); C 79b, fols. 4–7, and Z IV 5. There is an edition of the text in MS 1395 by Cuthbert Hamilton Turner, *The Oldest Manuscript of the Vulgate Gospels* (Oxford, 1931). Additional fragments were found and edited by Paul Lehmann and, especially, by P. Alban Dold; see Dold, "Neue Teile der ältesten Vulgata-Evangelienhandschrift aus dem 5. Jahrhundert," *Biblica* 22 (1941), 105–146.

Gospels and were intended, apparently, to disclose slight liberties in translation. Parts of this critical apparatus came to be copied in other Bibles transcribed during the ninth century.[22] Two St. Gall manuscripts have a few of the Greek notes.

There are four in MS 49. On p. 143, the text of Luke 1.2, "ipsi viderunt," is glossed with "ΛΥΤΟΠΤΑΙ." On the same page, Luke 1.4, "eruditus es," is glossed "ΚΛΤΝΧΗΘΗС." On p. 144, Luke 1.18, "processit," is glossed "ΠΡΟΒΕΒΗΚΥΙΛ." On p. 162, finally, Luke 6.1, "secundoprimo," is glossed "ΔΥΤΕΡΟΠΡШΤΟ." (Note the confusion of "Λ" and "A" in the first three examples.)[23] MS 50 has two notes. On p. 232, Mark 13.15, "super tectum," is glossed "ЕПΙ ΤΟΥ ΔШΜΑΤΟС." On p. 283, Luke 6.1, "secundoprimo," is glossed "ΔΕΥΤΕΡΟΠΡΟΤΟΝ."[24]

Three of the St. Gall Scriptures stand apart from the rest, and together they form a single editorial unit. Irishmen copied the Basel Psalter, the Gospels in MS 48, and the Epistles in the *Codex boernerianus*. They wished, it seems clear, to provide for a bilingual collection of the most important and most familiar books of the Bible. The *Codex boernerianus*, probably the last of the three to be copied, contains marginal references to its predecessors: on fol. 90v, someone wrote "ΕΥΑΓΓΕΛΙΟΝ ΕΛΛΙΝΙΚΟΝ" (for "εὐαγγέλιον Ἑλληνικόν"); and, on fol. 92v, "ΨΑΛΤΕ [corrected to Η] ΡΙΟΝ" (for "ψαλτήριον").

Paleographically, the Irish bilinguals present a unified appearance. All were written in the middle of the ninth century. They are similar in their physical format, with approximately the same measurements for the size of the pages, the surface used for writing, and the number of lines per page. The Greek text is written in Greek majuscules; the Latin, in neat small minuscules. Indeed, a single scribe wrote portions of each manuscript.[25]

---

22. Bernhard Bischoff, "Zur Rekonstruktion des Sangallensis (Σ) und der Vorlage seiner Marginalien," *Biblica* 22 (1941), 147–158, identifies the manuscripts in which the notes appear and provides a reconstruction of them.

23. Bischoff, "Zur Rekonstruktion," pp. 150, 156, relied on a list of readings in MSS 49 and 50 prepared for him by J. Müller, but the list is imprecise. The fourth note of MS 49 does not appear on p. 166, as Müller indicates (there is no Greek on the page), but rather on p. 162.

24. I have added the note on p. 283 to the list printed by Bischoff, "Zur Rekonstruktion," pp. 150, 156.

25. On the physical format, see the comparative table of measurements in Frede, *Altlateinische Paulus-Handschriften*, p. 68. On the script, see Bieler, *Psalterium graeco-latinum*, pp. xix–xxi. The hand of the Dresden Epistles is the main hand of the Interlinear Gospels, which is, in turn, identical with one of two hands of the Basel Psalter. Characteristic

The interlinear arrangement of text and translation was characteristically Irish. Continental scribes preferred to copy Greek and Latin texts in parallel columns, in the traditional arrangement for bilingual material. The difference in the two procedures is illustrated by the history of the prototype of the Pauline Epistles shared by the monks of Reichenau and St. Gall. The Swabian scribe of the *Codex paulinus augiensis* retained the parallel columns found in the prototype, while the Irish scribe of the *Codex boernerianus* put the material into an interlinear form.[26]

The Irish left their imprint on the bilingual manuscripts in other ways as well. In the margins there are Irish verses and allusions to Ireland and, most especially, references to numerous Irish and continental figures. The personal names serve as bibliographical guides, as reminders of the doctrines of particular teachers, and as criticisms or approbations of the views of contemporary scholars. They have long interested modern scholars, for they seem to suggest the possibility of an identification of the Irishmen responsible for the bilingual books.

Ludwig Traube, the first to provide a list of the names, believed that they described the Irishmen of Liège. He grouped together four Irish manuscripts: the Interlinear Gospels, the Dresden Epistles, the "St. Gall Priscian" (MS 904), and the "Bern Horace," and connected them with a fifth, a bilingual Psalter containing the autograph of Sedulius Scottus (Paris, Bibliothèque de l'Arsenal, Cod. 8407). The entire group, Traube concluded, should be attributed to Sedulius Scottus and the members of his Liège circle. But more recent paleographical inquiry has demonstrated that the "St. Gall Priscian" does not belong to the original group of four. The Basel Psalter should be added in its stead. Moreover, there is no paleographical basis for associating any of these books with the Sedulius Psalter. Scholars today therefore reject the attribution to Sedulius and view more favorably the hypothesis that the bilinguals were the work of Bishop Marcus, his nephew Moengal, and their immediate circle at St. Gall. Hermann Frede suggests that the plan for the three bilingual volumes was conceived during the Roman pilgrimage by Bishop Marcus and was later administered by Moengal. The first gathering of the Interlinear Gospels is written in northern Italian minuscules, so that it is likely the copying was begun in northern Italy (from Italian prototypes) and completed at

---

of the scribe's Greek hand are his forms of lambda, psi, and omega. Furthermore, the corrector (or later owner) of the Interlinear Gospels and the Basel Psalter appears also to be the scribe of the greater portion of the "Bern Horace" (Bern, Burgerbibliothek, Cod. 363).

26. Frede, *Altlateinische Paulus-Handschriften*, p. 84.

St. Gall.[27] Perhaps the Greek-Latin Psalter, Gospels, and Epistles were among the volumes that Ekkehard IV reported were brought to the monastery by the Irish pilgrims.[28]

The remaining St. Gall Scriptures were the work of Frankish monks. The Psalters in MSS 17, 1395, and Bamberg, Msc. Bibl. 44, the New Testament fragments in MSS 18, 45, and Zurich C 57, and the Greek marginal notes in MSS 49 and 50 were copied in continental hands. Unlike the Irish bilinguals, they do not represent the outcome of a single editorial directive. These manuscripts are more diverse. The Greek and Latin Psalter texts, while in some cases related, were drawn from a range of sources. The Greek text of MS 17 is written in fine Greek majuscules, but the Greek texts of MS 1395 and the Bamberg Psalter are written in Latin letters. The quality of the texts is uneven.

The best of all of the St. Gall Greek Psalter texts is given by MS 17, and it is by far the most accurately written. As Frede observes, the manuscript is "impressive testimony that a knowledge of Greek existed in St. Gall during the mid-ninth century independently of the Irish influence. . . ."[29] Where the prototype was obtained is not entirely clear. The most likely possibility is that it came from southern Italy, for at least one text in the manuscript originated there. The text was the *Te Deum*, included in the Canticle sequence that followed the Psalms. Curiously, it was not an authentic Greek version, but a retranslation into Greek from Latin—a Neapolitan composition of the ninth century.[30] Bilingual Psalters copied afterwards in Italy frequently made use of the text, but MS 17 was the first northern manuscript to do so. One of the Italian bilinguals, then, was likely its immediate model. The Bamberg Psalter and MS 1395, pp. 336–361, were copied within a few decades of MS 17. Their texts are closely related. Because the two manuscripts share even orthographical

27. The bibliography on the issue is extensive, and it begins with Traube, "*O Roma nobilis*," pp. 350–351. For more recent developments, see Bischoff, "Irische Schreiber im Karolingerreich," *Mittelalterliche Studien* (Stuttgart, 1981), 3:45–47, and Frede, *Altlateinische Paulus-Handschriften*, pp. 50–77. The marginal notes of the Bern Horace have been edited by John J. Contreni, "The Irish in the Western Carolingian Empire (According to James F. Kenney and Bern, Burgerbibliothek 363)," in *Die Iren und Europa im früheren Mittelalter*, ed. Heinz Löwe, Veröffentlichungen des Europa Zentrums Tübingen, Kulturwissenschaftliche Reihe (Stuttgart, 1982), (Teilband 1), pp. 758–798.
28. *Casus 2.*
29. *Altlateinische Paulus-Handschriften*, p. 79.
30. See Schneider, "Die biblischen Oden," pp. 480, 483. Frede's notion that the prototype of MS 17 was a minuscule codex from Constantinople (*Altlateinische Paulus-Handschriften*, p. 79) seems to be based on a misunderstanding.

and scribal errors, Alfred Rahlfs concluded that MS 1395 was either a direct copy of the Bamberg manuscript (made before it was corrected) or that both manuscripts derived from the same archetype.[31] Allgeier gave evidence for the second hypothesis. He identified two sources for the Latin text of the Psalters: an early-ninth-century tripartite Psalter from Reichenau (Karlsruhe, Badische Landesbibliothek, Aug. XXXVIII) and, for a third column of Canticles, a bilingual Psalter edited by the Milanese monk Symeon in the second half of the ninth century (East Berlin, Deutsche Staatsbibliothek, Hamilton 552). There were also two sources for the Greek text: Symeon's Psalter and MS 17. The manuscripts were not collated, but were followed in an apparently random alternation. As a result, the Bamberg Psalter does not present a Greek text that is internally consistent, and the arrangement of the Canticles is rather odd.[32]

The distinctive quadripartite format of the Bamberg Psalter became a model for scholars elsewhere on the Continent. According to a story based on the *Casus S. Galli* of Ekkehard IV, the emperor Otto II, while on a visit to the monastery in 972, made a gift to himself of the quadripartite Psalter.[33] The book was among the treasures of the imperial court that Emperor Henry II later placed for safekeeping in the cathedral library of Bamberg. It seems to have enjoyed a high visibility while in the imperial possession. At the end of the tenth and the beginning of the eleventh centuries two remarkably exact copies were made. Cologne, Dombibliothek, Cod. 8 corresponds to the Bamberg exemplar page for page, line for line, and scribal error for scribal error. Essen, Münsterschatz S.N. is nearly identical, except that a different Latin text was used for the *Psalterium iuxta Hebraeos*. When Abbot Odo had the quadripartite Psalter copied at St-Martin in Tournai in 1105, he changed the text very slightly (Paris, BN nouv. acq. lat. 2195). Odo's Psalter, finally, was copied at St-Amand during the twelfth century (Valenciennes, Bibliothèque Municipale 14 [B.I.37]). In addition to these four books there are several surviving manuscript fragments that can be traced back to the original quadripartite codex from St. Gall.[34]

---

31. Alfred Rahlfs, *Septuaginta-Studien*, 2: *Der Text des Septuaginta-Psalters* (Göttingen, 1907), pp. 13, 38 – 39.

32. Allgeier, "Das Psalmenbuch," pp. 115 – 118. On the Canticles, see Heinrich Schneider, *Die altlateinischen biblischen Cantica*, Texte und Arbeiten 29 – 30 (Beuron, 1938), pp. 115 – 116, and "Die biblischen Oden," p. 485. For Symeon's Psalter, see Boese, *Die lateinischen Handschriften*, pp. 269 – 270.

33. *Casus* 16.

34. On the quadripartite manuscripts, see Allgeier, "Das Psalmenbuch," pp. 107 – 108. As for

In reviewing the St. Gall Scriptures it may be useful to underline once again the distinction between the three Irish bilinguals and the bilinguals produced by the Frankish scholars. Certainly Irish scribes on the Continent learned to write in continental hands, and they came eventually to participate in a generalized Carolingian culture. Their work, as a modern scholar puts it, "soon was absorbed into the Carolingian amalgam."[35] Despite the often-quoted objections of some contemporaries to the Irish presence, it would not do to assume that scholarly life was conducted as a sort of competition between Irishmen and Franks. In the school of St. Gall especially, which owed much to its early Irish teachers, scholars from many parts of Europe worked together in harmony. But in the case of Bible studies at the monastery I think we ought to draw particular attention to the contribution of the Franks. The spotlight so long cast on the Irish achievement seems to have obscured the work of other medieval scholars. Franks copied more bilinguals than Irishmen did. Moreover, the quality of their work stands up well in comparison, and—to judge by the reception of Bishop Solomon's innovative Psalter—their influence was longer lasting.

In their response to the Greek text of Scripture, however, Frankish and Irish scholars were in many ways alike. Two agents were responsible for the production of a bilingual codex: editor and scribe. The editor planned and directed the enterprise, selecting the Greek Scripture to be used, providing the Latin translation if one were not available, and rectifying errors in the drafts of text and translation. The scribe carried out the editor's plan, transferring the texts from their prototypes to the parchment before

---

the fragments, there are: (1) two very large leaves from the twelfth century in Freiburg i. B., Universitätsbibliothek, Cod. 629 (Allgeier, "Das Psalmenbuch," p. 108); (2) one leaf in Rome, Biblioteca Vaticana, Pal. lat. 39 (Rahlfs, *Verzeichnis*, p. 9); and (3) five leaves in Coburg, Bayer. Staatsarchiv (B. Fischer, "Bibelausgaben des frühen Mittelalters," in *La Bibbia nell'alto medioevo*, Settimane di Studio del Centro italiano di Studi sull'alto Medioevo, 10 [Spoleto, 1963], p. 544). See also Jürgen Erdmann, "Coburger und Bamberger Fragmente eines Psalterium Quadrupartitum: Teile einer Abschrift des Bamberger Codex Msc. Bibl. 44 aus dem Jahre 909?" *Bericht des Historischen Vereins Bamberg* 102 (1966), 63–80.

The Latin text of the Bamberg Psalter was also transmitted separately. For copies, see *Vetus Latina*, 312–315, and Henri de Sainte-Marie, *S. Hieronymi Psalterium iuxta Hebraeos*, Collectanea Biblica Latina 11 (Rome, 1954), pp. xlii–xliii. Schneider, *Die altlateinischen biblischen Cantica*, pp. 118–119, traces the route of the Latin Canticles of Symeon's Psalter through the quadripartite Psalters to some more recent Psalters simpler in form.

35. John J. Contreni, "Carolingian Biblical Studies," in *Carolingian Essays*, ed. Blumenthal, p. 94.

him. Although his task might appear to be straightforward, it was not really so, for scribes knew less Greek than editors, and the Greek of their sources might be difficult to read.

The Greek text of the prototype was, in all probability, written in *scriptio continua*, or connected writing. Divisions between the words were not indicated. The Carolingian scribes, in order to assist their readers, attempted to set the single words off from one another. The Frankish scribes did this by leaving spaces between the words, as is the modern custom. (The dots they sometimes used seem to be signs of punctuation rather than of word division.) The Irish scribes, on the other hand, made use of either blank spaces or of interposed dots. Incorrect placement of the dots resulted in a misshapen vocabulary. Compare a few readings of the Basel Psalter with those of the Septuagint:

Basel Psalter	Septuagint[36]
Ps. 18.2, OIPANOY.ΔIΓOYNTE. ΔOΞ AN.Θ̄Ῡ.ΠYHCHΔE. XHPON.AYTOY.ANAΓΓEΛI-TOCTE.PEωMA	οἱ οὐρανοὶ διηγοῦνται δόξαν Θεοῦ, ποίησιν δὲ χειρῶν αὐτοῦ ἀναγγέλλει τὸ στερέωμα
Ps. 18.4, OYKECHN.ΛAΛEIAI.OIΔE. ΛωΓHON.OYKE.XHAKAOYONTE AIΦONE.AYTON.	οὐκ εἰσὶν λαλιαὶ οὐδὲ λόγοι, ὧν οὐχὶ ἀκούονται αἱ φωναὶ αὐτῶν
Ps. 101.3, AΠE.MOY	ἀπ᾿ ἐμοῦ
Ps. 101.6, TOYC.TENAΓMOY	τοῦ στεναγμοῦ
Ps. 101.7, EPHMI.Kω. EΓENH.ΘHN	ἐρημικῷ, ἐγενήθην
Ps. 101.9, KATE.MOY	κατ᾿ ἐμοῦ

The same examples suggest that transcription at some point followed oral dictation. The pronunciation is itacistic; vowels are carelessly interchanged and diphthongs are reduced. Note, for instance, "ΔIΓOYNTE" for "διηγοῦνται," "ΠYHCH" for "ποίησιν," "XHPON" for "χειρῶν," "ANAΓΓEΛI" for "ἀναγγέλλει." There is a similar tendency in the Frankish texts. For example, MS 17, p. 133r (Ps. 101.3) gives "᾿EN I" for "ἐν ᾗ," "ΘΛIBOME" for "θλίβωμαι," "EΠIKAΛECOME" for "ἐπικαλέσωμαι," and more. Itacisms recur in the Latin transliterations of the

---

36. The Septuagint readings here and in the following tables are taken from the edition by Alfred Rahlfs, *Septuaginta, 2: Libri poetici et prophetici* (Stuttgart, 1935).

Greek in MS 1395 and the Bamberg Psalter. Somewhat surprisingly, there are far fewer itacistic spellings in the Gospel fragments in MSS 18, 45, and Zurich C 57.

The role of the editor was more complex than that of the scribe. The success of the work depended upon his understanding of the Greek text and his concept of its relation to the Latin. In the bilingual codices Greek was nearly always the leading text and Latin the accompanying text. In other words, Greek took the left side of the page when a columnar system was used, and it took the main line in a codex using an interlinear system. The mere placement of a text in either language in a bilingual edition had consequences for its style. When Latin was copied next to Greek it influenced Greek vocabulary and syntax; the Greek in turn determined even more strongly the quality of the Latin.

An obvious problem arose when the sources themselves were incomplete. If the editor of a bilingual volume wished to present consistently parallel readings, he had sometimes to procure new Greek or Latin texts. The problem was real. It is not unusual to find in these bilingual Scriptures that parts of texts in one or the other language are missing. (See the entries in Appendix 4 [below, pp. 127 – 130] for MSS 17, 48, 1395, and the Dresden Epistles for details.)

The treatment of the Canticles illustrates the difficulty. In the Latin-speaking West it had been customary since the fourth century to transcribe the Canticles, Old Testament hymns drawn chiefly from the Prophets, together with the Psalms in the church books. A western editor preparing a bilingual Psalter, then, would probably also wish to include Greek and Latin versions of the Canticles. But Greek texts of the Canticles would not be readily available. The Roman church used a collection of Canticles that differed in the number and arrangement of the hymns from the collection favored by the Greek church. Byzantine books would not be helpful. And since copies of the Septuagint were scarce in the medieval West, the editor could not simply look up the corresponding passages in that source.

The editor of MS 17 resolved the problem by providing new translations. He was faithful to the arrangement of Canticles prescribed by the Roman church, selecting only the Greek hymns that corresponded to those in the *Officium romanum* and placing them in the western sequence. Apparently he had no Greek model for the Canticle of Isaiah (Isa. 12.1 – 6), because the Greek text now in the manuscript is not a Greek original; it is a retranslation into Greek from the Latin, one probably composed at St. Gall.[37] The hymn *Te Deum*, transmitted together with the

---

37. Schneider, "Die biblischen Oden," pp. 483 – 484.

Canticles, is another retranslation. The text given in MS 17 represents a Neapolitan composition of the ninth century, and it was repeated in the Bamberg Psalter and the quadripartite manuscripts dependent on the Bamberg Psalter.[38] The ninth century saw several such retranslations: Sedulius Scottus added the Greek text of a further hymn from Isaiah (Isa. 5) to his bilingual Psalter, and scholars elsewhere retranslated the Canticle of the Three Youths (Dan. 3.51–90).[39]

Even where Greek texts were available, as for Psalms, Gospels, or Epistles, their language was affected by their nearness to the Latin. Rahlfs defined as *codices latinizantes*, or "Latinizing books," bilinguals containing recensions "so un-Greek that they can only be understood as maladroit adaptations to the Latin translation."[40] The Greek text of the Basel Psalter was frequently adapted to the Latin, as the following examples demonstrate:

Basel Latin	Basel Greek	Septuagint
Ps. 13.3, plenum est	ΠΛΥΡΟC.ECTIN	γέμει
Ps. 16.12, catulus leonis	CKYMNOC.ΛΕѠΝΤΟC	σκύμνος
Ps. 30.14, in circuitu	EN.KYKΛΟΘEN	κυκλόθεν
Ps. 48.16; 61.5, 6, 10 verumtamen	ΠΛΗΝ.ΤΑCYM (61.5 - CYN)	πλὴν
Ps. 72.27, qui elongant se	OI.MAKPYNONTEC CE.EAYTOYC	οἱ μακρύνοντες ἑαυτοὺς

"ΠΛΗΝ.ΤΑCYM" (Ps. 48.16 and elsewhere) is an aberrant neologism. The introduction into the Greek text of a pronoun corresponding to the Latin "se" (Ps. 72.27) is a characteristic way of bringing the two texts into closer alignment.

There are fewer changes in the Greek readings of the Frankish Psalters, but they are similar in intent. In MS 1395, for instance, we read:

MS 1395 Latin	MS 1395 Greek	Septuagint
Ps. 31.4, in aerumna mea	EIC TAΛAIΠѠPIAN MOY	εἰς ταλαιπωρίαν

38. MS 17, pp. 332–333, Latin and Greek fragment; Bamberg Psalter, fol. 162r–162v, Latin and Greek, Greek text incomplete. The *Te Deum* texts of all of these manuscripts are published by Cagin, *L'euchologie latine*, 1:147–152.

39. Schneider, "Die biblischen Oden," p. 491. See also Schneider, *Die altlateinischen biblischen Cantica*, pp. 181–182.

40. *Septuaginta-Studien*, pp. 95–97, with examples.

Again, a pronoun given by the Latin text but not by the Septuagint is brought into the Greek reading.

Perhaps the texts in the Irish bilinguals followed one another more literally because their interlinear format encouraged it. Or perhaps Rahlfs is correct when he attributes the restraint of the Franks to their greater sophistication: "The more scholarly spirit of the later St. Gall monastery school appears to have rejected the crude Latinization of the Greek text introduced by Moengal and his comrades and to have obliterated its traces as much as possible."[41]

The Greek text exerted a still more powerful influence on the Latin. It stood, after all, for the original recension of the New Testament and for a prior recension of the Old. In the Basel Psalter, the Latin interlinear seems to derive primarily from the Vulgate. But it is not an exact rendering of Jerome's text, for on many occasions the language is altered in order to conform more closely to the Greek:

Basel Greek	Basel Latin	Vulgate[42]
Ps. 1.1, ΛΟΙΜѠΝ	pestilentiarum	pestilentiae
Ps. 2.2; 4.9, ΕΠΙ.ΤΟ.ΑΥΤΟ	in id ipsum	in unum
Ps. 2.11, ΕΝ.ΤΡΟΜѠ	in tremore	cum tremore
Ps. 18.9, ΤΑ.ΔΙΚΕΟΜΑΤΑ ΚΥΡΙΟΥ ΕΥΘΙΑ	iustitia domini recta	iustitiae domini rectae

The editor's scrupulous regard for the Greek text leads him to offer a choice of translations when he considers the Vulgate reading too free. In the following examples, the editor offers both the Vulgate reading and a more literal equivalent:

Ps. 1.3, "ΔΙΕ.ΞΟΔΟΥC" is glossed with "decursus" (Vulgate) "vel exitus."

Ps. 2.1, "INA TI" is glossed with "utquid vel quare" (Vulgate).

Ps. 2.13, "Ο.ΘΥΜΟC" is glossed with "ira" (Vulgate) "vel furor."

Ps. 17.18, "ΕΚ.ΤѠΝ.ΜΙCΟΥΝΤѠΝ.ΜΕ" is glossed with "ab" (Vulgate) "vel ex odientibus me." (The complete Vulgate reading is "ab his qui oderunt me.")

---

41. *Septuaginta-Studien*, pp. 98–99.

42. The Vulgate readings here and in the examples following are taken from the *Biblia sacra iuxta Vulgatam clementinam*, ed. Alberto Colunga and Laurentio Turrado, in Biblioteca de Autores Cristianos, 4th ed. (Madrid, 1965).

There are very many more examples of double translation in the Basel Psalter, the Interlinear Gospels, and the Dresden Epistles.[43] The practice suggests that, for the Irish scholars at least, the value of the Latin text lay not so much in its role as an independent witness to the Word of God as in its ability to serve as a guide to understanding the Greek.

Further illustrations from the Basel Psalter make clear the ancillary role of the Latin text. At times even the syntax of the Latin is changed, although the result may be language that is clumsy or inappropriate:

> Ps. 3.7,
> non timebo vel perterrebor a x milibus populi
> ΟΥ ΦΟΒΗΘΗCΟΜΑΙ.ΑΠΟ.ΜΥΡΙΑΔѠΝ.ΛΑΟΥ.ΤѠΝ
> circundantis   me
> ΚΥΚΛѠCΥΝ.ΕΠΙ.ΤΙ.ΘΕΜΕΝѠΝ.ΜΟΙ . . .
> for the Vulgate reading: "Non timebo millia populi circumdantis me."

In another example the editor seems to have tried to match a Greek verb governing the accusative with a Latin verb governing the same case. When the effort failed he dropped the verb from his translation altogether:

> Ps. 9B.10,
> cum eum
> ΚΥΨΕΙ.CΕ.ΚΑΙ.ΠΕCΕΙΤΑΙ.ΕΝΤѠ.ΑΥΤΟΝ
> dominatus fuerit
> ΚΑΤΑΚΥΡΙΕΥCΑΙ.
> for the Vulgate reading: "Inclinabit se, et cadet cum dominatus fuerit pau-
>   perum."

To summarize, then, the interaction between Greek and Latin recensions in the bilingual books was mutual. Each recension underwent changes in wording that were not the result of some natural elaboration of the language itself, but were rather the consequence of its proximity to a text in another language. And so there are Latin constructions in the Greek texts and Greek constructions in the Latin. If the Greek exerted a stronger

---

43. The double translations were studied by Hermann Rönsch, "Zur biblischen Latinität aus dem cod. Sangallensis der Evangelien," *Romanische Forschungen* 1 (1883), 419–426, and "Die Doppelübersetzungen im lateinischen Texte des cod. Boernerianus der Paulinischen Briefe," *Zeitschrift für wissenschaftliche Theologie* 25 (1882), 488–509; 26 (1883), 73–99, 309–344. Since Rönsch based his study on Matthaei's defective edition (see n. 17 above), his readings should be compared with those in Reichardt's facsimile edition.

influence on the Latin, it was because the Greek Scripture was seen as the principal text, and the Latin viewed as an adjunct and a translation. It was probably also for the simple reason that the writers were not so fluent in Greek as in Latin, and they were therefore less confident in proposing alternative readings for it. But for both texts, the very fact of their inclusion in a bilingual volume was significant. It determined the construction of the language, and it also determined the uses to which the texts were put.

The bilingual Scriptures were not part of the biblical mainstream. It was not simply the problem of their language. They had been copied from out-of-the-way sources in the first place and even in the ninth century, these texts of the Bible were obsolete. Modern scholars preparing editions of Scripture have generally chosen not to use them.[44] Yet the very qualities that disappoint the biblical text critic—the contaminated language, the antiquated texts—make the bilingual manuscripts a "first-class source" for the historian interested in the study of Greek.[45]

They offer evidence for one of the important questions about the knowledge of Greek in Carolingian Europe. Where did ninth-century scholars find their Greek? Where did they obtain their texts? Most of the models for the St. Gall bilinguals have been identified, at least in terms of their geographical origin, and they came from Italy. The copying of the three Irish bilinguals was begun in northern Italy; hymns and Canticles in the Frankish Psalters were based on Italian translations; the Greek marginal notes in the Latin Gospels derived from a Veronese manuscript; and even the Catholic Epistles copied by Notker Balbulus had been lent to him by the bishop of Vercelli. This should come as no surprise, for St. Gall received many Italian manuscripts, and the route of transmission is well

44. Alfred Rahlfs did not include the western bilinguals in his collation of manuscripts for the Göttingen Septuagint. As he remarked in *Psalmi cum Odis*, Septuaginta Societas Scientiarum Gottingensis 10 (Göttingen, 1931), p. 32: "Diese Handschriften sind interessant, weil sie lehren, wie man sich auch im Abendlande um den griechischen Psalter bemüht hat. Aber in der vorliegenden Ausgabe habe ich sie bis auf wenige Stellen ... ganz beiseite gelassen, da ich mir von ihrer Benützung einen die Mühe lohnenden Nutzen nicht versprechen kann. Denn sie sind nicht nur recht inkorrekt geschrieben, sondern oft ist auch ihr griech. Text durch den dabei stehenden lateinischen beeinflusst, zuweilen in höchst sonderbarer Weise." Frede evaluated the Greek-Latin Pauline Epistles in *Altlateinische Paulus-Handschriften*, pp. 91–92, 98–101. He observed on p. 91, "Im ganzen ... ist ... ihr Text künstlich, konstruiert, tot und für die Textgeschichte des 9. Jahrhunderts nur von geringem Wert. Wirklich in Gebrauch waren ganz andere Texte."
45. Allgeier, "Exegetische Beiträge," p. 265. There is much work to be done on these manuscripts. I have recently undertaken a series of studies on them.

known. It ran from south to north, from Italy through St. Gall and the Alps, on to the rest of the Frankish realm. The bilinguals took the traditional route. The point is worth making, because scholars seem often inclined to suppose that Greek texts arrived at the monastery by some special path that began, for instance, in Constantinople. But there is no indication that Byzantium had anything to do with the transmission of these Scriptures. They are western texts, copied and used in western ways.

There are some references to Byzantine customs in the margins of the Irish manuscripts. They are polemical: notices *contra graecos* written alongside certain biblical texts. The Dresden Epistles have six of them. Two are specific charges against the Greeks. One draws attention to a scriptural injunction against long hair on men (fol. 32v, added to 1 Cor. 11.13 – 15, evidently directed against the bearded Orthodox clergy); the other, to a verse interpreted in support of the *filioque* (fol. 57v, to Gal. 4.6). The remaining four notices are written alongside scriptural verses that caution against the deception of empty arguments and the corruption of pure ideas (fol. 50r, twice, to 2 Cor. 11.3; fol. 66r, to Eph. 5.6; fol. 66v, to Eph. 5.15 – 16). The notes suggest an incipient awareness of differences in matters of worship and church discipline, but they hardly reflect a prolonged acquaintance with Byzantine texts. They are notes written in the workroom of a western scholar, and it was in the libraries and classrooms of the West that the bilingual Scriptures had their proper sphere.

In the early centuries of the church, Greek-Latin Scriptures had provided texts for liturgical performance. Bilingual lessons, Psalms, and Canticles were recited or chanted in southern Italy and in other areas where congregations had members who used both languages. But the Greek-Latin Scriptures copied at St. Gall were not intended for use in public worship. Instead, they served the needs of the monastery's scholars. (Greek letters were a hindrance for public performance. When bilingual texts were transcribed for liturgical use—as in the examples discussed in the following chapter—they were written in Latin letters so that they could be read quickly and fluently.)

The editors of the bilingual volumes occasionally proclaimed their intentions in dedicatory verses or prologues. At the beginning of the Bamberg Psalter there is a poem of forty-four dactylic hexameters that explains the history and purposes of the edition. The author credits Solomon III with the plan for the book. He observes that there are four routes to the hidden meaning of Scripture, and that the four texts in the quadripartite edition represent them. Learned men should use the book to study the Bible:

> ... hoc et psalterium docte collegit in unum,
> pandens lectori studioso mente sagaci
> auctorum sensus vario sermone secretos. . . .[46]

An anonymous scholar of the ninth century produced another such text. The *Litterae de psalterio transferendo*, a treatise in the form of a letter, introduces a critical edition of the Milanese Psalter. It addresses specifically textual problems, for the editor wished to establish the relationship of the Milanese text to the Septuagint and, in turn, to Jerome's *Psalterium gallicanum*. His goal, he wrote, was "to reject superfluous readings and to insert suitable ones in the chanting of the Psalms" ("reprobare superflua et inserere congrua in psalmorum cantibus").[47] For his textual emendations the editor devised a new set of symbols, abandoning Jerome's system and using instead a set partly derived from Isidore's *Etymologiae*.

There is more evidence that scholars occupied themselves with textual problems in order to further biblical exegesis. Isidore's introduction to the Mozarabic Psalter, Theodulf of Orléans' dedication of a Psalter to a woman named Gisela, and Florus of Lyons' letter to Abbot Hyldradus are all examples of essays that urge readers to refer to the *lingua praecedens* when the meaning of a biblical text is in doubt.[48] And when Bede, or Christian of Stavelot, or John Scottus used the Greek-Latin books as a basis for biblical scholarship, the enterprise was crowned with success.

Even in the margins of the St. Gall bilinguals there are traces of exegetical pursuits. Many appear in the Dresden Epistles.[49] Some notes identify Old Testament quotations:

To Rom. 4.3,
"ΕΠΙCΤΕΥCΕΝ ΑΒΡΑΑΜ ΤШ ΘΕШ ΚΑΙ ΕΛΟΓΕΙCΘΗ ΑΥΤШ ΕΙC ΔΙΚΑΙ-OCΥΝΗΝ," is added "in ΓΕΝΕCΙ" (an evident reference to Gen. 15.6).
To Rom. 4.17,
"ΟΤΙ ΠΑΤΕΡΑ ΠΟΛΛШΝ.ΕΘΝШΝ ΤΕΘΕΙΚΑ CΕ," is added "in genesi" (a reference to Gen. 17.5).

---

46. Quoted here are lines 10–12. The entire poem is printed by Allgeier, "Das Psalmenbuch," pp. 104–105.
47. The text is edited by E. Dümmler (1925), MGH Epp 6:201–205. On the question of authorship, see Berschin, *Griechisch-lateinisches Mittelalter*, pp. 194–196.
48. For the texts, see Allgeier, "Das Psalmenbuch," pp. 111–114.
49. See Rönsch, "Die Doppelübersetzungen," 26:75–78, and Frede, *Altlateinische Paulus-Handschriften*, p. 62.

To Rom. 10.6,
> "TIC.ANABHCETAI.EIC TON.OYPANON," is added "in ΔEYTEPONOMIW" (a reference to Deut. 9.4; 30.12f.).

Some refer to the New Testament:

To Rom. 3.29–30,
> "H ÏOYΔAIWN O ΘEOC.MONON.OYXE KAI EΘNWN NAI KAI EΘNWN. EΠEIΠEP, EIC, O ΘEOC . . ." is added "KATA ΛOYKAN" (a reference to passages such as Luke 2.30–32, emphasizing the universality of God's will for salvation).

To 1 Cor. 11.24,
> "TOYTO MOY ECTIN TO.CWMA TO.YΠEP YMWN KΛWMENON," is added "EN MATΘEW" (a reference to Matt. 26.26–29).

Others summarize the adjacent text:

To 1 Cor. 6.4,
> "BIWTIKA ΓOYN.KPHTHPIA.EAN EXHTAI . . ." is added "de iudicibus."

To 1 Tim. 3.11–12,
> "ΓYNAIKAC WCAYTWC.CEMNAC.MH ΔIABOΛOYC NHΦAΛAIOYC ΠICTAC EN ΠACIN," is added "ΠEPI TWN ΓYNAIKWN."

The Greek notes in the Latin Gospels of MSS 1395, 49, and 50, which we have already discussed, demonstrate similar concerns.

On a more fundamental level the manuscripts served as sources for the study of Greek. Medieval readers were accustomed to learn from Psalters, and the bilinguals were no exception. They were often laid out like schoolbooks, with such pedagogical devices as Latin, Greek, or Hebrew alphabets and numerals, Latin and Greek prayers, grammatical exercises, and vocabulary lists. Bilingual versions of Scripture provided excellent material for reading practice. The Greek text was rendered all the more accessible by the familiarity of the Latin. Together with the *Hermeneumata*, these Scriptures were among the few really useful sources of Greek prose or poetry available to medieval students.

Again, marginal notes in the St. Gall manuscripts show that these books were used for instruction in the language. Most of the grammatical information given in the Irish books is quite elementary. The notes identify parts of speech, the voice or tense of verbs, the gender or case of nouns. If a noun is given in an oblique case in the text, the note may restore the nominative form.

Interlinear Gospels

To Matt. 21.5, "TH ΘΥΓΑΤΡΙ," is added "filiae id est dativus."
To Luke 18.24, "ΔΥСΚΟΛѠС," is added "difficile id est adverbium."
To John 3.2, "ΔΙΔΑСΚΑΛΟС," is added "magister id est nominativus."

Dresden Epistles

To 1 Cor. 15.10, "ΠΤѠΧΗ," is added "pauper id est femininum."
To Phil. 1.10, "ΕΙС ΤΟ Λ[for Δ]ΟΚΙΜΑΖΕΙΝ," is added "ad probandos vel in probando id est infinitivus vel ut probetis."
To 2 Tim. 4.8, "Ο," is added "id est articulus."

The New Testament manuscripts also refer to such school authors as Porphyry, Martianus Capella, Donatus, and Lucan. The pedagogy of the Basel Psalter is rather more sophisticated, and the notes comment on style and etymology as well as syntax.[50]

In the ninth and early tenth centuries St. Gall monks assumed a leading role in the composition of bilingual Scriptures. Surely these books were the pride of their owners. Not only were they helpful to beginners in Greek, but they were used by more experienced men to further the study of Scripture. Of all the different texts prepared by medieval scholars with an interest in Greek—the grammars, the glossaries, the liturgies—it seems that the scholarship engendered by the study of the Greek Bible was the most accomplished. Perhaps this is because it was in some ways the most purposeful.

---

50. Additional examples and discussion in Rettig, *Antiquissimus quatuor evangeliorum*, pp. xxii, xxxi–xxxii, xxxvi (MS 48); Rönsch, "Die Doppelübersetzungen," 25:489–90, and 26:73–76, and Frede, *Altlateinische Paulus-Handschriften*, p. 62 (Dresden Epistles); Allgeier, "Exegetische Beiträge," pp. 265–267 (Basel Psalter).

VIII

Liturgies

Perhaps the most noticeable manifestation of Greek in medieval Latin culture occurred in the liturgy. Indeed, there are Greek elements in the Latin liturgy to the present day, surviving either as traces of the traditional Roman liturgical language or as more symbolic assertions of the ideal of the universality of the church. The Kyrie Eleison of the mass and the Trisagion of the service for the Adoration of the Cross on Good Friday are familiar to everyone who has taken part in the liturgy of the Roman rite.

Greek was the first ecumenical language of the Christian church. From the time of the Apostolic preaching until the second half of the second century, Koine, the common dialect of Hellenistic Greek, was the language in which most Christians worshiped. But as the Christian communities of the West began to drift apart from those in the East they turned increasingly to their own colloquial Latin. In North Africa and in Rome Latin came to be used ever more frequently in the performance of liturgical acts, and eventually it was even employed in the celebration of the Eucharist. The transition from Greek to Latin was gradual, and it is likely that for a time the liturgy was celebrated in both languages. Between the years 360 and 382, however, Latin displaced Greek as the liturgical language of the church in Rome.[1]

The Latinization of the Roman liturgy meant that thereafter the forms of worship developed in the West would be different from those developed in the East. But it did not imply that Greek would no longer play a role in public worship. Greek was too important to be forgotten. It was the historical language of the Christian community, and Greek-speaking populations continued in Italy throughout the Middle Ages. It

---

1. T. Klauser, "Der Uebergang der römischen Kirche von der griechischen zur lateinischen Liturgiesprache," in *Miscellanea Giovanni Mercati*, Studi e Testi 121 (Vatican City, 1946), 1:467–482. See also Christine Mohrmann, "Les origines de la latinité chrétienne à Rome," *Vigiliae christianae* 3 (1949), 67–106, 163–183, and *Liturgical Latin: Its Origins and Character* (London, 1957), pp. 45–46. Sources and bibliography on the liturgical language of the early church are reviewed by Cyrille Vogel, *Introduction aux sources de l'histoire du culte chrétien au moyen âge* (Spoleto, 1966; repr. Spoleto, 1975), pp. 241–247.

was the "sacred language" of Scripture and was therefore held in reverence. And the texts of the Septuagint and Greek New Testament, which were made accessible even to people who did not know the language through bilingual codices, were nearly inexhaustible sources of material for those who wished to prepare new pieces for liturgical performance.

At Rome there were several occasions on which readings from Scripture were given in both Greek and Latin. The ninth-century *Ordo* of St-Amand, for example, prescribed that the *lectiones* and *cantica* before mass on Holy Saturday be recited in both languages.[2] Bilingual readings were prescribed for other feasts as well: Gospel and Epistle were read in Greek and Latin on the first day of Christmas, the first and second days of Easter, the Saturday before Pentecost, the Saturdays of the Ember weeks, and the mass for the installation of a pope.[3]

A later medieval commentator on the liturgy suggested that the Roman practice was due to the presence of bilingual congregations. According to the anonymous author of the *Speculum ecclesiae* in a thirteenth-century manuscript from Tours,

> We chant that [Gloria] in Greek according to the ancient custom of the Roman church, to which both Greeks and Latins once adhered. A very great part of Italy was inhabited by Greeks, so that the Greek language was not less known—even to the Latins—than the Latin. And also, the seventy interpreters of the Septuagint translated each Testament from Hebrew into Greek, and then it was translated into Latin. So on account of our esteem and reverence for the Greek language, we sing that Angelic Canticle in Greek during the first mass [on Christmas], but in Latin at the second. For it is appropriate that Greek precede Latin as a mother her daughter, and that Latin follow Greek as a daughter does her mother.[4]

2. *Ordo* XXX B, ed. M. Andrieu, *Les Ordines romani du haut moyen âge*, 5 vols. (Louvain, 1931–1956), 3:472.

3. For references to the *Ordines romani*, see Vogel, *Introduction*, p. 247, and Caspari, *Geschichte des Taufsymbols*, 3:466–472.

4. *Speculum ecclesiae* 3.2, ed. E. Martène, *De antiquis ecclesiae ritibus* (Rouen, 1700), 1:102: "Nos canimus illud graece juxta morem antiquum Romanae ecclesiae, cui tam graeci, quam latini solebant antiquitus deservire, et a graecis habitabatur maxima pars Italiae, unde lingua graeca non minus erat nota etiam latinis, quam latina, et quia LXX. interpretes utrumque testamentum transtulerunt ex hebraeo in graecum, et inde translatum est in latinum, ob honorem et reverentiam linguae graecae cantamus canticum angelicum illud graece in prima quidem missa, sed in secunda latine. Decet enim, ut graeca praecedat latinam tanquam mater filiam, graecamque latina sequatur ceu filia matrem." For background on the text, see A.-G. Martimort, *La documentation liturgique de Edmond Martène* (Vatican City, 1978), pp. 222–223.

Bilingual recitations of the Nicene-Constantinopolitan Creed were part of the Roman catechumenate. The sources indicate considerable variation in the method of performance. The creed might be recited in either Greek or Latin, depending on the language normally spoken by the candidates or their sponsors. The Rite of Scrutiny of the Gelasian Sacramentary instructed an acolyte to chant the creed over the head of an infant first in Greek and then in Latin. In a Fulda Sacramentary of the tenth century, the creed was chanted in Greek over boys and in Latin over girls.[5] Honorius of Autun described a similar gender-differentiated ceremony in the late eleventh or early twelfth century.[6]

Throughout the Middle Ages expressions of a liturgical interest in Greek took many forms.[7] Some Graecisms are known to us through only one or two examples, and so it is difficult to assess their real importance in the liturgical life of the time. Other texts, however, appear regularly in the manuscripts, and we may suppose that they were performed in a number of monasteries and cathedrals.

One series of bilingual texts occurs frequently in music manuscripts of the ninth through the eleventh centuries. The texts have come to be regarded as a group by modern scholars and are known collectively as the *Missa graeca*. They are chants for the Ordinary of the mass: "Doxa en ipsistis theo" ("Δόξα ἐν ὑψίστοις Θεῷ," "Gloria in excelsis Deo," the Greater Doxology), "Pisteuo eis ena theon" ("Πιστεύω εἰς ἕνα Θεόν," "Credo in unum Deum," the Nicene-Constantinopolitan Creed), "Pisteuo eis theon" ("Πιστεύω εἰς Θεόν," "Credo in Deum," the Apostles' Creed), "Agios, agios, agios" ("Ἅγιος, Ἅγιος, Ἅγιος," the Sanctus), and

---

5. On the Gelasian Sacramentary (as well as *Ordo romanus* XI), see Andrieu, *Les Ordines romani*, 2:393–394, 434–435. On the Fulda Sacramentary (Göttingen, Universitäts-bibliothek cod. theol. 231), see *Sacramentarium Fuldense*, ed. A. Richter and A. Schön-felder (Fulda, 1912), p. 339. For a full account of the bilingual creed in the Rite of Scrutiny, see Caspari, *Geschichte des Taufsymbols*, 3:480–489. For a discussion of the creedal formulas used in the baptismal liturgy, see Bernice M. Kaczynski, "Creeds, Liturgical Use of," in Joseph R. Strayer, ed., *Dictionary of the Middle Ages* (New York, 1983), 3:675–677. Many of the manuscripts that transmit the instructions for the Rite of Scrutiny simply give the incipits of the creeds and not the full texts. Professor Bernhard Bischoff kindly called my attention to a manuscript that appears to be an exception: Paris, Bibliothèque de l'Arsenal MS 227, a late-ninth-century pontifical from Saint-Pierre de Vierzon.

6. *Gemma animae* 3.67, PL 172:661.

7. For an overview of texts and liturgical practices, see Bischoff, "Das griechische Ele-ment," pp. 262–263; Berschin, *Griechisch-lateinisches Mittelalter*, pp. 33–37; Jeau-neau, "Jean Scot Erigène et le grec," pp. 37–40.

"O amnos tu theu" ("'Ο ἀμνὸς τοῦ Θεοῦ," the Agnus Dei).[8] (The titles have been given first in the transliterated form in which they usually appear in the manuscripts.)

The term "Missa graeca" is an unfortunate label for this series of pieces, but it seems to be firmly entrenched in the secondary literature. In fact, it is anachronistic and imprecise. The medieval books do not describe their contents in this way; only the individual texts are given titles. The concept of the *Missa graeca* entered the literature as a description of a particular Greek service assembled at St-Denis in the thirteenth century and celebrated annually thereafter on 16 October, the octave of the monastery's patron.[9] The service, which underwent several revisions in later years, was performed at St-Denis down to the time of the French Revolution. The term misleads when it is applied to the chants of an earlier period, for it implies a system and a unity that simply were not there. Very few Carolingian manuscripts transmit a complete set of Greek chants for the mass Ordinary. They generally give only one or two pieces—most often the Doxa and the Agios. The manuscript tradition of the Greek chants therefore offers little support for the notion of a codified *Missa graeca* in the ninth century. Instead, it more closely resembles the apparently capricious transmission of the corresponding Ordinary chants in Latin.

The question of the origin of the Greek Ordinary chants has been of great interest to musicologists. Were they remnants of the period of transition in liturgical language at Rome, that is, early Christian texts either in more or less continual use since their inception or reintroduced into the liturgy at some later date? Were they borrowed from the contemporary Greek liturgies of the Orthodox church in Byzantium? Or were they fashioned anew in the medieval West either as translations or retranslations from the Latin to the Greek or as revisions of existing Greek texts?

Peter Wagner and Otto Ursprung set the main lines of the debate in the early 1900s when they proposed that the immediate source of the Greek chants in the West was Rome. But while Wagner believed that the Roman liturgy had taken over the chants from Byzantium, Ursprung claimed that they represented indigenous Roman musical practice. He rejected the

---

8. Since the Kyrie Eleison is a Greek text that became embedded in the Latin liturgy on its own, it is not normally counted among the pieces of the *Missa graeca*.

9. The bibliography on St-Denis is extensive. See Michel Huglo, "Les chants de la *Missa greca* de Saint-Denis," in *Essays Presented to Egon Wellesz*, ed. Jack Westrup (Oxford, 1966), p. 83, and, for a review of the scholarship, see Berschin, *Griechisch-lateinisches Mittelalter*, pp. 35–36.

possibility of Byzantine models and saw the chants instead as the deliberate affectations of western Graecophiles. In Ursprung's view the Greek chants of the late Carolingian liturgical books were the outcome of a purely western evolution.[10]

The discussion became more complicated as scholars turned their attention to particular melodies. As the manuscript tradition should make clear, the case for the historical development of each piece must be made separately. Michel Huglo and Kenneth Levy have argued that the western Doxa, Pisteuo, and Agios depend upon Byzantine models. Levy went on to suggest that the Greek chants of the Ordinary, together with a translated Introit and the Byzantine hymn *I ta Cherubim* (Οἱ τὰ χερουβίμ) as an Offertory, were assembled into a *Missa graeca* sometime between 790 and 814, during the reign of Charles the Great.[11] But scholars disagree. According to Jean Deshusses, Charles the Bald had a group of seven manuscripts copied at St-Amand for distribution to the churches and monasteries of his empire.[12] One of them (Paris, Bibliothèque Nationale lat. 2290, fols. 7v–8v) is the oldest extant manuscript with four complete Greek chants. It is this codex, copied at St-Amand for St-Denis in about 867, that has led some scholars to look to St-Denis and others to St-Amand as the place where the Greek chants originated. Most recently Charles Atkinson has argued, primarily on the basis of the manuscript tradition of the O amnos, for the reign of Louis the Pious and a date of

---

10. Peter Wagner, *Einführung in die gregorianischen Melodien*, 3 vols. (Leipzig, 1911–1921; repr. Hildesheim, 1962), 1:51–52, 263, and "Morgen- und Abendland in der Musikgeschichte," *Stimmen der Zeit* 114 (1927), 131–145. Otto Ursprung, "Alte griechische Einflüsse und neuer gräzistischer Einschlag in der mittelalterlichen Musik," *Zeitschrift für Musikwissenschaft* 12 (1930), 193–219, and "Um die Frage der Echtheit der Missa greca," *Die Musikforschung* 6 (1953), 289–296.

11. Michel Huglo, "La mélodie grecque du 'Gloria in excelsis' et son utilisation dans le Gloria XIV," *Revue grégorienne* 29 (1950), 30–40; "Origine de la mélodie du Credo 'authentique' de la Vaticane," *Revue grégorienne* 30 (1951), 68–78; "La tradition occidentale des mélodies byzantines du Sanctus," in *Der kultische Gesang der abendländischen Kirche*, ed. F. Tack (Cologne, 1950), pp. 40–46. For a critique of this work, see Neil K. Moran, *The Ordinary Chants of the Byzantine Mass* (Hamburg, 1975), pp. 12–16. Moran remarks on p. 14, "All these projects and studies have, however, one weakness in common. They were conceived without knowledge of the Greek Ordinary chants as they were sung in the medieval Byzantine Church." Kenneth Levy, "The Byzantine Sanctus and Its Modal Tradition in East and West," *Annales musicologiques* 6 (1958–1963), 7–67.

12. Jean Deshusses, "Chronologie des grands sacramentaires de Saint-Amand," *Revue bénédictine* 87 (1977), 230–237.

sometime between 827 and 835.[13]

Let us set aside these hypotheses for the moment and turn to the manuscripts themselves. Greek chants for the mass Ordinary appear in some sixty manuscripts from the eighth through the fourteenth centuries.[14] Not all the sources are liturgical; the texts sometimes appear in Psalters, grammars, and miscellaneous collections. The heaviest concentration, of course, is found in music manuscripts, especially in tropers and graduals of the tenth and eleventh centuries.

Thirteen of the manuscripts have been attributed to St. Gall. This figure is high in proportion to the total surviving deposit. It seems that more specimens have survived from St. Gall than from any other monastery. Its role in the history of the *Missa graeca* is significant, and its position becomes more interesting yet when we remind ourselves that the Ordinary chants represent only part of the Greek *liturgica* in circulation at the time.[15] The full complement of St. Gall sources is varied and rich.

Appendix 5 (below, pp. 131 – 135) describes the Greek and Greek-Latin texts prepared at the monastery. They occur in music manuscripts, in bilingual Scriptures, and in a few grammatical and other books. Eight tropers and two graduals contain Greek chants for the mass Ordinary. The tropers range in date from the ninth through the twelfth centuries; most are from the eleventh century. The graduals are from the eleventh century. (The dates of some manuscripts are disputed: see Appendix 5.)

13. Charles M. Atkinson puts forward this hypothesis in two fine articles: "*O amnos tu theu*: The Greek Agnus Dei in the Roman Liturgy from the Eighth to the Eleventh Century," *Kirchenmusikalisches Jahrbuch* 65 (1981), 7 – 30, and "Zur Entstehung und Ueberlieferung der 'Missa graeca,'" *Archiv für Musikwissenschaft* 39 (1982), 113 – 145.

14. Atkinson, "*O amnos tu theu*," pp. 9 – 14, and "Zur Entstehung," pp. 120 – 125, lists the manuscripts. There are certainly more texts to be found. The state of scholarship with reference to music manuscripts is reviewed by Gunilla Björkvall, Gunilla Iversen, and Ritva Jonsson, eds., *Tropes du propre de la messe*, 2: *Cycle de Pâques*, Acta Universitatis Stockholmiensis, Studia latina stockholmiensia, 25; Corpus Troporum, 3 (Stockholm, 1982), pp. 24 – 27. Cagin, *L'euchologie latine*, 1:532 – 536, lists occurrences of Greek liturgical pieces in the bilingual Psalters. Jeauneau, "Jean Scot Erigène et le grec," p. 38, gives additional references. I have seen the Doxa, Pisteuo eis theon, and O amnos in Zurich, Zentralbibliothek C 58, fol. 158v, a collectanea manuscript of the twelfth century (L. C. Mohlberg, *Katalog der Handschriften der Zentralbibliothek Zürich*, 1 [1932; repr. Zurich, 1951], pp. 31 – 33).

15. Atkinson's lists are restricted to occurrences of the pieces of the *Missa graeca* as it has been defined by modern scholars. As a result, they do not take into account the presence of other Greek liturgical material that is transmitted in the same manuscripts. The Lord's Prayer, for instance, is very often copied together with the Ordinary chants—at least in the St. Gall books.

MS 381 contains the fullest set, with paired texts in Greek and Latin of the Greater Doxology, the Apostles' Creed (in Greek only), the Lord's Prayer, the Nicene-Constantinopolitan Creed, the O amnos tu theu, and the Agios. The manuscript is perhaps the most spectacular of the St. Gall sources, for it also contains Notker's letter to Lantpert with the greeting from the "ellinici fratres," as well as liturgical verses by Notker and Hartmann embellished with Greek words and letters.

MS 382 has the same set of Ordinary chants, but omits the O amnos and the Agios. Plate 7 illustrates its treatment of the Greater Doxology. MS 484 omits the Lord's Prayer. Three additional tropers, MSS 376, 378, and 380, contain the Greater Doxology, the Apostles' Creed (in Greek only), the Nicene-Constantinopolitan Creed (in Greek only), and the O amnos. An eleventh-century troper bound in a collectanea volume, Zurich, Zentralbibliothek Rh. 97, has the Apostles' Creed in Greek.

St. Gall monks probably prepared the "Minden Troper" (formerly Berlin, Deutsche Staatsbibliothek theol. lat. qu. 11; now Krakow, Bibliotheca Jagiellonska, MS 783) for Bishop Sigebert of Minden between 1024 and 1027. The art-loving bishop commissioned many works from monasteries in the area of the Lake of Constance; this one has a unique ivory binding with portraits of St. Gall poets. It contains bilingual versions of the Greater Doxology, the Nicene-Constantinopolitan Creed, the Lord's Prayer, the Agios, and the O amnos.

As for the graduals, MSS 338 and 340 contain the Greater Doxology, the Apostles' Creed (in Greek only), and the Nicene-Constantinopolitan Creed (in Greek only). The texts in MS 340 are fragmentary.

Greek texts in the liturgical books were generally written in Latin letters, a method that made it possible to perform them fluently in public. With the exception of the Apostles' Creed (and some supplementary versions of the Greater Doxology), the prayers were presented in both Greek and Latin. This was done in one of several ways: the complete Greek text might be joined by a complete Latin text; it might be supplied with a Latin interlinear version; or it might be followed clause by clause with a Latin translation. The Greek prayers in the tropers and graduals were normally provided with musical notations (sometimes missing from the Latin), and so it is fair to conclude that they really were chanted during some masses at St. Gall.

Not all of the manuscripts containing Greek prayers were specifically intended for use in the liturgy. Two Greek-Latin Psalters, which antedate the tropers and graduals by about a century, contain the texts. MS 17 has bilingual versions of the Lord's Prayer, the Apostles' Creed, and a litany of the saints. The Bamberg Psalter has bilingual versions of the Lord's

OXA EN IPSISTIS THEO

GLORIA IN EXCELSIS DEO

Keepus irini enandropis edochias

Et in terra pax homnib, bone uoluntatis

Enumense Elogumense

Laudamus te Benedicim te

Proskinumense Dorologumense

Adorani te glorificamus te

Euckaristumensi diatin megalin sudoxan

Gratias agim tibi ppt magna glam tua.

kyrie basileu epuranie teepatir pantocrator

Dne ds rex celestis dspat omnip otens

kyrie pie monogeni ihcu xpiete

Dne fili unigenite ihcu xpiete

kyrie otheos oamnos tutheu oyos tupatros

Domine ds agnus di filius patris

Oeromin amathyan tucosinu eleyson imas

Plate 7. Greater Doxology in Greek and Latin.
St. Gall, Stiftsbibliothek, MS 382, p. 5.

Prayer, the Apostles' Creed, the Greater Doxology, the Nicene-Constantinopolitan Creed, and the litany. In both Psalters Greek majuscules are used for most of the texts. In neither are there neumes.

That the litanies were copied, if not composed, at St. Gall is suggested by invocations to the local patrons. The litany of MS 17 invokes St. Gall and St. Otmar:

SANCTE GALLE   ΑΓΙΕ ΓΑΛΛΕ

SANCTE OTMARE   ΑΓΙΕ ΟΤΜΑΡΕ

The litany of the Bamberg Psalter invokes St. Gall, St. Otmar, and St. Pirminius, the founder of Reichenau:

ΑΓΙΕ ΓΑΛΛΕ ΕΥΧΟΥ ΥΠΕΡ ΗΜΟΝ   SANCTE GALLE ORA PRO NOBIS
ΑΓΙΕ ΟΤΜΑΡΕ ΕΥΧΟΥ ΥΠΕΡ ΗΜΟΝ   SANCTE OTMARE ORA PRO NOBIS
ΑΓΙΕ ΠΕΡΜΙΝΙΕ   Sancte Permini[16]

Dom Paul Cagin has demonstrated that the litanies were composed for the Latin rite and have nothing of the Byzantine liturgy about them.[17] The litany of the Bamberg Psalter was repeated in the four derivative quadripartite Psalters of the eleventh and twelfth centuries.

Two study books contain Greek prayers. In London, British Library Harley 5642, Greek texts of the Greater Doxology and the Agios follow upon the *Hermeneumata pseudo-dositheana* and other grammatical material assembled in the manuscript. The Greek Lord's Prayer appears on the flyleaf of MS 237, a ninth-century copy of Isidore's *Etymologiae*.

There are also more trivial indications of an interest in Greek. A tenth- or eleventh-century martyrology (MS 342, p. 13) gives Latin and Greek titles for the feast of the Transfiguration: "Transfiguratio domini. Metamophorseon [*sic*] tutheu." In a calendar of the saints composed at St. Gall in the tenth century (MS 459, pp. 47–50, 56) Greek majuscules are used for the names of Saints Stephen, Hippolytus, Agapetus, Bartholomew the Apostle, Matthew Apostle and Evangelist, Stephen Protomartyr, and the Theotokos.

A St. Gall manuscript from the end of the ninth century (Zurich, Zentralbibliothek C 78) is our oldest source for a Latin translation of the *Akathistos Hymnos*. The *Akathistos Hymnos*, the "hymn during which one does not sit," is the most celebrated of the Byzantine Marian hymns,

---

16. Fol. 165v. The full texts are printed by Cagin, *L'euchologie latine*, 1:502, 542.
17. *L'euchologie latine*, 1:563–568.

extravagant in its praises of Mary and her attributes. It was written in thanksgiving for her protection of the city of Constantinople, possibly by Romanos Melodos in the sixth century. The hymn comprises twenty-four strophes, each strophe corresponding to a letter of the alphabet and arranged in alphabetical order.

This manuscript gives a historical prologue on the office of the *Akathistos* and then presents Latin translations of the *kontakion*, or refrain, and the first *oikos*, or strophe. The translation is incomplete, for the scribe declares himself unimpressed by its quality. He refers to the portion of the text omitted—"which we have passed over, because, having been poorly translated from Greek into Latin, it possessed nothing of the truth."[18] If the writer himself felt able to criticize the translation, it is likely that he had the complete original before him. Indeed, the manuscript gives evidence of contact with Byzantine models, for on fol. 157r it displays the Byzantine cross "ΦѠC—ZѠH," surrounded by the legend "iħs—xp̄c—NI—KA."

Where was the Greek text first translated? Michel Huglo has suggested that it was the work of Hilduin's St-Denis scholars in about 825 and that it came to St. Gall from northeastern France, but the issue is far from settled.[19] In any case the St. Gall manuscript remains the earliest witness to the prologue and the Latin version of the hymn.

The translation of the *Akathistos Hymnos* is the only one of the St. Gall texts to suggest an immediate contact with Byzantine sources; for the most part these liturgical pieces are western creations. In thinking about Greek texts in medieval Europe, it is important to remember that the use of the language does not in itself imply an acquaintance with contemporary Byzantium. For the biblical sources from which the liturgical pieces most often derive were part of an early Christian deposit common to both East and West.

Despite the many questions that remain about the melodic origins of the Greek Ordinary chants, there is no doubt that the series took shape

18. Text printed by G. G. Meersseman, *Der Hymnos Akathistos im Abendland* (Freiburg, Switzerland, 1958), 1:58: "Qui propterea pretermissus est a nobis, qui male de greco in latinum versus, nihil habuit veri[ta]tis."

19. "L'ancienne version latine de l'hymne acathiste," *Le Muséon* 64 (1951), 59–60. For a critical assessment of this and other works, see Berschin, *Griechisch-lateinisches Mittelalter*, pp. 164–166. Another Latin translation of three Byzantine tropes in honor of the Virgin was discovered in a Laon manuscript (Paris, BN lat. 10307, fol. 95v) by John J. Contreni; see Contreni, *The Cathedral School*, p. 70, and Jeauneau, "Jean Scot Erigène et le grec," pp. 39–40.

according to the requirements of the Latin liturgy. This direction is evident both in the general pattern of their use in the mass and in specific details of their texts.

They seem to have been brought into the liturgy as companion pieces for the Latin Ordinary chants. For example, in the Byzantine church the Greater Doxology did not form part of the Eucharistic liturgy but belonged to the office, where it was recited as the liturgical morning prayer. In the West, however, it became customary to recite the Doxology at masses of a festive nature, and it is this practice that was furthered by the Doxa en ipsistis theo.

The Nicene Creed was performed in the Eucharistic liturgies of both Byzantium and Rome, but at different times and in different ways. In the eastern liturgies it was recited after the Prayer of the Faithful and the Great Entry; in the western liturgies it was recited or sung after the reading of the Gospel.[20] Again, the St. Gall Pisteuo eis ena theon is in the western mode. There are well-known differences too in the texts of the eastern and western creeds. The most important is the western addition of the controversial *filioque* to the article on the Holy Spirit ("I believe in the Holy Spirit, Lord and Giver of life, who proceeds from the Father *and the Son*"). In the bilingual St. Gall creeds the *filioque* of the Latin version is translated into Greek ("καὶ υἱοῦ") and added to the Greek text of the article.

The case for the Apostles' Creed is straightforward. Carolingian reformers encouraged its use, because they believed that it was well suited for the religious instruction of the laity, but in the East it was little known. (So unaccustomed were the Greeks to the Apostles' Creed that in 1438 Mark Eugenicus shocked the Latin clerics at the Council of Florence by claiming that he had never heard of it.)[21] The Greek text of the Apostles' Creed in the St. Gall manuscripts is not a Greek original; it is a translation from the Latin into Greek.[22]

It should be evident that the Greek chants of the mass Ordinary do not represent a transposition of the liturgical practices of the eastern rites to the Frankish kingdoms. While it would be foolhardy to rule out the possibility of a Byzantine contribution to either melodies or texts, it is doubtful that the Byzantine role could be described as anything more than episodic.

20. Joseph A. Jungmann, *The Mass of the Roman Rite: Its Origins and Development (Missarum Sollemnia)*, trans. Francis X. Brunner (New York, 1961), 1:569–584.
21. J. Hardouin, *Acta conciliorum et epistolae decretales ac constitutiones summorum pontificum (34–1714)*, 11 vols. in 12 (Paris, 1715), 9:842–843.
22. Caspari, *Geschichte des Taufsymbols*, 3:204–234.

Some melodies and some texts may have come from visiting Greeks, as Notker's account of the translation of the *Veterem hominem* antiphons makes clear.[23] The history of the Christian liturgy is complex, with the various rites acting upon one another in ways that are often obscure. But these St. Gall pieces are for the most part the consequence of the elaboration of the Latin rites.[24] The liturgists quite intentionally sought to introduce Greek elements to the public worship of the West. Why?

Of the approximately sixty western manuscripts that contain Greek Ordinary chants, sixteen assign them to the feast of Pentecost.[25] (In a majority of the liturgical books, including those from St. Gall, the chants are not rubricked.) Their time of appearance within the liturgical year seems to have been chosen with purpose, for the feast of Pentecost commemorates the descent of the Holy Spirit upon the Apostles:

> And when the day of Pentecost was now come they were all together in one place. And suddenly there came from heaven a sound as of the rushing of a mighty wind, and it filled all the house where they were sitting. And there appeared unto them tongues distributed among them like fire; and they sat upon each one of them. And they were all filled with the Holy Spirit and began to speak with other tongues, as the Spirit gave them utterance. Now there were dwelling at Jerusalem Jews, devout men, from every nation under heaven. And when this sound was heard, the multitude came together, and were confounded, because every man heard them speaking in his own language ... [and they] exclaimed: ". . . We do hear them speaking in our tongues the mighty works of God."[26]

23. In *Gesta Karoli* 2.7, Notker Balbulus reported that when Byzantine visitors sang for Charles the Great on the octave of the Epiphany, the emperor was delighted and ordered his clerics to translate their antiphons. He was so eager for the Latin text that they were compelled to work through the night and were denied breakfast until they had finished. As a result of their haste, Notker commented somewhat maliciously, they made several mistakes (among them, the substitution of *conteruit* for *contrivit*). Indeed, musicologists have found that the Latin *Veterem hominem* cycle corresponds to a Greek cycle for the octave of the Epiphany; for a review of the scholarship see Berschin, *Griechisch-lateinisches Mittelalter*, pp. 141–142.

24. Of course the pattern of transmission of texts and melodies in the western sources was by no means uniform. For a discussion of variations in the transmission of Greek Ordinary chants in the eastern and western regions of the Frankish Empire see Atkinson, *"O amnos tu theu,"* pp. 19–30, and "Zur Entstehung," pp. 126–132.

25. See Atkinson, "Zur Entstehung," p. 132.

26. From Acts 2.1–11. On the response of medieval thinkers to the scriptural text see Borst, *Der Turmbau von Babel,* 2.1:483–541.

The New Testament account signaled an end to the confusion of tongues that had resulted from the Tower of Babel. "It did not do this by returning to a single language," observes Philippe Wolff, "but by a mysterious inter-comprehension amongst God's people."[27] And so Pentecost called to mind all of the languages spoken by Christians. To sing the mass in Greek and Latin, then, was to celebrate the feast in a way that was singularly appropriate.

Medieval writers on the liturgy commented on the presence of the two languages. One of them was Amalarius of Metz (ca. 775 – ca. 850), whose allegorical interpretations of the mass were popular at St. Gall.[28] In his explanation of the reasons for bilingual lessons on a particular Sabbath, he said: "Six lessons were read by the ancient Romans in Greek and Latin, and this practice is still kept in Constantinople today, for—if I am not mistaken—two reasons: first, because Greeks to whom the Latin language was unknown were present, and Latins were present to whom Greek was unknown; second, on account of the unanimity of both peoples. . . ."[29]

Remigius of Auxerre (ca. 841 – ca. 908) expressed the same sentiment in almost the same words.[30] In his discussion of the Kyrie Eleison, he went on to add: "The Kyrie Eleison is professed by the Latins in Greek and by the Greeks in Latin, both because certain of its words sound more creditable in Greek than in Latin, and certain of them sound more pleasing in Latin than in Greek, and [also] so that we may show that we are His [the Lord's] one people, and that each people believes in one God."[31]

Honorius of Autun (ca. 1080 – ca. 1137) suggested that the two languages were complementary. During the Rite of Scrutiny the creed was

---

27. *Western Languages*, p. 107.
28. Today there are seven manuscripts. See *Amalarii Episcopi opera liturgica omnia*, 1 – 3, ed. J. M. Hanssens, Studi e Testi 138 – 140 (Vatican City, 1948 – 1950), 1:83 – 91, on the manuscript tradition.
29. *Liber officialis* 2.1, in *Amalarii Episcopi opera*, 2:197. Perhaps Amalarius witnessed the bilingual readings during the course of his diplomatic mission to Constantinople. For an account of the reception of his work in the Carolingian Empire see Franz Brunhölzl, *Geschichte der lateinischen Literatur des Mittelalters* (Munich, 1975), 1:437 – 440 and Rosamund McKitterick, *The Frankish Church and the Carolingian Reforms, 789 – 895* (London, 1977), pp. 148 – 151.
30. *De celebratione missae*, in PL 101:1228. The authorship of this portion of the treatise is disputed; Migne publishes it under the name of pseudo-Alcuin. On the attribution to Remigius of Auxerre, see McKitterick, *The Frankish Church*, p. 148.
31. *De celebratione missae*, in PL 101:1248. Remigius of Auxerre's authorship of this portion of the treatise is not in question. For an account of his work, see Brunhölzl, *Geschichte*, pp. 486 – 489.

chanted in Greek and Latin because "through these two [languages] every language is designated. For in fact the Greeks surpassed all peoples in philosophy, but the Romans governed all peoples. Therefore wise men are understood through the Greek tongue; princes, through the Latin. And so the faith is chanted in Greek and Latin, so that every tongue may acknowledge the Lord."[32]

The theme of the unanimity of the peoples, as expressed by the conjunction of their languages, was a favorite of the medieval commentators. Despite their differences, the Christian people were members of a single church. In the words of Remigius, ". . . We are His [the Lord's] one people, and . . . each people believes in one God."

A worrying question remains. If the bilingual performance was to provide a symbolic demonstration of Christian unity, for whom was the demonstration intended? The Greeks? One Byzantine who recorded his impression was Photius, patriarch of Constantinople (858–867, 877–886). When the patriarch observed that Pope Leo III had ordered the creed to be recited in Greek, he made no reference to Christian unity. Leo, he said, had turned to Greek "on account of the deficiency of his own language, which does not stretch forth so expansively as the Greek." Latin was not a suitable medium for theological discourse, and the addition of the Greek creed was necessary, in Photius's words, "so that the deficiency of the [Latin] language might be restored and cleansed."[33]

There is another way to look at the Greek pieces. Liturgical language is not the same as social language, and it need not be understood by all who use it. In her discussion of the phenomenon of sacred languages Christine Mohrmann observes that prayer more often lies within the domain of expression than in that of communication: "In prayer considered as expression . . . the dominant element is no longer that of intelligibility, as in human dialogue. This is replaced, at least in part, by more subtle elements, partly spiritual, partly affective, which can be crystallized in the rhythm, the tone of delivery, or in the style. There often appears a certain hankering after archaism—essentially a traditional stylistic phenomenon, a

32. *Gemma animae* 3.67, PL 172:661. See above, n. 6.
33. *Mystagogy Concerning the Doctrine of the Holy Spirit* 87, in PG 102:376. See Jaroslav Pelikan, *The Christian Tradition: A History of the Development of Doctrine*, vol. 2, *The Spirit of Eastern Christendom (600–1700)* (Chicago and London, 1974), p. 180 for an account of some sharp exchanges between Greek and Latin theologians on the relative merits of their languages: "It became a commonplace of Byzantine polemics to observe that Latin-speaking barbarians did not have the same capacity for theological precision that Greek writers had acquired."

preference for older modes of expression no longer current in everyday linguistic usage. Such archaizing and stylizing tendencies can be carried so far that the language of religious expression becomes incomprehensible for outsiders."[34]

In the liturgical pieces of the medieval West, Greek served as a sacral or hieratic language. It was used in order to give an impression of solemnity, of formality, and of mystery. The authors of Latin tropes and sequences sought the same effect when they brought Greek words into their verse. From the ninth century onward, religious poets delighted in Greek vocabulary. Words like "melodema," "ierurgia," "hymnologia," and "euprepia" came from John Scottus Eriugena's translations of pseudo-Dionysius and his commentary on the *Celestial Hierarchy*, while "deo ipsistis," "agius," and "kyrie" came from the liturgy itself.[35] Notker Balbulus and Hartmann in the ninth century and Ekkehard I and Ekkehard IV in the tenth and eleventh were among the St. Gall poets who contributed to the monastery's reputation as a center of the new liturgical verse.

It did not seem to matter that few people knew the language. For if the words of the Greek chants were not accessible to the intellect, they were accessible to the senses. Whenever medieval writers used Greek—whether in the liturgy, or in religious verse, or even in grammars and glossaries—they took evident pleasure in its foreign sounds and rhythms. Greek belonged to their liturgy perhaps because it was a token of Christian unity, perhaps because it was a sacred tongue, but certainly because they thought that it was beautiful.

---

34. *Liturgical Latin*, pp. 5–6.

35. For a sample of liturgical Graecisms in Latin verse, see MGH Poet 5.1:55 ("patri summo KAI YΩ eum pneumate doxa"), 91 ("deo ipsistis"), 398 ("agius"), 441 ("doxa en ipsistis theo"), 467 ("kyrie"), 515 ("agius"), 628 ("ICKIPOC AΘANATOC" and "ΔOΣA patri KE YΩ, pneumate cum sancto, nunc et perpetuo").

St. Gall and the Pursuit of the Knowledge of Greek

From the early ninth through the early eleventh centuries the use of Greek at St. Gall was multiform: it appeared in alphabets and ornamental titles and diagrams, in grammars and glossaries, in Scriptures, in liturgies, and in a series of occasional and miscellaneous works. In themselves, some of the texts are dreary indeed. The faulty lists of letters and numbers and the misshapen script used for transcribing *Graeca* in Latin books indicate little more than a trivial curiosity about the language. Yet other texts demonstrate serious concerns. The grammars and *Hermeneumata* were used in the classroom, and the bilingual Scriptures offer sure evidence of a scholarly interest in Greek. When they are all gathered together, these texts form an exceptional collection. They give us a comprehensive account of the Greek materials prepared and used by the scholars of a leading center of learning during the Carolingian period. And so they inform us, with some authority, of the nature of one monastery's preoccupation with Greek.

The study of Greek at St. Gall was a collective enterprise. It was not dominated by a single brilliant figure in the way that John Scottus presided over the court of Charles the Bald. Nor were Greek studies directed by a prominent teacher, as was the case with Martin Hiberniensis in Laon or Sedulius Scottus in Liège. There were many at St. Gall who were interested in the language. A few are known by name: Marcus, Moengal-Marcellus, and the Irishmen who prepared the set of bilingual Scriptures; Notker Balbulus with his verses and Catholic Epistles; Solomon III and his quadripartite Psalter; and Ekkehard I, Ekkehard IV, and the other liturgical poets who employed a Greek vocabulary. But who copied the *Ars grammatica*, the *Hermeneumata*, the glossaries, the various incidental texts? Perhaps Notker's maddening offhand reference to the "ellinici fratres" is the best description after all.[1] They were simply Latin monks who had a taste for Greek.

Few of them succeeded in mastering the language. They might learn the letters of the alphabet, memorize words from vocabulary lists, and

---

1. See Cagin, *L'euchologie latine*, 1:159, for a philological analysis of the term "ellinici."

follow Greek prose with the help of Latin translations. But they suffered because they did not have a foundation in elementary grammar. The Carolingian world had few resources for the study of Greek, and although St. Gall monks had access to most of what seems to have been available at the time, they were not able to overcome its limitations.

It would not do, however, to dismiss the Greek and Greek-Latin texts transcribed at the monastery because the quality of their language is often poor. They represent a unique body of sources. They are more numerous and more diverse than one might have supposed from glancing over the better-known monuments of Carolingian scholarship. And they suggest that for medieval scholars, Greek texts—whatever their quality—were very much a part of traditional monastic culture. They are Greek texts fashioned by Latin hands, and they give support to Walter Berschin's view that the history of the knowledge of Greek in the West is in fact the literary history of the Latin Middle Ages "sub specie graecitatis."[2]

Very little of this material came from the medieval Greek empire. Some few texts give evidence of direct contact with Byzantine sources— two or three alphabetical diagrams, the letter of Lazaros, a glossary of colloquial Greek, a Latin translation of the *Akathistos Hymnos*—but they are exceptions. At St. Gall, the study of Greek was a bookish pursuit, conducted without much knowledge of the spoken language of Byzantium.

For the most part, the Greek material transcribed at St. Gall was drawn from Scripture, from early Christian commentaries, or from the school texts of late Antiquity. The monastery's geographical position was fortunate, because it received many manuscripts that had been preserved in Italy. In copying these works, the monks sought to recover a legacy they believed was rightfully theirs, for had not St. Jerome urged them to study the biblical languages? If Jerome's ideal remained out of reach, it was nevertheless pursued with fervor, and perhaps it served to remind them of their intellectual possibilities as well as their limitations.

---

2. *Griechisch-lateinisches Mittelalter,* p. 9.

Appendix 1

Alphabets and Numerals

This appendix gives a sample, rather than a complete, listing of Greek alphabets found in such conventional sources as Isidore's *Etymologiae*, Bede's *De temporibus* and *De temporum ratione*, the computus, and the *epistolae formatae*. More pertinent to the issue of Greek scholarship are alphabets transcribed independently, and here the appendix attempts to be complete.

St. Gall, Stiftsbibliothek

MS 17

P. 133r: Greek majuscule alphabet. (The numeration of the manuscript here is anomalous. Two sides of a single leaf are identified as p. 133. I have used p. 133r and p. 133v to distinguish them.)

Second half of the ninth century.
Bruckner, *Scriptoria*, 3:57.
See the entries for this manuscript in Appendices 4 and 5, below.

MS 18

P. 4: Two Greek alphabets, majuscule and minuscule, written by a foreign, possibly Byzantine, hand.

Tenth century (tentatively): Bruckner, *Scriptoria*, 3:57.
Ca. twelfth century: Bischoff, "Das griechische Element," p. 253, n. 35.
See the entry for this manuscript in Appendix 4, below.

MS 184

P. 242: Greek majuscule alphabet, with names of the letters and their numerical values. Appears in the context of a discussion of the Greek computus.

End of the ninth century.
Bruckner, *Scriptoria*, 3:79–80.

MS 237

P. 327: Three alphabets, with the names of the letters and the corresponding letters of the Latin alphabet. The alphabets, untitled in the manuscript, are Hebrew, Greek, and the "Scythian" alphabet of the pseudonymous Aethicus Ister. Scherrer's tentative identification of the first alphabet as Slavic is mistaken (Scherrer, *Verzeichnis*, p. 86, relying upon a notation written by Ildefons von Arx on the flyleaf of the manuscript).

Ninth century.
Bruckner, *Scriptoria*, 3:85.
See the entries for this manuscript in Appendices 3 and 5, below.

MS 251

P. 2: Greek majuscule alphabet, with numerical values of the letters. Appears at the end of a discussion of the computus.

Ca. 830.

Bruckner, *Scriptoria*, 2:75.

P. 48: Greek majuscule alphabet, with numerical values of the letters. Appears in Bede's *De temporibus*.

Ca. 830.

Bruckner, *Scriptoria*, 2:75.

MS 397

P. 25: Greek majuscule alphabet, with names of the letters.

Ninth century.

Bruckner, *Scriptoria*, 3:102.

Pp. 78–79: Greek majuscule alphabet, with names of the letters and their numerical values. Also included are three Greek diphthongs, with phonetic Latin equivalents.

Ninth century.

Bruckner, *Scriptoria*, 3:102.

See the entry for this manuscript in Appendix 3, below.

MS 459

P. 111: Following upon discussions of digital computation (*De compoto articulari*) and phonetics (*De enigmaticis notis et loquelis de vocalibus*) appears a full-page chart of letters and numbers. Represented are the letters of the Greek majuscule alphabet (and several numerical signs) together with their names, as well as the numerical values of the letters together with the names of the numbers. (See Plate 1.)

Late ninth or early tenth century.

Bruckner, *Scriptoria*, 3:107.

P. 154: Greek majuscule alphabet. Appears in Bede's *De temporum ratione*.

End of the ninth century.

Bruckner, *Scriptoria*, 3:107.

MS 671

P. 207: Greek majuscule alphabet, with numerical values of the letters and the names of the numbers. Appears in discussion of *epistolae formatae*.

Beginning of the ninth century.

Bruckner, *Scriptoria*, 2:79–80.

MS 751

P. 36: Greek majuscule alphabet. Appears in a discussion of weights and measures (*De ponderibus et mensuris*).

Ninth century.

According to Scherrer, *Verzeichnis*, p. 247, the manuscript is from Italy or France.

MS 876

Pp. 278 – 280: Five alphabets (Hebrew, Greek, Latin, the "Scythian" alphabet of the pseudonymous Aethicus Ister, and Anglo-Saxon runes). All are written in large majuscules and accompanied by a Latin commentary. For the role of this manuscript in the transmission of the *De inventione litterarum* text, see Derolez, *Runica Manuscripta*, pp. 290 – 295. Added to the Greek alphabet (including numerical signs) are the corresponding letters of the Latin alphabet, the names of the Greek letters, and their numerical values.

End of the eighth or beginning of the ninth century.
Bruckner, *Scriptoria*, 2:80 – 81.

MS 877

Pp. 63 – 64: Three alphabetical and numerical series: (1) Greek numerals (Greek majuscules) with their Greek names. Numerical values of the letters differ from those customarily assigned. The names of the numbers 70, 80, 90, and 100 ("obdoenta," "octointa," "enenta," "eccaton," for "ἐβδομή-κοντα," "ὀγδοήκοντα," "ἐνενήκοντα," "ἑκατόν") lack the corresponding symbols. (2) Greek majuscule alphabet (including numerical signs), with names of the Greek letters, the numerical values of the letters, and the names of the Greek numbers (as above). (3) Twenty-three letters of the Latin alphabet, with their numerical values.

Beginning of the ninth century: Bruckner, *Scriptoria*, 2:81.

Bischoff, however, in *Historisches Jahrbuch* 57 (1937), 695, ascribes the manuscript to a northern French scriptorium. Whatever its provenance, the manuscript was soon acquired by the St. Gall library.

See the entry for this manuscript in Appendix 3, below.

MS 878

P. 319: Greek majuscule alphabet. Appears in Isidore's *Etymologiae*.

Mid-ninth century: Bischoff, "Eine Sammelhandschrift Walahfrid Strabos (Cod. Sangall. 878)," in *Mittelalterliche Studien*, 2:35 – 36.

Eleventh century: Scherrer, *Verzeichnis*, p. 307.

The manuscript was not written at St. Gall, but may have been an early addition to the library.

Pp. 320 – 321: Four alphabets: Hebrew (entitled in the manuscript "hebraice littire"), Greek ("ALFABETUM GRECE . . ."), Anglo-Saxon runes ("ANGULISCUM"), and Norse runes ("ABECEDARIUM NORD<MANNICUM>"). For the role of the manuscript in the transmission of the *De inventione litterarum* text, see Derolez, *Runica Manuscripta*, pp. 73 – 83. To the Greek majuscule alphabet (including numerical signs) are added the names of the Greek letters and their numerical values. Also listed are four Greek diphthongs with the corresponding Latin phonetic equivalents.

Date and origin: see above.

MS 902

P. 153: Greek majuscule alphabet. Appears in the context of a Greek computus.
First third of the ninth century. The last of four codices bound in the volume.
Perhaps not from St. Gall.
Bruckner, *Scriptoria*, 3:122.
See the entries for this volume in Appendices 2 and 3, below.

MS 1026

P. 7: Greek majuscule alphabet (including numerical signs), with the corresponding Latin letters, names of the Greek letters, and their numerical values.
Thirteenth century.
Scherrer, *Verzeichnis*, p. 389.

ZURICH, ZENTRALBIBLIOTHEK

C 62

Fol. 211v: Greek majuscule alphabet, with numerical values of the letters.
Appears in a discussion of the computus.

Tenth century; perhaps not from St. Gall.
Bruckner, *Scriptoria*, 3:125.

Appendix 2

Grammatical Texts

London, British Library

MS Harley 5642

Fols. 1r–4r: Alphabetized Greek-Latin glossary similar to (but not identical with) the *Leidensia*, book 1 (*Glossae*). The text is printed in part by Krumbacher, "Eine neue Handschrift," pp. 194–195.

Fols. 4r–8v: *Declinationes Graecorum*, new recension.

Fols. 9r–23v, 34r, 35r–39v: Dositheus, *Ars grammatica*, portions of the first half of the text. (The manuscript appears to have been taken apart and carelessly reassembled: the contents of fols. 9r–15r are disordered.)

Fols. 24r–29r, 39v–47r: Selections from the *Hermeneumata pseudo-dositheana*, as follows:

> Fols. 24r–25v contain topical Greek-Latin glosses corresponding to the *Leidensia*, book 2 (*Capitula*), ch. 33 (middle) to ch. 39.
>
> Fols. 25v–29r contain the *Leidensia*, book 3 (*Divi Hadriani sententiae et epistolae*).
>
> Fol. 29r contains a fragment of the *Leidensia*, book 4 (*Fabulae Aesopiae*).
>
> Fols. 39v–47r contain topical Greek-Latin glosses corresponding to the *Leidensia*, book 2 (*Capitula*), ch. 4 (middle) to ch. 33 (middle).

Fols. 29r–33v: *Colloquium harleianum*. Printed by Goetz, *CGL* 3:108–116.

The Greek is written in Latin characters until fol. 4r, thereafter in Greek majuscules. Latin and Greek texts are copied in parallel columns.
End of the ninth or beginning of the tenth century.
Krumbacher, "Ein neuer Codex," p. 349.
See the entry for this manuscript in Appendix 5, below.

Munich, Bayerische Staatsbibliothek

Clm 601

Fols. 59r–66v: Selections from the *Hermeneumata pseudo-dositheana*, as follows:

> Fols. 59r–61r contain topical Greek-Latin glosses corresponding to the *Leidensia*, book 2 (*Capitula*), ch. 33 (middle) to ch. 39.
>
> Fols. 61r–66v contain a fragment of the *Leidensia*, book 3 (*Divi Hadriani sententiae et epistolae*).

Fols. 67r–82v: Dositheus, *Ars grammatica*, portions of the second half of the text.

Greek majuscules are used throughout.
End of the ninth or beginning of the tenth century.
Krumbacher, "Ein neuer Codex," p. 349.

St. Gall, Stiftsbibliothek

MS 902

Pp. 8–43: Dositheus, *Ars grammatica*.

Pp. 43–59: Selections from the *Hermeneumata pseudo-dositheana*, as follows:
   Pp. 43–51 contain topical Greek-Latin glosses corresponding to the *Leidensia*, book 2 (*Capitula*), ch. 4 (middle) to ch. 39.
   Pp. 51–59 contain the *Leidensia*, book 3 (*Divi Hadriani sententiae et epistolae*).
   P. 59 contains a fragment of the *Leidensia*, book 4 (*Fabulae Aesopiae*).
   P. 60 is blank.

Pp. 61–68: *Declinationes Graecorum*, in a new recension (see Plate 2). Among the additions to the text given in Laon MS 444 is a brief glossary of Greek terms used by St. Jerome (see Appendix 3, below).

Greek majuscules are used throughout. Two hands appear in the manuscript, apparently those of a teacher and his pupil. The first, more practiced hand transcribed the *Ars* and the *Hermeneumata*. The second hand, large and awkward, transcribed the *Declinationes*. Corrections in the *Declinationes* are made in the teacher's hand. On pp. 8–49 the bilingual text is written continuously, each Latin term followed by its Greek translation. From p. 50 onward the Latin and Greek texts are copied in separate columns.
Second half of the ninth century.
Bruckner, *Scriptoria*, 3:122.
See the entries for this volume in Appendices 1 and 3.

Appendix 3

Glossaries and Word Lists

St. Gall, Stiftsbibliothek

MS 196

Front flyleaf, recto: Glossary listing Greek names of charitable institutions and giving Latin definitions. Six lemmata. Greek words written in Latin letters. Text edited by Kaczynski, "Some St. Gall Glosses," pp. 1010–1011.

Front flyleaf, recto: List of the Greek names of the twelve signs of the zodiac. Greek names written in Greek majuscules. Each Greek name is preceded by the initial letter of the corresponding Latin sign. Transcription above, in Chapter 6.
Ninth century.
Bruckner, *Scriptoria*, 3:80.

MS 237

P. 326: Glossary of Greek metrical and grammatical terms with Latin definitions. Twenty-six lemmata. Greek terms written in Latin letters.
Ninth century.
Bruckner, *Scriptoria*, 3:85.
See the entries for this manuscript in Appendices 1 and 5.

MS 249

Pp. 5, 11: Two marginal notes on the text of Bede's *De orthographia* contain Greek terms with Latin definitions. Greek terms written in Greek minuscules (!) by two hands. Transcription above, in Chapter 6.
Beginning of the ninth century.
Bruckner, *Scriptoria*, 2:74.

MS 270

Pp. 55–68: Lengthy composite glossary of which some portions appear to be bilingual:
P. 57 contains a Greek-Latin glossary of biblical terms, many from Gen. 1–3. Twenty-nine lemmata. Greek words written in Latin letters with occasional use of Greek letters.
Pp. 60–62 contain Greek-Latin glosses with many biblical and ecclesiastical terms. On p. 60 Greek terms are written in Greek majuscules; on pp. 61–62, in Latin letters.
Pp. 62–64 contain a glossary of Greek terms derived from Jerome's *De viris illustribus* together with Latin translations. Greek terms for the

"

most part are written in Greek majuscules.
Ninth century.
Bruckner, *Scriptoria*, 3:90 and plate 26.

MS 299

Pp. 281–283: Glossary of Greek terms derived from Jerome's commentaries and epistles with Latin translations. Greek terms written in Greek majuscules.

Pp. 288–292: Glossary of Greek terms derived from Jerome's *De viris illustribus* with Latin translations. (See Plate 4.) On p. 292 there is also a list of seven terms derived from Gennadius's *De viris illustribus*. Greek terms written in Greek majuscules.

Pp. 292–293: Attached to the preceding text is a glossary listing Greek names of charitable institutions and giving Latin translations, as in MS 196.
Second half of the ninth century.
Bruckner, *Scriptoria*, 3:94.

MS 397

P. 37: Glossary of four Greek theological terms with Latin explanations derived from Boethius's *Contra Eutychen et Nestorium*. Greek terms written in Greek majuscules.

P. 38: Glossary listing Greek names of charitable institutions and giving Latin definitions, as in MS 196.
Ninth century.
Bruckner, *Scriptoria*, 3:102.
See the entry for this manuscript in Appendix 1, above.

MS 877

Pp. 65–66: Greek-Latin glossary with many colloquial terms and phrases. Fifty-seven lemmata. Greek terms written in Latin letters. Text edited above, in Chapter 6.
Date: see the entry for this manuscript in Appendix 1, above.

MS 899

P. 84: Greek-Latin list of Neoplatonic terms taken from Victorinus. Nineteen lemmata. Most Greek terms are written in Greek majuscules. See the transcription in Chapter 6, above.

P. 107: Glossary of four Greek theological terms with Latin explanations derived from Boethius's *Contra Eutychen et Nestorium*, as in MS 397.
End of the ninth or beginning of the tenth century.
Bruckner, *Scriptoria*, 3:122.

MS 902

P. 68: A glossary of Greek terms derived from Jerome's *De viris illustribus* with Latin translations is inserted between the lists of adverbs and conjunctions in the *Declinationes Graecorum*. Greek terms written in Greek majuscules.

Second half of the ninth century.

Bruckner, *Scriptoria*, 3:122.

See the entries for this volume in Appendices 1 and 2, above.

Appendix 4

Biblical Texts

For ready identification of the Greek texts within the context of biblical criticism, references are given to the sigla in Alfred Rahlfs, *Verzeichnis der griechischen Handschriften des Alten Testaments*, Mittheilungen des Septuaginta-Unternehmens der Königlichen Gesellschaft der Wissenschaften zu Göttingen 2 (Berlin, 1914), and in C. R. Gregory, *Die griechischen Handschriften des Neuen Testaments* (Leipzig, 1908). Latin texts are indicated by the sigla in the Beuron edition of Petrus Sabatier's *Vetus Latina: Die Reste der altlateinischen Bibel*, 1: *Verzeichnis der Sigel* (Freiburg, 1949).

OLD TESTAMENTS (PSALTERS)

BAMBERG, STAATSBIBLIOTHEK

Msc. Bibl. 44 (A.I.14). Quadripartite Psalter.

> Fols. 12r–150r: Ps. 1–150. The manuscript gives, in four parallel columns, the three Latin versions of St. Jerome and the Septuagint. The Greek text of the Septuagint is written in Latin letters.

> Fols. 150v–161v: Canticles, as above. The Greek text is written in Latin letters.

> Fol. 162r–v: *Te Deum*, in Greek and Latin. Greek text incomplete. Text printed by Cagin, *L'euchologie latine*, 1:147–152.
> 909.
> Bruckner, *Scriptoria*, 3:51.
> Rahlfs, 1037.
> *Vetus Latina*, 311.
> See the entry for this manuscript in Appendix 5, below.

BASEL, UNIVERSITÄTSBIBLIOTHEK

A.VII.3. Greek-Latin Psalter.

> Fols. 4r–97v: Ps. 1–146.2. Greek text written in Greek majuscules. Latin interlinear translation.

> Fol. 98r: Ps. 151, added later. Greek text written in Greek majuscules. Latin interlinear translation.
> Middle of the ninth century.
> Bruckner, *Scriptoria*, 3:51 and plate 14.
> Rahlfs, 156.
> *Vetus Latina*, 334.

St. Gall, Stiftsbibliothek

MS 17. Greek-Latin Psalter.

> Pp. 133r–296: Ps. 101–150. (See Plate 5.) Greek text written in Greek majuscules with minuscule psi. Latin translation copied in a parallel column.

> Pp. 296–333: Canticles, as above. The initial letters of the Latin are often missing. The Latin text itself is not always complete: see pp. 139–176, 178–273, 300–314, and 324–325 (nearly complete). Some Latin lines are missing on pp. 177, 274, and 309.
>
> Second half of the ninth century.
> Bruckner, *Scriptoria*, 3:57 and plate 26.
> Rahlfs, 1053.
> *Vetus Latina*, 335.
> See the entries for this manuscript in Appendices 1 and 5.

MS 1395. Collectanea.

> Pp. 336–361: Fragments of a Greek-Latin Psalter, containing Ps. 30–34, 39–40, and 43–47 (with some portions of the text incomplete). Ten of the thirteen leaves are complete. The Greek text is written in Latin letters on the recto; the Latin text is on the verso. The initial letters of the Greek verses are often missing.
>
> Ninth century.
> Rahlfs, 1054.

NEW TESTAMENTS

Dresden, Sächsische Landesbibliothek

A.145b. Greek-Latin Pauline Epistles ("Codex boernerianus").

> Fols. 1r–99v: Thirteen Pauline Epistles, given in the traditional sequence: Rom., 1 Cor., 2 Cor., Gal., Eph., Phil., Col., 1 Thess., 2 Thess., 1 Tim., 2 Tim., Titus, Philem. The Epistle to the Hebrews is missing. There are no prologues or summaries. The prototype of the manuscript was defective; as a result several verses in the Greek text are missing (Rom. 1.1–5, 2.16–25; 1 Cor. 3.8–16, 6.7–14; Col. 2.1–8; Philem. 21–25). Greek text in Greek majuscules. Latin interlinear translation.
>
> Middle of the ninth century.
> Gregory, G 012.
> *Vetus Latina*, 77.

St. Gall, Stiftsbibliothek

MS 18

> Pp. 143–146: Fragments of a Greek Gospel book. Other fragments from the same book survive in St. Gall MS 45 and Zurich, Zentralbibliothek, MS C 57 (see the entries below). The seven leaves that have been recovered contain Mark 1.31–2.16 and Luke 1.20–32, 1.64–79, and 2.24–48. Most

of the leaves are palimpsests. The underlying Greek text was written in Greek uncials. The upper text in MS 18, copied during the twelfth century, contains Latin Psalms. P. 146 of MS 18 contains a half column of Greek that was not erased and therefore remains legible.

Ninth century.
Bruckner, *Scriptoria*, 3:57, 60, 124–125.
Gregory, O 130.
See the entry for this manuscript in Appendix 1, above.

MS 45

Pp. 1–2: See the preceding entry. The upper text in this manuscript was copied during the thirteenth century. Two photographs of the pages made by the Palimpsest Institute of the Archabbey of Beuron are bound in the manuscript.

MS 48

Pp. 19–407: Greek-Latin "Interlinear Gospels." Greek text written in Greek majuscules. Latin interlinear translation. The Greek text of John 8.11 is missing, but a space on p. 348 was left blank for it. (See Plate 6.)

Middle of the ninth century.
Bruckner, *Scriptoria*, 3:60–61 and plates 13–14.
Gregory, Δ (δ = Latin text) 037.

Zurich, Zentralbibliothek

C 57

Fols. 5r, 74r, 93r, and 135r: See the entries above in this section concerning St. Gall MSS 18 and 45. The upper text here was copied during the thirteenth century.

GREEK MARGINAL NOTES IN LATIN GOSPELS

St. Gall, Stiftsbibliothek

MS 49

Pp. 143 (*bis*), 144, and 162: Four Greek notes in the margins of a Latin Gospel book.

End of the ninth century. The manuscript may have been copied at St. Gall.
Bischoff, "Zur Rekonstruktion," p. 150.

MS 50

Pp. 232 and 283: Two Greek notes in the margins of a Latin Gospel book.

End of the ninth century.
Bruckner, *Scriptoria*, 3:61.

MS 1395

Pp. 7–327: The "St. Gall Gospel Fragments." Vulgate Gospels with contemporary marginal notes taken from a Greek text. The original codex was dismembered in 1461, and the fragments are now widely scattered. The ninety leaves and leaf fragments of this manuscript represent the largest surviving portion. Greek notes are found on pp. 75, 80, 82, 101, 102, 104, 105, 111, and 179.

End of the fifth century. The manuscript was copied in Verona but soon arrived at St. Gall.

Dold, "Neue Teile," p. 105.

Gregory, Σ.

Appendix 5

Liturgical Texts

An asterisk before a shelfmark indicates a music manuscript.

BAMBERG, STAATSBIBLIOTHEK

Msc. Bibl. 44 (A.I.14). Quadripartite Psalter.

> Fol. 162r: Lord's Prayer, in Greek and Latin. The bilingual liturgical texts in this manuscript are copied in parallel columns. The Greek texts are written in Latin letters until fol. 162r; beginning with the Litany on fol. 163r they are written in Greek majuscules.

> Fol. 162r: Apostles' Creed, in Greek and Latin.

> Fols. 163r–167r: Litany, in Greek and Latin. Text printed by Cagin, *L'euchologie latine*, 1:537–546.

> Fol. 167r: Greater Doxology, in Greek and Latin. Text printed by Cagin, *L'euchologie latine*, 1:568.

> Fols. 167r–168r: Nicene-Constantinopolitan Creed, in Greek and Latin. 909.
> See the entry for this manuscript in Appendix 4, above.

BERLIN, DEUTSCHE STAATSBIBLIOTHEK

*Theol. lat. qu. 11. "Minden Troper." See the next entry.

KRAKOW, BIBLIOTHECA JAGIELLONSKA

*MS 783 (Theol. lat. qu. 11). "Minden Troper." The manuscript, long thought to have been lost during World War II, has now come to light in Poland. Dr. Gerard Achten, of the Staatsbibliothek Preussischer Kulturbesitz in West Berlin, drew my attention to its reappearance, and Dr. Paul E. Szarmach, of the State University of New York at Binghamton, verified further details during a recent visit to Krakow.

> Fol. 91v: Greater Doxology, in Greek and Latin. The Greek texts in this manuscript are written in Latin letters.

> Fol. 92v: Greater Doxology, in Greek.

> Fol. 101r: Nicene-Constantinopolitan Creed, in Greek and Latin. Incorrectly identified in the manuscript as the Apostles' Creed.

> Fol. 105r: Lord's Prayer, in Greek and Latin.

Fol. 105v: Agios/Sanctus.

Fol. 109r: O amnos tu theu/Agnus Dei.

Copied between 1024 and 1027, probably at St. Gall, for Bishop Sigebert of Minden. On the contents see V. Rose, *Verzeichniss der lateinischen Handschriften [der Kgl. Bibliothek zu Berlin]*, 2.2 (Berlin, 1903), cols. 684–686 (no. 694). See also Heinrich Husmann, *Tropen- und Sequenzenhandschriften* (Munich and Duisburg, 1964), pp. 62–63.

LONDON, BRITISH LIBRARY

MS Harley 5642

Fol. 47v: Greater Doxology, in Greek. Text written in Latin letters.
Printed by Krumbacher, "Ein neuer Codex," p. 358.

Fol. 47v: Agios, in Greek. Text written in Greek majuscules.
Printed by Krumbacher, "Ein neuer Codex," p. 358.
End of the ninth or beginning of the tenth century.
Krumbacher, "Ein neuer Codex," p. 349.
See the entry for this manuscript in Appendix 2, above.

ST. GALL, STIFTSBIBLIOTHEK

MS 17. Greek-Latin Psalter.

P. 334: Lord's Prayer, in Greek and Latin. The bilingual liturgical texts in this manuscript are copied in parallel columns, the Greek texts written in Greek majuscules.

Pp. 334–336: Apostles' Creed, in Greek and Latin.

Pp. 336–341: Litany, in Greek and Latin. Text printed by Cagin, *L'euchologie latine*, 1:501–505.
Second half of the ninth century.
See the entries for this manuscript in Appendices 1 and 4, above.

MS 237

P. 326: Lord's Prayer, in Greek. Text written in Latin letters.
Ninth century.
Bruckner, *Scriptoria*, 3:85.
See the entries for this manuscript in Appendices 1 and 3, above.

*MS 338. Gradual.

Pp. 178–179: Trisagion. Greek verses in Greek majuscules.

Pp. 307–308: Greater Doxology, in Greek. This text and the remaining Greek texts in the manuscript are written in Latin letters.

P. 309: Apostles' Creed, in Greek. Text printed by Caspari, *Geschichte des Taufsymbols*, 3:11.

Pp. 310–312: Greater Doxology, in Greek and Latin. Verse of Greek followed by verse of Latin.

Pp. 312–313: Nicene-Constantinopolitan Creed, in Greek. Incorrectly identified in the manuscript as the Apostles' Creed. Text printed by Caspari, *Geschichte des Taufsymbols*, 1:240–241.

Eleventh century.
Bruckner, *Scriptoria*, 3:96–97.

*MS 339. Gradual.

P. 102: Trisagion. Greek verses in Greek majuscules.

Eleventh century.
Bruckner, *Scriptoria*, 3:97.

*MS 340. Gradual.

Pp. 39 and 212: Fragments of the Greater Doxology, in Greek and Latin. The Greek texts in the manuscript are written in Latin letters.

Pp. 40 and 212: Fragments of the Nicene-Constantinopolitan Creed, in Greek.

P. 212: Fragment of the Apostles' Creed, in Greek.

Eleventh century.
Bruckner, *Scriptoria*, 3:97.

*MS 359. Gradual.

P. 100: Trisagion. Greek verses in Greek majuscules.

Ninth or tenth century.
Bruckner, *Scriptoria*, 3:98–99.

*MS 374. Gradual.

P. 96: Trisagion. Greek verses in Greek majuscules.

Eleventh century.
Bruckner, *Scriptoria*, 3:99.

*MS 376. Troper.

Pp. 68–69: Greater Doxology, in Greek. Most of the Greek texts in this manuscript are written in Latin letters.

Pp. 69–70: Greater Doxology, in Greek and Latin. Verse of Greek followed by verse of Latin.

Pp. 70–71: Apostles' Creed, in Greek.

Pp. 71–72: Nicene-Constantinopolitan Creed, in Greek.

P. 76: O amnos tu theu.

P. 190: Trisagion. Greek verses in Greek majuscules.

Eleventh century.
Bruckner, *Scriptoria*, 3:99–100.

*MS 378. Troper.

Pp. 106–108: Greater Doxology, in Greek and Latin. Verse of Greek followed by verse of Latin. The Greek texts in this manuscript are written in Latin letters.

Pp. 109 – 110: Greater Doxology, in Greek. Text written in Latin letters, except for imitation Greek majuscules in the first line.

Pp. 110 – 112: Apostles' Creed, in Greek.

Pp. 112 – 115: Nicene-Constantinopolitan Creed, in Greek.

P. 126: O amnos tu theu.

Twelfth century: Bruckner, *Scriptoria*, 3:100.
Between 1034 and 1070: scholarship reviewed by Husmann, *Tropen- und Sequenzenhandschriften*, pp. 35 – 37.

*MS 380. Troper.

Pp. 90 – 92: Greater Doxology, in Greek. Most of the Greek texts in this manuscript are written in Latin letters.

Pp. 92 – 94: Greater Doxology, in Greek and Latin. Verse of Greek followed by verse of Latin.

Pp. 94 – 96: Nicene-Constantinopolitan Creed, in Greek.

Pp. 97 – 98: Apostles' Creed, in Greek.

P. 101: O amnos tu theu.

P. 333: Trisagion. Greek verses in Greek majuscules.

Eleventh century: Bruckner, *Scriptoria*, 3:100.
Ca. 1054: scholarship reviewed by Husmann, *Tropen- und Sequenzenhandschriften*, p. 40.

*MS 381. Troper.

Pp. 13 – 14: Greater Doxology, in Greek. The Greek texts in this manuscript are written in Latin letters.

Pp. 14 – 15: Apostles' Creed, in Greek.

Pp. 15 – 17: Greater Doxology, in Greek and Latin. Verse of Greek followed by verse of Latin.

Pp. 17 – 18: Lord's Prayer, in Greek and Latin. Verse of Greek followed by verse of Latin.

Pp. 18 – 22: Nicene-Constantinopolitan Creed, in Greek and Latin. Verse of Greek followed by verse of Latin. Incorrectly identified in the manuscript as the Apostles' Creed.

P. 311: O amnos tu theu/Agnus Dei.

P. 315: Agios.

Eleventh century: Bruckner, *Scriptoria*, 3:100.
Tenth century: scholarship reviewed by Husmann, *Tropen- und Sequenzenhandschriften*, pp. 42 – 43.

*MS 382. Troper.

P. 3: Greater Doxology, in Greek. Most of the Greek texts in this manuscript are written in Latin letters.

P. 4: Apostles' Creed, in Greek.

Pp. 5–6: Greater Doxology, in Greek and Latin. Verse of Greek followed by verse of Latin. (See Plate 7.)

Pp. 6–7: Lord's Prayer, in Greek and Latin. Verse of Greek followed by verse of Latin.

Pp. 7–11: Nicene-Constantinopolitan Creed, in Greek and Latin. Verse of Greek followed by verse of Latin. Incorrectly identified in the manuscript as the Apostles' Creed.

P. 255: Trisagion. Greek verses in Greek majuscules.
Eleventh century: Bruckner, *Scriptoria*, 3:100–101.
Early eleventh century or middle of the tenth century: scholarship reviewed by Husmann, *Tropen- und Sequenzenhandschriften*, pp. 44–45.

*MS 484. Troper.

Pp. 1 and 234–235: Fragments of the Nicene-Constantinopolitan Creed, in Greek. The line on p. 1 also appears (copied by the same hand and supplied with a Latin translation) in MS 40, p. 302.

Pp. 202–204: Greater Doxology, in Greek.

Pp. 205–207: Apostles' Creed, in Greek.

P. 244: O amnos tu theu.

Pp. 298–302: Greater Doxology, in Greek and Latin. Verse of Greek followed by verse of Latin.

Pp. 303–304, 317–318, and 305: Nicene-Constantinopolitan Creed, in Greek. The pages were disarranged when the codex was rebound. Incorrectly identified in the manuscript as the Apostles' Creed.

Pp. 305–306: Agios.
Ninth century: Bruckner, *Scriptoria*, 3:107.
Tenth century: Husmann, *Tropen- und Sequenzenhandschriften*, p. 47.

Zurich, Zentralbibliothek

C 78

Fols. 47v–48v: Fragment of a Latin translation of the *Akathistos Hymnos*.
End of the ninth century.
Bruckner, *Scriptoria*, 3:126.

*Rh. 97

Fol. 36v: Apostles' Creed, in Greek. Text written in Latin letters. Printed by Wagner, *Einführung*, 1:102–103.
This portion (troper) of the collectanea manuscript may have been copied at St. Gall during the eleventh century.
L. C. Mohlberg, *Katalog der Handschriften der Zentralbibliothek Zürich*, 1: *Mittelalterliche Handschriften* (1932; repr. Zurich, 1951), p. 206.

Bibliography

PRIMARY SOURCES

The list of published primary sources includes facsimile editions of St. Gall manuscripts, editions of complete texts or significant fragments of texts, and editions of the medieval authors whose works are most germane to the study of St. Gall and of Greek. It does not include references to the many classical and medieval authors whose works are cited in the course of the book in order to document specific points. These references are given in the footnotes according to standard editions.

Allgeier, Arthur. "Bruchstücke eines altlateinischen Psalters aus St. Gallen in Codd. 1395 St. Gallen, C 184 Zürich, und 587 Wien." *Sitzungsberichte der Heidelberger Akademie der Wissenschaften, phil.-hist. Klasse* 2 (1928 – 1929), 62 – 141.

Amalarius of Metz. *Amalarii Episcopi opera liturgica omnia.* 3 vols. Edited by Joannes Michael Hanssens. Studi e Testi 138 – 140. Vatican City, 1948 – 1950.

Biblia sacra iuxta Vulgatam clementinam. 4th ed. Edited by Alberto Colunga and Laurentio Turrado. Biblioteca de Autores Cristianos. Madrid, 1965.

Bieler, Ludwig, ed. *Psalterium graeco-latinum: Codex Basiliensis A.VII.3.* Umbrae Codicum Occidentalium 5. Amsterdam, 1960.

Dold, P. Alban. "Neue Teile der ältesten Vulgata-Evangelienhandschrift aus dem 5. Jahrhundert." *Biblica* 22 (1941), 105 – 146.

————, and Arthur Allgeier. *Der Palimpsestpsalter im Codex sangallensis 912.* Texte und Arbeiten 21 – 24. Beuron, 1933.

Dositheus Magister. *Ars grammatica.* Edited by Heinrich Keil in *Grammatici latini* 7:365 – 436. Leipzig, 1880; repr. Hildesheim, 1961.

————. *Dosithei Ars grammatica.* Edited by Iohannes Tolkiehn. Leipzig, 1913.

Ekkehard IV. *Casus s. Galli.* Edited by Ildefons von Arx (1829) in MGH SS 2:77 – 147.

————. *Casus s. Galli.* Edited by Gerold Meyer von Knonau in *Mittheilungen zur vaterländischen Geschichte* 15 – 16 (N.F. 5 – 6) (1877), 1 – 450.

————. *Die Geschichten des Klosters St. Gallen.* Translated by Bruno Helbling. Graz, 1958.

————. *Der Liber Benedictionum Ekkehards IV. nebst den kleineren Dichtungen aus dem Codex Sangallensis 393.* Edited by Johann Egli. St. Gall, 1909.

Ermenrich of Ellwangen. *Epistola ad Grimaldum abbatem.* Edited by Ernst Dümmler (1899) in MGH Epp 5:536–579.

Das Formelbuch des Bischofs Salomo III von Konstanz. Edited by Ernst Dümmler. Leipzig, 1857; repr. Osnabrück, 1964.

Goetz, Georg, ed. *Corpus glossariorum latinorum.* 7 vols. Leipzig, 1888–1923; repr. Amsterdam, 1965.

Jerome. *Hieronymus liber de viris inlustribus. Gennadius liber de viris inlustribus.* Edited by Ernest C. Richardson. Leipzig, 1896.

Notker Balbulus. *Einhard and Notker the Stammerer: Two Lives of Charlemagne.* Translated by Lewis Thorpe. Harmondsworth, 1969.

————. *Gesta Karoli.* Edited by Hans F. Haefele (1959) in MGH SSrG N.S. 12.

————. *Notker der Dichter und seine geistige Welt.* 2 vols. Edited by Wolfram von den Steinen. Bern, 1948.

Poggio Bracciolini. *Two Renaissance Book Hunters: The Letters of Poggius Bracciolini to Nicolaus de Niccolis.* Translated by Phyllis W. G. Gordan. New York and London, 1974.

Rahlfs, Alfred, ed. *Psalmi cum Odis.* Septuaginta Societas Scientiarum Gottingensis 10. Göttingen, 1931.

————. *Septuaginta, 2: Libri poetici et prophetici.* Stuttgart, 1935.

————. *Septuaginta-Studien, 2: Der Text des Septuaginta-Psalters.* Göttingen, 1907.

Ratpert. *Casus s. Galli.* Edited by Ildefons von Arx (1829) in MGH SS 2:61–74.

————. *Casus s. Galli.* Edited by Gerold Meyer von Knonau in *Mittheilungen zur vaterländischen Geschichte* 13 (N.F. 3) (1872), 1–64.

Reichardt, Alexander, ed. *Der Codex Boernerianus der Briefe des Apostels Paulus (Msc. Dresd. A 145b) in Lichtdruck nachgebildet.* Leipzig, 1909.

Rettig, Hans Christian Michael, ed. *Antiquissimus Quatuor Evangeliorum canonicorum Codex sangallensis graeco-latinus interlinearis.* Zurich, 1836.

Roger Bacon. *The Greek Grammar of Roger Bacon and a Fragment of His Hebrew Grammar.* Edited by Edmond Nolan and Samuel Abraham Hirsch. Cambridge, Eng., 1902.

Scrivener, Frederick H., ed. *An Exact Transcription of the Codex Augiensis, a Graeco-Latin Manuscript of St. Paul's Epistles, Deposited in the Library of Trinity College, Cambridge.* Cambridge, Eng., 1859.

Stokes, Whitley, and John Strachan. *Thesaurus Palaeohibernicus: A Collection of Old-Irish Glosses, Scholia, Prose and Verse.* 2 vols. Cambridge, Eng., 1903.

Turner, Cuthbert Hamilton, ed. *The Oldest Manuscript of the Vulgate Gospels.* Oxford, 1931.

von Matthaei, Christian Friedrich, ed. *XIII epistolarum Pauli codex graecus cum versione latina veteri vulgo antehieronymiana olim boernerianus nunc bibliothecae electoralis dresdensis summa fide et diligentia transcriptus et editus . . . cum tabulis aere expressis. Accessit ex eodem codice fragmentum Marci Monachi.* Meissen, 1791; editio minor Meissen, 1818.

SECONDARY SOURCES

Aland, Kurt. *Kurzgefasste Liste der griechischen Handschriften des Neuen Testaments, 1: Gesamtübersicht.* Arbeiten zur neutestamentlichen Textforschung 1. Berlin, 1963.

————. *Materialien zur neutestamentlichen Handschriftenkunde, 1.* Arbeiten zur neutestamentlichen Textforschung 3. Berlin, 1969.

Allgeier, Arthur. "Exegetische Beiträge zur Geschichte des Griechischen vor dem Humanismus." *Biblica* 24 (1943), 261–288.

————. "Das Psalmenbuch des Konstanzer Bischofs Salomon III. in Bamberg: Eine Untersuchung zur Frage der mehrspaltigen Psalterien." In *Jahresbericht der Görresgesellschaft 1938*, pp. 102–121. Cologne, 1939.

Ammann, Hektor, and Karl Schib, eds. *Historischer Atlas der Schweiz.* 2nd ed. Aarau, 1958.

Atkinson, Charles M. "*O amnos tu theu*: The Greek Agnus Dei in the Roman Liturgy from the Eighth to the Eleventh Century." *Kirchenmusikalisches Jahrbuch* 65 (1981), 7–30.

————. "Zur Entstehung und Ueberlieferung der 'Missa graeca.'" *Archiv für Musikwissenschaft* 39 (1982), 113–145.

Becker, Gustav. *Catalogi bibliothecarum antiqui.* Bonn, 1885; repr. Hildesheim, 1973.

Berger, Samuel, "De la tradition de l'art grec dans les manuscrits latins des Evangiles." *Mémoires de la Société nationale des antiquaires de France* 52 (1891), 144–154.

————. *Histoire de la Vulgate pendant les premiers siècles du moyen âge.* Nancy, 1893.

Berschin, Walter. "Drei griechische Majestas-Tituli in der Trier-Echternacher Buchmalerei." *Frühmittelalterliche Studien* 14 (1980), 299–309.

————. *Griechisch-lateinisches Mittelalter: Von Hieronymus zu Nikolaus von Kues.* Bern and Munich, 1980.

————. "Griechisches bei den Iren." In *Die Iren und Europa im früheren Mittelalter*, edited by Heinz Löwe, vol. 1, pp. 501–510. Stuttgart, 1982.

————. "Liudprands Griechisch und das Problem einer überlieferungsgerechten Edition." *Mittellateinisches Jahrbuch* 20 (1985), 112–115.

Bikel, Hermann. *Die Wirtschaftsverhältnisse des Klosters St. Gallen von der Gründung bis zum Ende des XIII. Jahrhunderts.* Freiburg im Breisgau, 1914.

Bischoff, Bernhard. *Anecdota novissima: Texte des vierten bis sechzehnten Jahrhunderts.* Quellen und Untersuchungen zur lateinischen Philologie des Mittelalters 7. Stuttgart, 1984.

————. *Mittelalterliche Studien: Ausgewählte Aufsätze zur Schriftkunde und Literaturgeschichte.* 3 vols. Stuttgart, 1966–1981. See especially vol. 2, pp. 227–245 ("The Study of Foreign Languages in the Middle Ages"), vol. 2, pp. 246–275 ("Das griechische Element in der abendländischen Bildung des Mittelalters"), and vol. 3, pp. 39–54 ("Irische Schreiber im Karolingerreich").

__________. *Paläographie des römischen Altertums und des abendländischen Mittelalters*. Berlin, 1979.

__________. "Zur Rekonstruktion des Sangallensis (Σ) und der Vorlage seiner Marginalien." *Biblica* 22 (1941), 147–158.

Björkvall, Gunilla; Gunilla Iversen; and Ritva Jonsson, eds. *Tropes du propre de la messe, 2: Cycle de Pâques*. Acta Universitatis Stockholmiensis, Studia latina stockholmiensia 25, Corpus Troporum 3. Stockholm, 1982.

Blass, Friedrich, and Albert Debrunner. *Grammatik des neutestamentlichen Griechisch*. 15th ed. rev. by Friedrich Rehkopf. Göttingen, 1979.

Boese, Helmut. *Die lateinischen Handschriften der Sammlung Hamilton zu Berlin*. Wiesbaden, 1966.

Booth, Alan D. "Elementary and Secondary Education in the Roman Empire." *Florilegium* 1 (1979), 1–14.

Borst, Arno. *Der Turmbau von Babel: Geschichte der Meinungen über Ursprung und Vielfalt der Sprachen und Völker*. 4 vols. Stuttgart, 1957–1963.

Browning, Robert. *Medieval and Modern Greek*. London, 1969.

Bruckner, Albert. *Scriptoria medii aevi helvetica: Denkmäler schweizerischer Schreibkunst des Mittelalters*. Vol. 2, *Schreibschulen der Diözese Konstanz: St. Gallen I* (Geneva, 1936). Vol. 3, *Schreibschulen der Diözese Konstanz: St. Gallen II* (Geneva, 1938).

Brunhölzl, Franz. *Geschichte der lateinischen Literatur des Mittelalters*. Vol. 1. Munich, 1975.

Bullough, D. A. "The Educational Tradition in England from Alfred to Aelfric: Teaching *Utriusque Linguae*." In *La Scuola nell'Occidente latino dell'alto Medioevo*. Vol. 2, pp. 453–494. Settimane di Studio del Centro italiano di Studi sull'alto Medioevo 19. Spoleto, 1972.

Cagin, Paul. *L'euchologie latine, étudiée dans la tradition de ses formules et de ses formulaires, 1: Te Deum ou Illatio? Contribution à l'histoire de l'euchologie latine à propos des origines du Te Deum*. Scriptorium Solesmense 1.1. Solesmes, 1906.

Cahn, Walter. *Romanesque Bible Illumination*. Ithaca, 1982.

Cames, Gérard. *Byzance et la peinture romane de Germanie*. Paris, 1966.

Cappelli, Adriano. *Dizionario di abbreviature latine ed italiane*. 6th ed. from the 3rd ed. of 1929. Milan, 1961.

Cappuyns, Maïeul. *Jean Scot Erigène: Sa vie, son oeuvre, sa pensée*. Paris, 1933.

Caspari, Carl Paul. *Ungedruckte, unbeachtete und wenig beachtete Quellen zur Geschichte des Taufsymbols und der Glaubensregel*. 3 vols. Kristianstad, 1866–1875; repr. Brussels, 1964.

Clark, James Midgeley. *The Abbey of St. Gall as a Centre of Literature and Art*. Cambridge, Eng., 1926.

Coens, Maurice. "'Utriusque linguae peritus': En marge d'un prologue de Thierry de Saint-Trond." *Analecta bollandiana* 76 (1958), 118–150.

Contreni, John J. "The Biblical Glosses of Haimo of Auxerre and John Scottus Eriugena." *Speculum* 51 (1976), 411–434.

__________. "Carolingian Biblical Studies." In *Carolingian Essays*, edited by Uta-

Renate Blumenthal, pp. 71–98. Andrew W. Mellon Lectures in Early Christian Studies. Washington, D.C., 1983.

————. *The Cathedral School of Laon from 850 to 930: Its Manuscripts and Masters*. Münchener Beiträge zur Mediävistik und Renaissance-Forschung 29. Munich, 1978.

————. "The Irish in the Western Carolingian Empire (According to James F. Kenney and Bern, Burgerbibliothek 363)." In *Die Iren und Europa im früheren Mittelalter*, edited by Heinz Löwe, vol. 1, pp. 758–798. Veröffentlichungen des Europa Zentrums Tübingen, Kulturwissenschaftliche Reihe. Stuttgart, 1982.

————. "John Scottus, Martin Hiberniensis, the Liberal Arts, and Teaching." In *Insular Latin Studies: Papers on Latin Texts and Manuscripts of the British Isles, 550–1066*, edited by Michael W. Herren, pp. 23–44. Papers in Mediaeval Studies 1. Toronto, 1981.

————. "Three Carolingian Texts Attributed to Laon: Reconsiderations." *Studi medievali* 17 (1976), 797–813.

Cuissard, Charles. *L'étude du grec à Orléans depuis le IXe siècle jusqu'au milieu du XVIIIe siècle*. Mémoires de la Société archéologique et historique de l'Orléannais 19. Orléans, 1883.

Delaruelle, Etienne. "La connaissance du grec en occident du Ve au IXe siècle." *Mélanges de la Société toulousaine d'études classiques* 1 (1946), 207–226.

Derolez, R. *Runica Manuscripta: The English Tradition*. Bruges, 1954.

Deshusses, Jean. "Chronologie des grands sacramentaires de Saint-Amand." *Revue bénédictine* 87 (1977), 230–237.

Dinneen, Lucilla. *Titles of Address in Christian Greek Epistolography to 527 A.D.* Washington, D.C., 1929.

Dionisotti, Anna Carlotta. "From Ausonius' Schooldays? A Schoolbook and Its Relatives." *Journal of Roman Studies* 72 (1982), 83–125.

————. "From Stephanus to Du Cange: Glossary Stories." *Revue d'histoire des textes* 14–15 (1984–1985), 303–336.

————. "On Bede, Grammars, and Greek." *Revue bénédictine* 92 (1982), 111–141.

Drögereit, Richard. "Griechisch-Byzantinisches aus Essen." *Byzantinische Zeitschrift* 46 (1953), 110–115.

Duft, Johannes. "Die Handschriften-Katalogisierung in der Stiftsbibliothek St. Gallen vom 9. bis zum 19. Jahrhundert." In *Die Handschriften der Stiftsbibliothek St. Gallen: Codices 1726–1984 (14.–19. Jahrhundert)*, by Beat Matthias von Scarpatetti, pp. 9*–26*. St. Gall, 1983.

————. "Irische Handschriftenüberlieferung in St. Gallen." In *Die Iren und Europa im früheren Mittelalter*, edited by Heinz Löwe, vol. 2, pp. 916–937. Stuttgart, 1982.

————. "Iromanie—Irophobie." *Zeitschrift für schweizerische Kirchengeschichte* 50 (1956), 241–262.

————, and Peter Meyer. *The Irish Miniatures in the Abbey Library of St. Gall*. Olten, Switzerland, 1954.

Eckstein, Friedrich A. "Ein griechisches Elementarbuch aus dem Mittelalter." In *Programm der Lateinischen Hauptschule in Halle für das Schuljahr 1860–1861*, pp. 1–11. Halle, 1861.

Erdmann, Jürgen. "Coburger und Bamberger Fragmente eines Psalterium Quadrupartitum: Teile einer Abschrift des Bamberger Codex Msc. Bibl. 44 aus dem Jahre 909?" *Bericht des Historischen Vereins Bamberg* 102 (1966), 63–80.

Fischer, Bonifatius. "Bibelausgaben des frühen Mittelalters." In *La Bibbia nell'alto medioevo*, pp. 519–600. Settimane di Studio del Centro italiano di Studi sull'alto Medioevo 10. Spoleto, 1963.

Frakes, Jerold C. "Griechisches im frühmittelalterlichen St. Gallen: Ein methodologischer Beitrag zu Notker Labeos Griechischkenntnissen." *Zeitschrift für deutsche Philologie* 106 (1987), 25–34.

Frede, Hermann Josef. *Altlateinische Paulus-Handschriften.* Vetus Latina: Aus der Geschichte der lateinischen Bibel 4. Freiburg, 1964.

Gardthausen, Viktor. *Griechische Palaeographie.* 2 vols. 2nd ed. Leipzig, 1911–1913; repr. Leiden, 1979.

—————. "Die griechische Schrift des Mittelalters im Westen Europas." *Byzantinisch-neugriechische Jahrbücher* 8 (1930), 114–135.

Gianola, Giovanna M. *Il Greco di Dante: Ricerche sulle dottrine grammaticali del Medioevo.* Venice, 1980.

Goetz, Georg. "Glossographie." In Pauly-Wissowa, *Real-Encyclopädie der Classischen Altertumswissenschaften.* Vol. 7, cols. 1433–1466. Stuttgart, 1910.

Grabar, André. "Les fresques de Castelseprio et l'occident: Art du haut moyen âge." In *Actes du IIIe congrès international pour l'étude du haut moyen âge*, pp. 85–93. Olten and Lausanne, 1954.

Hattemer, Heinrich. *St. Gallens altdeutsche Sprachschätze.* 3 vols. St. Gall, 1844–1848.

Havet, Louis. *Manuel de critique verbale appliquée aux textes latins.* Paris, 1911; repr. Rome, 1967.

Herren, Michael W., ed. *The Sacred Nectar of the Greeks: The Study of Greek in the West in the Early Middle Ages.* King's College London Medieval Studies 2. (Forthcoming.)

Holtz, Louis. *Donat et la tradition de l'enseignement grammatical.* Paris, 1981.

Horn, Walter, and Ernest Born. *The Plan of St. Gall: A Study of the Architecture and Economy of, and Life in a Paradigmatic Carolingian Monastery.* 3 vols. Berkeley and Los Angeles, 1979. See the review article by Warren Sanderson, "The Plan of St. Gall Reconsidered," *Speculum* 60 (1985), 615–632.

Huglo, Michel. "L'ancienne version latine de l'hymne acathiste." *Le Muséon* 64 (1951), 27–61.

—————. "Les chants de la *Missa greca* de Saint-Denis." In *Essays Presented to Egon Wellesz*, edited by Jack Westrup, pp. 74–83. Oxford, 1966.

—————. "La mélodie grecque du 'Gloria in excelsis' et son utilisation dans le Gloria XIV." *Revue grégorienne* 29 (1950), 30–40.

—————. "Origine de la mélodie du Credo 'authentique' de la Vaticane." *Revue grégorienne* 30 (1951), 68–78.

————. "La tradition occidentale des mélodies byzantines du Sanctus." In *Der kultische Gesang der abendländischen Kirche*, edited by Franz Tack, pp. 40–46. Cologne, 1950.

Husmann, Heinrich. *Tropen- und Sequenzenhandschriften*. Munich and Duisburg, 1964.

Irigoin, Jean. "La culture grecque dans l'occident latin du VIIe au XIe siècle." In *La cultura antica nell'occidente latino dal VII all'XI secolo*. Vol. 1, pp. 425–446. Settimane di Studio del Centro italiano di Studi sull'alto Medioevo 22. Spoleto, 1975.

————. "Survie et renouveau de la littérature antique à Constantinople (IXe siècle)." *Cahiers de civilisation médiévale* 5 (1962), 287–302.

Jeauneau, Edouard. "Les écoles de Laon et d'Auxerre au IXe siècle." In *La Scuola nell'Occidente latino dell'alto Medioevo*. Vol. 2, pp. 495–522, 555–560. Settimane di Studio del Centro italiano di Studi sull'alto Medioevo 19. Spoleto, 1972.

————. "Jean Scot Erigène et le grec." *Archivum Latinitatis Medii Aevi (Bulletin du Cange)* 41 (1979), 5–50.

————. "Pour le dossier d'Israel Scot." *Archives d'histoire doctrinale et littéraire du moyen âge* 52 (1985), 7–71.

————. "Pseudo-Dionysius, Gregory of Nyssa, and Maximus the Confessor in the Works of John Scottus Eriugena." In *Carolingian Essays*, edited by Uta-Renate Blumenthal, pp. 137–149. Andrew W. Mellon Lectures in Early Christian Studies. Washington, D.C., 1983.

————. *Quatre thèmes érigéniens*. Montreal, 1978.

Jungmann, Joseph A. *The Mass of the Roman Rite: Its Origins and Development (Missarum Sollemnia)*. 2 vols. Translated by Francis X. Brunner. New York, 1961.

Kaczynski, Bernice M. "Greek Glosses on Jerome's *Ep. CVI, Ad Sunniam et Fretelam*, in MS Berlin (East), Deutsche Staatsbibliothek, Phillipps 1674." In *The Sacred Nectar of the Greeks: The Study of Greek in the West in the Early Middle Ages*, edited by Michael W. Herren. King's College London Medieval Studies 2. (Forthcoming.)

————. "Some St. Gall Glosses on Greek Philanthropic Nomenclature." *Speculum* 58 (1983), 1008–1017.

————, and Haijo Jan Westra. "Aesop in the Middle Ages: The Transmission of the Sick Lion Fable and the Authorship of the St. Gall Version." *Mittellateinisches Jahrbuch* 17 (1982), 31–38.

————, and Haijo Jan Westra. "The Motif of the Hypocritical Wolf in Medieval Greek and Latin Animal Literature." In *The Sacred Nectar of the Greeks: The Study of Greek in the West in the Early Middle Ages*, edited by Michael W. Herren. King's College London Medieval Studies 2. (Forthcoming.)

Kapsomenos, Stylianos G. "Die griechische Sprache zwischen Koine und Neugriechisch." In *Berichte zum XI. Internationalen Byzantinisten-Kongress*, pp. 1–39. Munich, 1958.

Kenney, James F. *The Sources for the Early History of Ireland.* Vol. 1, *Ecclesiastical. An Introduction and Guide.* New York, 1929; repr. New York, 1968.

Klauser, Theodor. "Der Uebergang der römischen Kirche von der griechischen zur lateinischen Liturgiesprache." In *Miscellanea Giovanni Mercati.* Vol. 1, pp. 467–482. Studi e Testi 121. Vatican City, 1946.

Koder, Johannes, and Thomas Weber. *Liutprand von Cremona in Konstantinopel: Untersuchungen zum griechischen Sprachschatz und zu realienkundlichen Aussagen in seinen Werken.* Byzantina Vindobonensia 13. Vienna, 1980.

Kramer, Johannes. *Glossaria bilinguia in papyris et membranis reperta.* Papyrologische Texte und Abhandlungen 30. Bonn, 1983.

Krause, Wilhelm. "Das Fragment einer griechischen Grammatik des Cod. Vindob. 114 und das griech.-lat. Glossar der St. Pauler Handschrift XXV D/65." *Jahrbuch der Österreichischen Byzantinischen Gesellschaft* 5 (1956), 7–25.

Krumbacher, Karl. "Eine neue Handschrift der Grammatik des Dositheus und der Interpretamenta Leidensia (Codex Harleianus 5642)." In *Sitzungsberichte der Akademie der Wissenschaften, phil.-hist. Classe.* Vol. 3, pp. 193–203. Munich, 1883.

————. "Ein neuer Codex der Grammatik des Dositheus." *Rheinisches Museum für Philologie* 39 (1884), 348–358.

Laistner, Max Ludwig Wolfram. "Notes on Greek from the Lectures of a Ninth-Century Monastery Teacher." *Bulletin of the John Rylands Library* 7 (1923), 421–456.

————. "The Revival of Greek in Western Europe in the Carolingian Age." *History* 9 (1924), 177–187.

————. *Thought and Letters in Western Europe, A.D. 500 to 900.* 2nd ed. London, 1957.

Lapidge, Michael. "The Hermeneutic Style in Tenth-Century Anglo-Latin Literature." *Anglo-Saxon England* 4 (1975), 67–111.

Law, Vivien. *The Insular Latin Grammarians.* Studies in Celtic History 3. Woodbridge, Eng., 1982.

Leclercq, Henri. "Gall (Saint-)." In *Dictionnaire d'archéologie chrétienne.* Vol. 6.1, cols. 80–248. Paris, 1924.

Lehmann, Paul. "Konstanz und Basel als Büchermärkte während der grossen Kirchenversammlungen." In *Erforschung des Mittelalters: Ausgewählte Abhandlungen und Aufsätze.* Vol. 1, pp. 253–280. Stuttgart, 1959.

————, and Paul Ruf. *Mittelalterliche Bibliothekskataloge Deutschlands und der Schweiz.* Vol. 1. Munich, 1918.

Leitschuh, Friedrich, and Hans Fischer. *Katalog der Handschriften der Königlichen Bibliothek zu Bamberg.* 1 vol. in 2 pts. Bamberg, 1895–1906; repr. Wiesbaden, 1966.

Lemerle, Paul. *Le premier humanisme byzantin: Notes et remarques sur enseignement et culture à Byzance des origines au Xe siècle.* Paris, 1971.

Lesne, Emile. *Histoire de la propriété ecclésiastique en France.* Vol. 4, *Les livres, "scriptoria" et bibliothèques du commencement du VIIIe à la fin du XIe siècle*. Vol. 5, *Les écoles de la fin du VIIIe siècle à la fin du XIIe siècle*. Lille, 1938–1940.

Levy, Kenneth. "The Byzantine Sanctus and Its Modal Tradition in East and West." *Annales musicologiques* 6 (1958–1963), 7–67.

Lindsay, Wallace Martin, and Henry John Thomson. *Ancient Lore in Medieval Latin Glossaries*. St. Andrews University Publications 13. Oxford, 1921.

Löwe, Heinz. "Aethicus Ister und das alttürkische Runenalphabet." *Deutsches Archiv* 32 (1976), 1–22.

Lowe, Elias Avery. *Codices Latini Antiquiores: A Palaeographical Guide to Latin Manuscripts Prior to the Ninth Century*. Vol. 7, *Switzerland*. Oxford, 1956.

McKitterick, Rosamund. *The Frankish Church and the Carolingian Reforms, 789–895*. London, 1977.

McNally, Robert E. "The 'Tres Linguae Sacrae' in Early Irish Bible Exegesis." *Theological Studies* 19 (1958), 395–403.

Mansion, Augustin. "Disparition graduelle des mots grecs dans des traductions médiévales d'Aristote." In *Mélanges Joseph de Ghellinck*. Vol. 2, pp. 631–645. Louvain, 1951.

Marrou, Henri. *Histoire de l'éducation dans l'antiquité*. 6th ed. Paris, 1965.

Mayer, Theodor. "Konstanz und St. Gallen in der Frühzeit." *Schweizerische Zeitschrift für Geschichte* 2 (1952), 473–524.

Meersseman, Gérard Gillis. *Der Hymnos Akathistos im Abendland*. 2 vols. Freiburg, Switzerland, 1958–1960.

Merton, Adolf. *Die Buchmalerei in St. Gallen vom neunten bis zum elften Jahrhundert*. 2nd ed. Leipzig, 1923.

Miller, M. E. "Glossaire grec-latin de la bibliothèque de Laon." *Notices et extraits des manuscrits de la Bibliothèque Nationale* 29.2 (1880), 1–230.

Mirambel, André. "Pour une grammaire historique du grec médiéval: Problèmes et méthodes." In *Actes du XIIe congrès international des études byzantines*. Vol. 2, pp. 391–403. Ochride, 1961.

Mohlberg, Leo Cunibert. *Katalog der Handschriften der Zentralbibliothek Zurich*. Vol. 1, *Mittelalterliche Handschriften*. Zurich, 1932; repr. Zurich, 1951.

Mohrmann, Christine. "Les emprunts grecs dans la latinité chrétienne." *Vigiliae christianae* 4 (1950), 193–211.

————. *Liturgical Latin: Its Origins and Character*. London, 1957.

————. "Les origines de la latinité chrétienne à Rome." *Vigiliae christianae* 3 (1949), 67–106, 163–183.

Moran, Neil K. *The Ordinary Chants of the Byzantine Mass*. Hamburg, 1975.

Näf, J. B. "Die Bibliothek des ehemaligen Benediktinerstiftes St. Gallen." *Studien und Mitteilungen zur Geschichte des Benediktinerordens*, N.F. 1 (1911), 205–228.

Neff, Karl. *Die Gedichte des Paulus Diaconus*. Quellen und Untersuchungen zur lateinischen Philologie des Mittelalters 3.4. Munich, 1908.

Ó Cróinín, Dáibhí. "Mo-Sinnu moccu Min and the Computus of Bangor." *Peritia* 1 (1982), 281–298.

__________. "A Seventh-Century Irish Computus from the Circle of Cummianus." *Proceedings of the Royal Irish Academy*, sect. C, vol. 82, C, no. 11 (1982), 405–430.

Ohnsorge, Werner. "Byzanz und das Abendland im neunten und zehnten Jahrhundert: Zur Entwicklung des Kaiserbegriffes und der Staatsideologie." *Saeculum* 5 (1954), 194–220.

Omont, Henri. "Glossarium Andegavense. MS. 477 (461) de la bibliothèque municipale d'Angers." *Bibliothèque de l'Ecole des Chartes* 59 (1898), 665–688.

__________. "Grammaire grecque du IXe siècle." *Bibliothèque de l'Ecole des Chartes* 42 (1881), 126–127.

Opelt, Ilona. "Die Essener 'Missa Greca' der liturgischen Handschrift Düsseldorf D 2." *Jahrbuch der Österreichischen Byzantinischen Gesellschaft* 23 (1974), 77–88.

Oskamp, Hans. "The Irish Material in the St. Paul Irish Codex." *Eigse* 17.3 (1978), 385–391.

Pelikan, Jaroslav. *The Christian Tradition: A History of the Development of Doctrine.* Vol. 2, *The Spirit of Eastern Christendom (600–1700).* Chicago and London, 1974.

Perret, Franz. "Von der vornehmen Bedeutung des Stiftsarchivs St. Gallen." In *Gallus-Stadt 1971: Jahrbuch der Stadt St. Gallen.* St. Gall, 1971.

Pertusi, Agostino. "Bisanzio e l'irradiazione della sua civiltà in Occidente nell'alto medioevo." In *Centri e vie di irradiazione della civiltà nell'alto medioevo*, pp. 75–133. Settimane di Studio del Centro italiano di Studi sull'alto Medioevo 11. Spoleto, 1964.

Pfister, Rudolf. *Kirchengeschichte der Schweiz.* Vol. 1. Zurich, 1964.

Portmann, Marie-Louise. *Die Darstellung der Frau in der Geschichtsschreibung des früheren Mittelalters.* Basler Beiträge zur Geschichtswissenschaft 69. Basel and Stuttgart, 1958.

Psaltes, Stamatios B. *Grammatik der Byzantinischen Chroniken.* Göttingen, 1913.

Raasted, Jørgen. "A Byzantine Letter in Sankt Gallen and Lazarus the Painter." *Cahiers de l'Institut du moyen âge grec et latin* 37 (1981), 124–138.

Rahlfs, Alfred. *Verzeichnis der griechischen Handschriften des Alten Testaments.* Mittheilungen des Septuaginta-Unternehmens der Königlichen Gesellschaft der Wissenschaften zu Göttingen 2. Berlin, 1914.

Reichmann, Viktor. *Römische Literatur in griechischer Uebersetzung.* Leipzig, 1943.

Reynolds, Leighton Durham, ed. *Texts and Transmission: A Survey of the Latin Classics.* Oxford, 1983.

Riché, Pierre. *Les écoles et l'enseignement dans l'occident chrétien de la fin du Ve siècle au milieu du XIe siècle.* Paris, 1979.

Rönsch, Hermann. "Die Doppelübersetzungen im lateinischen Texte des cod. Boernerianus der Paulinischen Briefe." *Zeitschrift für wissenschaftliche Theologie* 25 (1882), 488–509; 26 (1883), 73–99, 309–344.

__________. "Zur biblischen Latinität aus dem cod. Sangallensis der Evangelien." *Romanische Forschungen* 1 (1883), 419–426.

Sabbadini, Remigio. *Le Scoperte dei codici latini e greci ne' secoli XIV e XV.* 2 vols. Florence, 1905–1914; new ed. Florence, 1967.

Salmon, Amédée. "Notice sur l'abbaye de Saint-Loup, près Tours." *Bibliothèque de l'Ecole des Chartes* 6 (1844), 444–445.

Scherrer, Gustav. *Verzeichnis der Handschriften der Stiftsbibliothek von St. Gallen.* Halle, 1875; repr. Hildesheim, 1975.

————. *Verzeichnis der Manuskripte und Inkunabeln der Vadianischen Bibliothek in St. Gallen.* St. Gall, 1864.

Schneider, Heinrich. *Die altlateinischen biblischen Cantica.* Texte und Arbeiten 29–30. Beuron, 1938.

————. "Die biblischen Oden im Mittelalter." *Biblica* 30 (1949), 479–500.

Schneider, Johannes. "Die Geschichte vom gewendeten Fisch." In *Festschrift Bernhard Bischoff.* Stuttgart, 1971.

Schubiger, Anselm. *Die Sängerschule St. Gallens vom 8. bis ins 12. Jahrhundert.* Einsiedeln and New York, 1858.

Siegmund, Albert. *Die Ueberlieferung der griechischen christlichen Literatur in der lateinischen Kirche bis zum 12. Jahrhundert.* Munich, 1949.

Smalley, Beryl. *The Study of the Bible in the Middle Ages.* 2nd ed. Oxford, 1952.

Stanford, William Bedell. *The Sound of Greek: Studies in the Greek Theory and Practice of Euphony.* Sather Classical Lectures 38. Berkeley, 1967.

Teodorsson, Sven-Tage. *The Phonology of Ptolemaic Koine.* Göteborg, Sweden, 1977.

Teuffel, Wilhelm Sigismund. *Geschichte der römischen Literatur.* 6th ed. rev. by Wilhelm Kroll and F. Skutsch. Vol. 3. Leipzig, 1913; repr. Aalen, 1965.

Thompson, James Westfall. *The Medieval Library.* Chicago, 1939.

Thürer, Georg. *St. Galler Geschichte: Kultur, Staatsleben und Wirtschaft in Kanton und Stadt St. Gallen von der Urzeit bis zur Gegenwart.* 2 vols. St. Gall, 1953.

Traube, Ludwig. "*O Roma nobilis*: Philologische Untersuchungen aus dem Mittelalter." *Abhandlungen der philosophisch-philologischen Classe der königlichen bayerischen Akademie der Wissenschaften* 19.2 (1892), 338–363.

Tristram, Hildegard L. C. "Ohthere, Wulfstan und der Aethicus Ister." *Zeitschrift für deutsches Altertum und deutsche Literatur* 111 (1982), 153–168.

Ursprung, Otto. "Alte griechische Einflüsse und neuer gräzistischer Einschlag in der mittelalterlichen Musik." *Zeitschrift für Musikwissenschaft* 12 (1930), 193–219.

————. "Um die Frage der Echtheit der Missa greca." *Die Musikforschung* 6 (1953), 289–296.

van Doren, Rombaut. *Etude sur l'influence musicale de l'abbaye de Saint-Gall.* Brussels, 1925.

Vogel, Cyrille. *Introduction aux sources de l'histoire du culte chrétien au moyen âge.* Spoleto, 1966; repr. Spoleto, 1975.

von Arx, Ildefons. *Berichtigungen und Zusätze.* St. Gall, 1830.

————. *Geschichten des Kantons St. Gallen.* 3 vols. St. Gall, 1810–1813.

von Schanz, Martin. *Geschichte der römischen Literatur bis zum Gesetz-*

gebungswerk des Kaisers Justinian. 2nd ed. rev. by Carl Hosius and G. Krüger. Part 4, vol. 1. Munich, 1914; repr. Munich, 1959.

Wagner, Peter. *Einführung in die gregorianischen Melodien.* 3 vols. Leipzig, 1911–1921; repr. Hildesheim, 1962.

————. "Morgen- und Abendland in der Musikgeschichte." *Stimmen der Zeit* 114 (1927), 131–145.

Wattenbach, Wilhelm, and Wilhelm Levison. *Deutschlands Geschichtsquellen im Mittelalter bis zur Mitte des dreizehnten Jahrhunderts.* Vol. 1. Weimar, 1952.

Weidmann, Franz. *Geschichte der Bibliothek von St. Gallen.* St. Gall, 1841.

Weiss, Roberto. "Lo Studio del greco all'abbazia di San Dionigi durante il Medioevo." *Rivista di storia della Chiesa in Italia* 6 (1952), 426–438. Repr. in *Medieval and Humanist Greek*, pp. 44–59. Padua, 1977.

Wolff, Philippe. *Western Languages, A.D. 100–1500.* Translated by Frances Partridge. New York and Toronto, 1971.

Wuttke, Heinrich. *Die Kosmographie des Istriers Aithikos.* Leipzig, 1853.

Index of Manuscripts

Index of *Graeca*
and *Graecolatina*

The terms are given here as they are spelled in the manuscripts and texts from which they are derived. There are two listings: one of terms given mostly in Greek letters, the other of terms rendered mostly in Latin. Minuscule entries in the first listing generally refer to material presented only in edited form. (Normalized forms suggested in editorial apparatus, however, are not repeated here.)

KYPIN, TON; κύριος; KYPIOY; KYP-
PIE

lalo, 17
lauta, 38

ma, 70
me, 20, 71. *See also* ME, MOI, MOY, μου
melodema, 113
metamophorseon, 107
mi, 38
mith, 70
moechus, 58
mucrus, 71. *See also* μικροτάτη

nechros, 17
neon, 17
ni, 38
nia, 38. *See also* ennea
nomu, 71. *See also* νόμου
nosochomium, 61

obdoenta, 119
octointa, 119
odon, 21
oenon, 17
oenus, 71. *See also* aeones
oftalmos, 70
ogda, 38
omo, 70. *See also* ἐμοί, ἐμο(ῦ), EMOY
oranus, 70. *See also* OIPANOY; OYPA-
NON, TON
orphanotrophium, 61
os, 20
ota, 70

paleon, 17
pant, 20. *See also* pantes, παντός, πᾶσι,
ΠΑCΙΝ
pantes, 19. *See also* pant, παντός, πᾶσι,
ΠΑCΙΝ
pantocrator, 19, 21
partenu, 21. *See also* ΠΑΡΘΙΝΟC
penta, 38
philacas, 63

philoponia, 17
phisa, 17
phronimos, 17
phrontistes, 17
physin, 21
pigon, 21
piisson, 70. *See also* ΠΥΗϹΗ
pimelin, 17
pisteucus, 70. *See also* pisteuo, theon
pisteuo, 101. *See also* pisteucus
pneoma, 71. *See also* pneuma; pneumate;
pneumati; pneumati, to; pogma; Π͞ΝΑ;
πνευματικοῦ; πνευματικῷ
pneuma, 21. *See also* pneoma; pneumate;
pneumati; pneumati, to; pogma; Π͞ΝΑ;
πνευματικοῦ; πνευματικῷ
pneumate, 113 n. 35. *See also* pneoma;
pneuma; pneumati; pneumati, to;
pogma; Π͞ΝΑ; πνευματικοῦ; πνευματικῷ
pneumati, 21. *See also* pneoma; pneuma;
pneumate; pneumati, to; pogma; Π͞ΝΑ;
πνευματικοῦ; πνευματικῷ
pneumati, to, 21. *See also* pneoma, pneuma, pneumate, pneumati, pogma, Π͞ΝΑ,
πνευματικοῦ, πνευματικῷ
poesis, 62
pogma, 70. *See also* pneoma; pneuma;
pneumate; pneumati; pneumati, to;
Π͞ΝΑ; πνευματικοῦ; πνευματικῷ
potami, 21. *See also* ΠΟΤΑΜΟΙ
prathema, 63
prosince, 70
Ψychen, 63
ptochotrophium, 61
pudas, 70
pullas, 70. *See also* ΠΟΛΛⲰΝ

quercum, 71
quirius, 70, 71. *See also* kyrie; kyrion, ton;
zuiri; zuiric; zuirie; zuuiron; K͞Ϲ;
KYPIN, TON; κύριος; KYPIOY; KYP-
PIE

rema, 17
ripho, 17
<r>unas, 70

sarcem, 71

selenen, 71

serenta, 38

simma, 38

sison, 17

sodisse, 19

sophia, 71. *See also* sopia

sopia, 70. *See also* sophia

soteria, 70

spermologos, 18

stuma, 70

su, 19, 21

talassum, 71. *See also* italasum, thalassi, ΘΑΛΑΣΣΑΙ

tantella, 71

taumastia, 71. *See also* transmascia

tauta, 20

tax, 70

te, 19

teon, teo, 70. *See also* theo; theon; theon, ton; theu, tu; theus, o; ΘΕΟΣ, Ο; ΘΕω, Τω; Θ̄Σ̄; Θ̄Ῡ

thalassi, 21. *See also* italasum, talassum, ΘΑΛΑΣΣΑΙ

theo, 101, 113 n. 35. *See also* teon, teo; theon; theon, ton; theu, tu; theus, o; ΘΕΟΣ, Ο; ΘΕω, Τω; Θ̄Σ̄; Θ̄Ῡ

theon, 20, 70, 101. *See also* pisteucus; teon, teo; theo; theon, ton; theu, tu; theus, o; ΘΕΟΣ, Ο; ΘΕω, Τω; Θ̄Σ̄; Θ̄Ῡ

theon, ton, 70. *See also* teon, teo; theo; theon; theu, tu; theus, o; ΘΕΟΣ, Ο; ΘΕω, Τω; Θ̄Σ̄; Θ̄Ῡ

theophania, 18. *See also* ΘΕΟΦΑΝΙΑ, ΘΕΟΦΑΝΙΑΕ, ΘΕΟΡΗΑΝΙΑΕ

theotocon, 18

theta, 38

theu, tu, 102, 107. *See also* teon, teo; theo; theon; theon, ton; theus, o; ΘΕΟΣ, Ο; ΘΕω, Τω; Θ̄Σ̄; Θ̄Ῡ

theus, o, 70, 71. *See also* teon, teo; theo; theon; theon, ton; theu, tu; ΘΕΟΣ, Ο; ΘΕω, Τω; Θ̄Σ̄; Θ̄Ῡ

topum, 71

transmascia, 70. *See also* taumastia

trinta, 38

troi, 70

uti, 70. *See also* OTI

xb, 41, 42

xenodochium, 61

xp̄c, 41, 42, 108. *See also* ΧΠΥΣΘΥΣ, Χ̄ΡΙ, ΧΡΙΣΤΕ, Χ̄ΡΜ, Χ̄ΡΣ, Χ̄Σ̄

ymas, 19. *See also* imon, ymon, HMON

ymnite, 21

ymon, 19. *See also* imon, ymas, HMON

ypnus, 63

yrge, 70

ysos, 19

zeta, 38

zoe, 71. *See also* ZOE, ΖωΗ

zui, 70

zuiri, 70. *See also* kyrie; kyrion, ton; quirius; zuiric; zuirie; zuuiron; Κ̄Σ̄; KYPIN, TON; κύριος; KYPIOY; KYPPIE

zuiric, 70. *See also* kyrie; kyrion, ton; quirius; zuiri; zuirie; zuuiron; Κ̄Σ̄; KYPIN, TON; κύριος; KYPIOY; KYPPIE

zuirie, 71. *See also* kyrie; kyrion, ton; quirius; zuiri; zuiric; zuuiron; Κ̄Σ̄; KYPIN, TON; κύριος; KYPIOY; KYPPIE

zuuiron, 71. *See also* kyrie; kyrion, ton; quirius; zuiri; zuiric; zuirie; Κ̄Σ̄; KYPIN, TON; κύριος; KYPIOY; KYPPIE

Index of Names
and Selected Subjects

Florus of Lyons, 96
Fulgentius, 57

Gaius, 46
Gall (saint), 9, 107
Gennadius, 64, 124
Glossarium andegavense. See Angers,
    Bibliothèque Municipale, MS 477
Gozbert (abbot of St. Gall), 11
Graeca collecta, 58, 63–67, 72, 123–124
Greater Doxology. See *Missa graeca*
Greek
    in Hellenistic and Byzantine periods,
        31–32, 99
    as sacred language, 2–3, 75, 100
    as transcribed in western manuscripts,
        27–31
Gregory of Nyssa, 5
Gregory of Tours, 27
Grimald (abbot of St. Gall), 11, 13, 17
Grosseteste, Robert, 2

Hadrian (Roman emperor), 46, 121–122
Hadwig (duchess of Swabia), 1, 21–22
Hartmann (monk of St. Gall), 19, 105, 113
Hartmut (abbot of St. Gall), 11, 13
Hebrew
    alphabets, 34–36, 117, 119
    as sacred language, 2–3, 75
Henry II (emperor), 87
Henry (duke of Bavaria), 22
Hermeneumata pseudo-dositheana
    as source of Greek grammar, 7, 44–47,
        50, 52–53, 56, 121–122
    as source of Greek vocabulary, 57–60,
        62, 69
Hilary of Poitiers, 2
Hilduin (abbot of St-Denis), 5, 108
Hincmar of Laon, 73–74
Hincmar of Reims, 73–74
Homer, 20, 46
Honorius of Autun, 101, 111–112
Hugh of St. Victor, 3
Hyginus, 45–46

Idiomata generum, 47
Interlinear Gospels. *See* St. Gall, Stifts-

bibliothek, MS 48
Irish scholars. *See also names of individual
    scholars*
    on the Continent, 3, 5, 23, 48–50, 85
    at St. Gall, 7–10, 13, 15, 23–25,
        84–86, 88–93
Isidore of Seville
    on Greek alphabet, 33, 35–36, 117, 119
    on sacred languages, 2, 75
    as source of Greek material, 4, 57,
        60–62, 67, 96
Iso (monk of St. Gall), 17, 23, 25
I ta Cherubim, 103

Jerome
    Graeca collecta of, 63–67, 72, 123–
        124
    Psalter translations of, 20, 75, 78, 92,
        96, 116
    as source of Greek material, 4, 28, 58,
        61
John (abbot of St. Gall), 10
John of Genoa, 61, 73
John Scottus Eriugena
    at court of Charles the Bald, 5, 25, 115
    his knowledge of Greek, 2, 19, 56, 76,
        96
    as source of Greek material, 47, 58, 67
Julian Antecessor, 61
Justinian, 61

Kyrie Eleison, 39 n. 13, 99, 113

Lactantius, 5, 58
Laon (cathedral school), 5–6, 8, 25, 47, 56,
    115
Latin
    alphabets, 35–36, 117, 119
    instruction in, 1
    knowledge of, at St. Gall, 12, 14
    as sacred language, 2–3, 75
    utriusque linguae peritus, 19–20
Lazaros (Byzantine letter writer), 53–54
Leo III (pope), 112
Libri scottice scripti, 13, 24–25
Liège, 5–6, 85, 115
Litany, 16, 78, 107, 131–132